ARMINDA ABERASTURY'S THEORY AND TECHNIQUE OF CHILD ANALYSIS

Edited by

Jill Savege Scharff and Lea Sofer de Setton

KARNAC

firing the mind

First published in 2025 by
Karnac Books Limited
62 Bucknell Road
Bicester
Oxfordshire OX26 2DS

The chapters by Arminda Aberastury were originally published in 1962 in *Teoría y técnica del psicoanálisis de niños* by Paidós, Buenos Aires

British Library Cataloguing in Publication Data

A C.I.P. for this book is available from the British Library

ISBN: 978-1-80013-319-8 (paperback)
ISBN: 978-1-80013-367-9 (e-book)
ISBN: 978-1-80013-366-2 (PDF)

Typeset by Medlar Publishing Solutions Pvt Ltd, India

www.firingthemind.com

MIX
Paper | Supporting responsible forestry
FSC® C007915
FSC
www.fsc.org

Karnac Books is committed to a sustainable future for our business, our readers, and our planet. This book is made from Forest Stewardship Council® certified paper.

Contents

Part IV
New perspectives on treatment and prevention of infantile neurosis

List of illustrations

Photos

Chapter 2

Chapter 7

Editors' note and acknowledgments

Arminda Aberastury was a pioneering child analyst, developing the field in Latin America in the mid-to-late twentieth century, and she is a profound inspiration to this day. Her work is outstanding, seminal, and admired, but little known in English-speaking analytic communities. We want to change that.

We knew of Arminda as the wife of Enrique Pichon-Rivière whose life and work on link theory (*el vínculo*) was the subject of a book by Roberto Losso, Lea Sofer de Setton, and David Scharff, through which Lea came to know Joaquín Pichon-Rivière, a social psychologist and one of the brothers who owned the rights to the work of their late parents. Joaquín shared beautiful photos and reminiscences of his parents and particularly his beloved mother, Arminda. That caught Jill's attention because she had heard of Arminda's work from Yolanda Varela in Panama, but she struggled to comprehend the chapter Yolanda sent. Then when visiting Virginia Ungar's traditional child analytic playroom in Argentina she heard of Arminda again. Of the four books by Arminda Aberastury, Virginia recommended *Teoría y técnica del psicoanálisis de niños* [*Theory and Technique of Psychoanalysis of Children*] (1962), which is, however, out of print, but Virginia introduced Jill to a bookseller who found her a battered pink copy of the fourth edition by Paidós, 1974, a copy formerly owned by Ángel Garma (Arminda's analyst), no less.

Already owning a copy, Lea began the work of translation and engaged Rafael Mendez to provide a professionally competent version for Jill to edit. We decided on a slightly abridged version, removing chapters by coauthors, and yet giving credit, as the author scrupulously did, to the work of collaborators who wrote chapters, shared in the research, and contributed clinical material. We made this decision to privilege Arminda's writing and thinking and to leave room for commentary by contemporary child analysts to show the global relevance today of Arminda's mid-century work in Argentina. We are grateful to these commentators for joining our project and to her son Joaquín, a dear friend, for arranging for his nephew Pedro Aberastury to review the contract, and for giving us permission to publish the English translation. We are grateful for Joaquín's support and friendship, for his generous and loving reminiscence of Arminda, his amazing mother, and his permission to reprint photographs from his photo essay about Enrique and Arminda presented in a gorgeous coffee-table book edited and designed with his daughter, Clara. With great appreciation we acknowledge the encouragement we received from Kate Pearce of Karnac Books who accepted our book proposal, believing that Arminda is another woman whose voice needs to be heard. We value the expertise of our production editor, Anita Mason and her team that shepherded this volume to publication. We want to express our gratitude and affection for all of them as they brought our book to life.

And so to the work of editing. We agreed to follow the author's arrangement of the sections, but included only Chapters 1–9, 11, and 14 (excluding those by coauthors). We wanted our volume to be accessible to the child analyst and child therapist, and so we rearranged some sentences and cut others to improve the flow and sense in English. We removed all the footnotes, especially those referring to articles available only in Spanish or without adequate citation, and integrated the essential ones into the text. It was not always possible to track down quotes in Spanish translation of English originals. Jill had one amazing success with a Freud quote Arminda gave in Spanish but had not cited: She took the quote in its Spanish-to-English translation, and fed it to artificial intelligence software. Even though the translated English she provided was obviously not a replica of the original, Chatbot GPT4 dated the quote 1897, then located it in a letter to "a colleague," narrowed it to "Letter to Fliess," and lastly gave the month and day of its writing!

As for other footnotes, the author's bibliography refers mainly to her sources in Spanish, and we could not provide access to English translations, so we left those in Spanish in her list of sources she consulted. She made a separate list of those sources she actually cited. We combined those lists and added corresponding English citations of major references, but in the end our bibliography could not be perfect. For any omissions, we take responsibility and apologize to the scholarly reader in advance. To orient readers, we might mention that prior to the divorce in 1958, Arminda authored her publications as Arminda A. de Pichon-Rivière. So her book *El juego de construir casas* (*The House Building Game*), written in 1950 by Arminda A. de Pichon-Rivière and published by Nova, appears in 1961 written by Arminda Aberastury and published by Paidós. We decided always to list the name that Arminda used in the original publication.

As for illustrations, in the 1962 book these were bunched together in sections, one on each side of a page. Nowadays, in 2024, it is technically possible to insert each illustration near the text to which it applies. So, we set about photocopying the children's drawings, but sadly the images were not clear because images on the other side of the page bled through. They were unusable, and we no longer had access to the originals. So, Jill traced each drawing faithfully and scanned it, and added typed translations of comments Arminda had written on two pages of drawings.

The progression of chapters in the opening section on theory shows how over time Arminda moved from a Freudian perspective closer to the Kleinian view of the stages of infant development, developed her own research into the mother–infant relationship, and refined her evolving signature clinical technique of child analysis (Bloj, 2014). The second section is highly practical, detailing the nuts and bolts of clinical practice, with numerous vignettes to illustrate her clinical technique—from parent work, to setting the frame, to play interpretation. This section lays the groundwork for the third section, surely the heart of the book. Arminda provides an immersive experience of two child analyses with detailed histories and narratives of their play and three vignettes of birth trauma revealed in symptoms and in play. We can feel Arminda's sensitivity and compassion, and learn from her brilliant capacity for following the child's play as a road to the unconscious. We see clearly the incorporation of Kleinian ideas and their development by Arminda's fertile mind and attentive clinical presence. The final section on infant development and the mothers who are learning to understand it, demonstrates her trust in the mothers' capacity, her fostering of fulfillment in motherhood, her belief in the power of psychoanalysis for treatment and prevention, and her commitment to the mental health and growth of children.

About the editors and contributors

Minnie Dastur (India) Senior training analyst of the Mumbai (formerly Bombay) Chapter of the Indian Psychoanalytical Society (IPA) and head of its Continued Professional Development Cell; child psychoanalytic psychotherapist trained at the Tavistock Institute, London; member of the China Committee of the IPA with projects in Wuhan, Beijing, and Shanghai; teacher and supervisor of some groups in China; presenter at psychoanalytic conferences in India and the Asia-Pacific; clinician and teacher of individual and child psychoanalysis and psychotherapy in practice in Mumbai.

Judith Edwards, PhD (UK) Senior teaching fellow of the UK Higher Academy of Education; formerly consultant child and adolescent psychotherapist teacher, tutor, and supervisor at the Tavistock Clinic; author and editor of psychoanalytic books, and coeditor of the *Journal of Child Psychotherapy* 1996–2000; 2010 winner of the Jan Lee memorial prize for the best paper linking psychoanalysis and the arts; author of *Pieces of Molly—An Ordinary Life* and *Grandmotherland*, both published by Karnac.

Jeanne Magagna, PhD (UK) Child, adult, and family psychotherapist trained at the Tavistock Clinic and formerly head of psychotherapy services at Great Ormond Street Hospital; specialist in infant observation and eating disorders; author of books including *The Silent Child, Intimate Transformations*, and *A Psychotherapeutic Understanding of Eating Disorders in Children and Young People.*

Elizabeth Palacios, MD (Spain) Psychiatrist, IPA training analyst; child and adolescent psychoanalyst; director of ASPADE, the Center for Vulnerable Adolescents; chair of the IPA Couple and Family Psychoanalysis Committee (COFAP); author of chapters on working analytically with children and families: in practice in Zaragoza, Spain.

Joaquín Pichon-Rivière, PhD (Argentina) Social psychologist, consultant for communication, management, and advertising in organizations, and senior qualitative researcher on psychosocial issues including education; director, Pichon-Rivière & Asociados 1998–2013; and three-term president of the Argentine Association of Social Psychologists and chair of its Ethics Tribunal.

Nydia Lisman Pieczanski, MD (Argentina and USA) Child and adult psychoanalyst, graduate and member of the British Psychoanalytical Society and Institute of Psychoanalysis; training and supervising analyst (child and adult) of the Washington Baltimore Center for Psychoanalysis (USA) and previously of the Buenos Aires Psychoanalytic Association (IPA); member of IPA, Association of Child Psychotherapists (UK) and Latin Association of Infant Observers; founding chair of the two-year Infant and Young Child Observation Program (Esther Bick/Tavistock Model) at the Washington School of Psychiatry, USA (2004–2019) and Beijing (2009), and author of *Infant and Young Child Observation in China* in Mandarin; scientific adviser and teacher at "Mind in Mind", Beijing; author, reviewer for JAPA and IJP journals, and coeditor of *The Pioneers of Psychoanalysis in South America: An Essential Guide* (in English/Spanish); in practice in Washington, DC.

Jill Savege Scharff, MD, FABP (USA) Cofounder, the International Psychotherapy Institute (IPI); founding chair and a supervising child and adult psychoanalyst in its analytic and child training programs; member APsA and IPA; clinical professor of psychiatry at Georgetown University School of Medicine; author, editor, and series editor of books on object relations theory, psychoanalytic child, couples, and family therapy, and teleanalysis; in private practice in Chevy Chase, MD; recipient of The Sigourney Award 2021; latest book, *An Introduction to Child and Adolescent Psychoanalytic Psychotherapy*, in English (2024) and Chinese (in press 2025).

David E. Scharff, MD, FABP (USA) Cofounder, the International Psychotherapy Institute (IPI), supervising child and adult psychoanalyst in IPI's analytic and child training programs and chair of its couple and family therapy training. Chair of family therapy programs in China and Russia; member APsA and IPA; clinical professor of psychiatry at Georgetown University School of Medicine; author, editor, and series editor of books on object relations theory, psychoanalytic child, couple, and family therapy, and psychoanalysis in China; in private practice in Chevy Chase, MD; recipient of The Sigourney Award 2021; latest book, *Marriage and Family in Modern China.*

Lea Sofer de Setton, PhD (Panama RP) Training analyst, member IPA, APsA, FEPAL; faculty member of the International Psychotherapy Institute (IPI) and supervising analyst at the International Institute of Psychoanalytic Training (IIPT) at IPI, Bethesda, Maryland; former chair of IPI-Panama; former faculty member of the Doctoral Program at the Catholic University in Panama; founding member and chair of the Panamanian IPA Provisional Psychoanalytic Society; coeditor of *The Linked Self in Psychoanalysis: The Work of Enrique Pichon-Riviere*; psychologist, psychoanalyst, and psychotherapist in private practice with individuals, couples, and families in Panama City, Panama RP.

Alan Sugarman, PhD (USA) Child, adolescent, and adult training and supervising analyst, San Diego Psychoanalytic Center; former assistant professor of psychology, Yale University School of Medicine and chief psychologist, Yale Psychiatric Institute; prolific author of journal articles on psychoanalysis; member IPA, APsA, and ACP (psychoanalysis, USA). He is in practice in San Diego, CA.

Virginia Ungar, MD (Argentina) Child, adolescent, and adult training analyst at the Buenos Aires Psychoanalytical Association; adjunct supervising analyst, IIPT; author; first woman president of the International Psychoanalytical Association (IPA) (2017–2023); recipient of The Sigourney Award 2023; in practice in Buenos Aires, Argentina.

Foreword

Virginia Ungar

Even though every time a book is published it brings forth a celebration, similar to the birth of a child, this volume calls for special recognition. Its editors, Jill Scharff and Lea Sofer de Setton, have enabled a broad English-speaking audience to access the legacy of the Argentine pioneer of child psychoanalysis, Arminda Aberastury. The *Merriam-Webster Dictionary* defines a *pioneer* as "a person or group that originates or helps open up a new line of thought or activity or a new method or technical development." *Theory and Technique of Child Psychoanalysis* introduces such a true pioneer.

In the sphere of child psychoanalysis, certain figures stand tall as impressive lighthouses, shedding light on the path of future generations of professionals. Aberastury looked to the first giants of child analysis in Europe, like Hermine Hug-Hellmuth, Sophie Morgenstern, Anna Freud, and Melanie Klein. Klein and Anna Freud especially left a profound impression and opened a path that was later pursued by numerous analysts who have considered them their inspiration. Among these European giants, Arminda Aberastury has a place of enormous importance. Her pioneer work expanded way beyond the borders of her native Argentina, to all of Latin America.

Melanie Klein had the greatest impact on Aberastury. Klein entered the psychoanalytic scene in Europe in the 1920s, and first presented the findings she had obtained from observation and then from her psychoanalytic work with children. By going into her own children's room to find some toys to offer to a patient, Klein took the first steps towards her revolutionary method and laid the foundations for what she eventually called "the play technique." In her paper titled "The psychoanalytic play technique: Its history and significance" (1955) Klein stated that her entire contribution to psychoanalytic theory resulted from the play technique for young children. She further clarified that her analytic work with adults did not entail implementing this technique. It was her work with children that had provided her with a deep understanding of early development, unconscious processes, and the nature of psychoanalytic interpretations, and the same can be said of Arminda herself.

The editors of this book, inspired by Aberastury's transforming contributions, embarked on the mission to take her works to a broader audience, overcoming linguistic barriers to make her teachings available to English-speaking analysts. They have tailored a selection of chapters to show the essence of Aberastury's theoretical framework and her clinical practice, enriched and elucidated by insightful, respectful commentary by renowned contemporary analysts. By means of this structure, not only has a close reading of the nodes of her theoretical contributions become possible, but also a close testing of their validity, endurance, and applicability to current clinical practice with children. As we browse the pages of the book, we embark on a journey into the rich fabric of the theoretical ideas and techniques of Aberastury. The abundant clinical materials presented allow us to see how the challenges of clinical practice provided the evidence of the value of therapeutic relationship and analytic interpretation and led her to make major contributions the theoretical corpus of psychoanalysis.

Aberastury's pioneer work was carried out with a strong conviction in the possibility of healing through the psychoanalytic treatment of children. In this endeavor, she had the collaboration of colleagues who drew inspiration from her passion in working with young selves in development. Together they had great impact on the dissemination of this practice in Argentina. This is something that still astonishes scholars in social sciences. In this regard, one of the factors that draws our attention is the great geographical distance of Argentina from the European hub of culture at the time when child psychoanalysis was being born. Argentina was far from the sophisticated thoughts and practices (surprisingly so, considering the times in which they took place) being developed at the end of the 1940s. But Aberastury found them. By reading the psychoanalytic literature and corresponding with Melanie Klein she extended the psychoanalytic culture to the world of childhood.

If we focus on child analysis and its penetration of the culture in Argentina today, it is safe to say that, if a survey were to be conducted in any primary or secondary school in a large city in the country, over half of the children and young people in the class would know the answer to the question, "What is a psychotherapist?" Either they themselves or a sibling, cousin, or friend will certainly have engaged—or will engage—in some kind of psychoanalytic treatment. Surely there are many reasons for this, but the main one is the social context.

Without meddling in the field of expertise of social sciences professionals, I, as a psychoanalyst, believe it is important to take into consideration the historical and sociocultural context in which the practice and teaching of psychoanalysis was born in Argentina by the late 1930s, when migrant pioneers arrived from Europe fleeing the threat of a thriving National Socialism. At that time, the population of Buenos Aires amounted to six million people, most of whom were immigrants. Their descendants—the majority being Spaniards and Italians—have maintained family traditions that have, to this day, always entailed sharing life with children at all times. The presence of children in shows, restaurants, family gatherings, and public spaces—not only during daytime, but also at night—has always been clearly observed as a feature of family life here.

Most immigrants came from a Europe that had been decimated by wars. As is understandable—taking into account the theory of narcissism—they naturally projected their ideal of the self onto their children. Parents sacrificed any immediate personal fulfillment by devoting their personal and economic efforts to the "good education" of their children, who were predestined to eventually carry the baton of progress forward. The place of the child as the center of the family structure, and the projection of the ideals of immigrant parents onto their children, allowed analytical treatment to take hold in these latitudes with unprecedented force.

It is in this context that Arminda Aberastury, the pioneer of child analysis in Argentina and throughout Latin America, stands out. "*La Negra*," as she was affectionately called by her close friends, was born in Buenos Aires in 1910 and died in the same city in 1972. She was a member of an aristocratic family in a time when studying medicine was frowned upon and a psychology degree (more acceptable for a woman from such a family) did not exist yet; so, she studied pedagogy. In 1933, she met Enrique Pichon-Rivière, master of psychiatry and psychoanalysis in Argentina, and married him four years later.

If we refer to a pioneer as one who leads the way, we can certainly apply this term to Aberastury as we revisit the story of her encounter with psychoanalysis, in what I have called the "context of discovery" in my commentary to Chapter 4 of this book. When we look back to the beginnings, which we admit are always somewhat mythical, we can imagine standing with Arminda in Hospicio de las Mercedes, a psychiatric institution, to which she went with her husband Enrique Pichon-Rivière where he provided daily treatment to a patient who attended that facility while her little daughter waited for her mother in the waiting room. The child was eight years old and had been diagnosed with oligophrenia. Coming upon this little girl, and noting such intelligence and anxiety in her eyes, Aberastury chose to offer her a pedagogical approach. She related as a tutor to the child, helping with her letters and numbers. However, this teaching method evolved to a clinical one as she applied new learning from her immersion in the reading of Anna Freud's discoveries on child analysis first expressed in German in 1927 and published in English as *Introduction to the Technic of Child Analysis* (1927a, 1928). This marked the beginning of Aberastury's exploration of learning disorder and psychiatric illness from a psychoanalytic perspective. Through this research, she laid the foundations for a practice that provided children's symptomatology with a human dimension. It was later known that this first girl she had treated developed normally and became a teacher as an adult.

Reading Melanie Klein, and maintaining a correspondence with her, Arminda became a follower and disseminator of Klein's thinking in Argentina. She translated Klein's work into Spanish and taught her theory in Argentina and several Latin American countries. Yet, she was able to follow her own theoretical path, without being bound to a dogmatic adherence to British ideas, for one important reason: Aberastury made personal developments according to her own unique interests, derived from her clinical work with her patients. She had a brilliant career as an analyst. We cannot fail to mention some of her most valuable contributions, such as her paper as associate member of the Argentine Psychoanalytic Association, including "Fobia a los globos en una niña de 11 meses" [Balloon phobia in an 11-month-old girl] (A. Pichon-Rivière, 1950b). Moreover, as full member, she published *El juego de construir casas. Su interpretación y valor diagnóstico* [*The House Building Game: Its Interpretation and Diagnostic Value*] (A. Pichon-Rivière, 1950a).

Following the Kleinian tradition, Aberastury built her theory on an empirical basis, on her analytic work with child and adult patients, her observation of infants, and her work with parents who provided her with detailed accounts of their children's sexual activities and who attended her parenting groups. In fact, she modified the scheme of development of infantile sexuality, already posited by Freud, by locating *la fase previa* (1964), a genital stage, which is prior to the anal stage. Always following her clinical observations, she took a step further on two issues: the assessment of genitality at the onset of the Oedipus complex, and the importance of dentition in the origin of the early genital stage.

In her original contribution on dentition, Aberastury (A. Pichon-Rivière, 1958b) postulates that the emergence of the teeth contributes to the creation of cannibalistic fantasies that appear regularly in the second half of the first year of life. She set forth her theory that the concrete appearance of teeth modifies anxiety, since what was, up to that point, a fantasy of possible destruction of the object and the self becomes the daily verification of having an instrument capable of destruction. Infants can bite the breast and make their mother cry or bleed; they can destroy inanimate objects, swallow them, and spit them out. This reality test of the capacity of teeth to cause an effect brings depressive anxiety to its peak, sets in motion the mechanisms of mourning, and drives the subsequent search for another form of unity. It thus takes the person from the oral stage to the early genital stage (prior to the anal stage), since their genital organs are the only means to recover the lost bond. In other words, when genital impulses emerge in the second half of the first year, the child fantasizes about an organ capable of satisfying them—girls will fantasize about something that will penetrate and fill up their vagina, and boys will fantasize about something that they can penetrate. According to Aberastury, the experience of teeth cutting through the gum to emerge also contributes to the construction of the image of genitalia, given that there is a cavity—the alveolus—and something that emerges and is penetrating—the tooth.

In Chapter 7 of this book, Aberastury offers an in-depth analysis of the "first playtime," a central tool in child psychoanalysis, later renamed "diagnostic playtime," a method still used today in the evaluation of a child's emotional state. The diagnostic playtime findings guide the analyst in assessing the possibility of initiating a treatment and in giving the parents evidence to back up the eventual recommendation. She placed great emphasis on the first meeting with a patient's parents, providing an excellent model for analysts who are starting their practice with children. Aberastury suggests that during the first meeting with the child, by offering them items to play and draw it is possible to detect both the unconscious fantasy of illness and that of healing. This idea deserves special consideration. It arises from the fact that, since children are always brought to the practice by adults, one may think that they are not conscious of being ill. The author argues very strongly that children know they are ill, and they have the will to heal. She elaborates extensively on transference and insists that young child patients are afraid when facing a new relationship with an analyst, because when they arrive at the analyst's practice, they relive the anxiety of separation that they have experienced at birth. That is why Aberastury also suggests that the therapist should interpret this anxiety from the outset.

Aberastury firmly follows Melanie Klein's method, equating play to free association and dreams in adult patients, and she recommends interpretation of play following the technique of dream analysis that Freud devised for reaching the unconscious. She goes on to share lengthy reflections on the relationship between the child analyst and the patient's parents. She describes the parent counseling groups she created as a way of working with parents of children undergoing analytic treatment. These groups help analysts to decompress the transference–countertransference field and break away from the projections that parents inevitably make when they entrust their children to us.

Each reader on their own journey as a child therapist can dive into child psychoanalysis in the voice of this author, who is so passionate about her work and about sharing her clinical practice. In her approach, there is a deep respect for the complex dynamics of the inner world of children. Her observational skills and empathic course of action allowed her to create a methodology to go beyond behavior and discover the latent meanings in children's play and symptoms. As we go through the chapters of this volume, we witness Aberastury's evolution from taking in Freud and Klein to arriving at her unique synthesis of Kleinian ideas, as she traces a path where theoretical rigor and engagement with developing minds intertwine. Similarly, the book adopts an evolutionary perspective that recognizes the formative influence of early experiences on the psychic structure as it invites us to reconsider traditional psychoanalytic paradigms. In this volume, readers will be both introduced to and guided through Arminda Aberastury's thinking by the insightful commentary of experienced child analysts.

It is in the realm of clinical practice that Aberastury's genius really shines, as she guides us through the complexities of child analysis and illustrates the therapeutic process with vivid narratives and evocative case studies. Each vignette serves as a testament to Aberastury's unwavering dedication to her young patients, and her profound insight into the dynamics of transference, countertransference, and symbolic communication. She so deftly conveyed her passion for psychoanalytic work with children to her disciples (whose collaboration and influence she generously acknowledges throughout this volume) that they took the baton and continued to develop child analysis in an impressive way, transcending the frontiers of Argentina. It is worth noting that in the original book in Spanish *Teoría y técnica del psicoanálisis de niños* (1962), Aberastury includes chapters by Susana L. de Ferrer, Elizabeth G. de Garma, and Pola I. de Tomás. In the English translation, the editors privilege only those chapters written by Arminda Aberastury herself.

Child psychoanalysis has had a great impact on other disciplines, such as pediatrics, pediatric dentistry, law, and education. Arminda was able to shape the interdisciplinary approach at a very early stage, and therefore, managed to push psychoanalytic thinking beyond child analysis, so as to help professionals in other disciplines related to child care to think analytically about the problems they face in their daily work with children.

By bringing Aberastury's work to a new audience, Scharff and Sofer de Setton have done a profound service to the field of child psychoanalysis. Thanks to their efforts, Aberastury's voice resonates across time and space, encouraging us to engage with her ideas, fight for them, and carry her legacy forward into the future. As we embark on this intellectual odyssey, may we be inspired by Aberastury's innovative spirit, her commitment to healing and her enduring belief in the transformative power of the human bond.

Arminda Aberastury, my mother: A personal reminiscence

Joaquín Pichon-Rivière

My mother Arminda Aberastury and my father Enrique Pichon-Rivière had three sons: Enrique Alfonso (1940) named after his father; Joaquín Pedro (1942) because Arminda liked the name Joaquín; Pedro from her older brother; and Marcelo Esteban (1944) named for her younger brother. Here[1] she is as a lively young mother responding with delight to her baby (Photo 1). Here I am Joaquín (Photo 2), the middle child, two years younger than Enrique and two years older than Marcelo. We all of us attended a state school that was only four blocks away on foot. It was our father's job to wake us in the morning before he went to work at the hospital or the Instituto Pichon-Rivière. Our mother managed the household and our food, in addition to being a tutor and then a psychoanalyst. We always returned from school at midday and ate lunch together in our dining room as a family. But in the evening, our hard-working mother and father stayed in their consulting rooms—sometimes until 9 pm—and so the children ate earlier in the television room.

---

[1] Photos in this chapter are from *A & E, Enrique and Arminda*, ed. Joaquín Pichon-Rivière. Buenos Aires: Capital Intellectual.

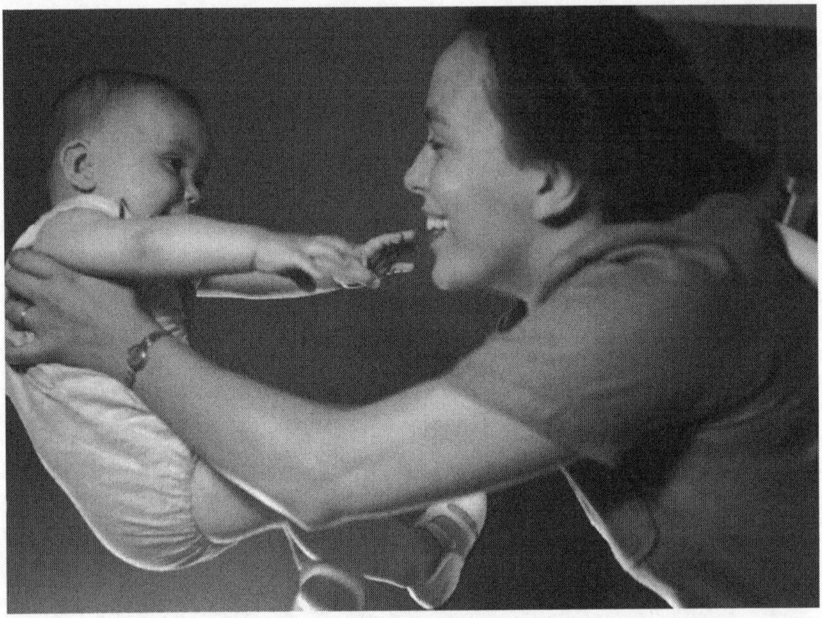

Photo 1. Arminda with firstborn, Enrique.

Photo 2. Joaquín at play.

Between the ages of eight and twelve, we boys loved building structures using the House Building Game. The game consisted of fitting together the necessary elements for construction of a house—doors, windows, railings, and vertical struts for fitting into a perforated horizontal base. She bought the game for use in her diagnostic and therapeutic work with child patients, but she let us play with it too. We built lots of different houses. In Photo 3, you can see Arminda playing with us (in the light-colored sweaters) and two of our cousins (in the dark sweaters) in her typical pose on the floor with her lower legs flexibly tucked underneath her thighs. Marcelo is on her lap, Enrique with his back to us in

Photo 3. Playing the House Building Game, Marcelo next to her.

the foreground is working on his house with Arminda, and I am fixing the railing on mine. Arminda developed this game as a psychological diagnostic tool for use in child assessment. I don't remember if she ever did an interpretive reading of the houses that we built! No doubt she got some information about us from what we were doing, but it was a group activity: at any moment my brother Enrique would put a roof on my house; so, she could not have made an individual interpretation.

Some of the houses we built were used as bases in a game of war with toy lead soldiers which Arminda had purchased for us at La Tour d'Argent when she was in Paris attending an international psychoanalytic congress with our father. We played with the soldiers on the floor, arranging them among the houses, pitting the Americans against the German army to reproduce the Second World War. After we saw the movie *The Day the Earth Stood Still* (1951) in which an alien lands in Washington, DC, and tells the people of Earth they must live peacefully by avoiding experimenting with the atomic bomb or they will be destroyed and be a danger to other planets, we added extra-terrestrials to the enemy forces and used our soldiers to fight off invasion and destruction. Arminda enjoyed our war games and approvingly called us boys "The Three Musketeers." One day she decided to show the lead soldiers she had found in Paris to the owner of a toy store she frequented in Buenos Aires, a few blocks from where we lived. He asked us to set up some of our scenes of soldiers shooting, being on the radio, marching, in hand-to-hand combat with the enemy, and so on. Thanks to Arminda's enthusiasm, he was inspired to make molds and put the toy soldiers into production locally. Probably not legal today, but back then there was no problem with that. To thank us, he gave us a set of boats to take home, and we then extended our battle fronts to include Normandy landing scenes.

On the first floor of our house on Copérnico Street in Buenos Aires, Arminda had a consulting room for adult patients and a playroom where she saw her child patients. The playroom had a low table and a floor to play on. It was characteristic of Arminda to attend to her younger patients sitting on the floor, drawing and putting together the houses, just as we did with her at home. Below the coffee table there were drawers, each one with different games and toys for each individual child patient undergoing treatment. For each patient she put together a box with the toys they usually used, and another with new toys. She was meticulous in choosing toys with an ordinary, everyday appearance, no characters from popular magazines or television, nothing overstimulating to the children. Those toys were the protagonists of the play.

On the ground floor of the house we had a dining room and kitchen, a room for the receptionist and a hallway for the patients to wait. Arminda let us play football (soccer) with a tennis ball in that hall. We had forty minutes to play while the patient was in. Then we'd go in the kitchen to eat something while the patient left or the next one arrived, and then we would continue for the next forty minutes. We managed our play around our mother's schedule. She used to play with us sometimes but she was bad at kicking the ball—she preferred tennis, and she excelled at swimming, completing one kilometer every Saturday and Sunday in the Olympic pool at the club she took us to.

When hearing these stories, perhaps you are wondering, as my children and nephews and nieces do, what kind of parents we had that we were allowed so much play and freedom without punishments. True, Arminda rarely got upset, and when she did, she did not yell. For instance, there was one time that one of her receptions ended late, and our parents slept in. My father didn't do his job of waking us up, and so we boys stayed asleep like them, and didn't go to school. Arminda was very upset with him and with us, but as usual more upset than angry. She spoke in a soft voice telling us what she was annoyed about. There were no harsh punishments but we did have consequences. If we were misbehaving, we got less pocket money. If we boys were playing at passing gas at the table or making scatological comments, we lost our weekly allowance altogether. Apart from that we enjoyed life with little parental control, but I also recognize beneath all the fun, a deep sorrow about the remoteness of our busy parents.

Sometimes during lunch, our mother would ask us about what we saw on TV or had read about in Mexican magazines and comics. She wanted to know all about the characters, what they were like, and their identifying characteristics and roles. As an adult, I'd say it was as if she were doing market research on media consumption and its content, but really she was always focused on the characters. She explained to us that sometimes the kids who came for treatment spoke or impersonated characters that appeared in magazines and especially on TV. She rarely had time to watch television herself, and so she had us tell her about them so that she would be able to understand who the characters were that her patients were talking to her about or personifying in their sessions. One of her patients had lost his mother, and in his sessions he referred to Bambi, the baby deer who lost his mother suddenly. (According to the story, the hunter's shot killed her, but the boy must have thought he lost her in the forest fire.) He skillfully and systematically drew all the scenes of the fire, one image per page. He was such a good artist, it made me feel envious, and there were thirty pages of the drawings!

Arminda was well known for her emphasis on working with the parents of the children who came to her for treatment. For those parents, she ran orientation groups (we might call them parent counseling groups today) where they could learn from her, share their stories of parenting, and find support from one another in realizing that they were not the only ones with problems. Trained in pedagogy, she gave well-attended talks on parenting in the anatomy room of the Buenos Aires University Faculty of Medicine. The anatomy room had a large blackboard on which Arminda wrote with white chalk in general and with colors when she wanted to highlight something in particular. Her handwriting was very clear and her graphics orderly and explanatory (Photo 4). As a teenager, I participated in many of my mother's activities, preparing transparencies of selected drawings from her child patients, installing sound equipment, or arranging a projector and screen for her slides.

Of great importance to Arminda were her receptions in our house where she brought together an interesting mix of movie directors, writers, and psychoanalytic colleagues whereby famous artists became part of the enriching field of psychoanalysis. Arminda was in her element as the hostess of these cultural events in which psychoanalysis was a valued element. She was much more than a psychoanalyst. She read many non-technical books, much of them in French. She read poetry and was herself a poet. She did not speak English fluently but she read psychoanalytic texts in English without a problem. Her English teacher was of German origin so he could help her with psychoanalytic terminology in German as well. With permission, she translated the complete works of Melanie Klein. She wrote three books of her own, two of which I designed for her, and I selected the photos and did the layout of photographs and copy for *El niño y sus juegos*.

Arminda was educated and cultured. She read poetry and novels in French, and loved Proust. She was not political (unlike our father). During the Cuban Revolution we had an Argentine and a Chilean writer at

Photo 4. Teaching at the university.

our table. They were talking about Castro, and my mother asked who this Mr. Castro was. She was not aware of the Cuban revolution because she did not read the newspapers daily or watch the news on television. That's why she had to ask us about the characters on television so she could understand what her child patients were talking about. She worked in a skirt and blouse appropriate to the setting with kids, but when there was a reception at the house she dressed in her elegant clothes. She was very well-dressed in the French fashion, and was an attractive woman with beautiful skin. From student to film director, they admired her and affectionately called her "*La Negra Aberastury.*" Her skin was not black: it was deeply tanned. Arminda was genuine and good-hearted. Open and innocent. Artistic. When a patient did not show up, she would go into her little piano room and play her favorite classical pieces (not popular music or Christmas carols for family singing) but we liked her playing piano because it made her happy—and then we could go off and have our fun.

We were teenagers when Arminda and Enrique were divorced in 1958, and he did not stay close to us. He wasn't the kind of person who would take the initiative to see us but his house was open to us and his new wife was kind and friendly. In a curious repetition of her childhood where she was the only girl with three brothers, Arminda found herself living as a woman alone with three adolescent males. It was hard for us to talk about guy stuff with her, especially sex, and we were left to deal with that the best we could by ourselves or with help from our friends, our older cousins, and our uncle who was like a father for me. On weekends she took us to a bookstore and to visit art galleries; in summer we went to the club. My older brother left at twenty to get married; I lived with Arminda after the divorce for only two years before I left to get married; and then she moved with Marcelo to an apartment. She kept her schedule, working a lot with patients and writing three books on her own and with her valued colleagues. When my brother and I began to have children, our mother was still fully engaged in her profession, so she was not in daily contact as a grandmother but she had the grandchildren to lunch now and then or came over to visit.

In those years, Arminda developed vitiligo, a patchy whitening of skin which destroyed the beloved evenly dark skin tone that was part of her identity as "*La Negra*". We all knew how upset she was, and how desperately she went from one doctor to another, in a futile search for treatment to reverse it. We did not realize how depressed she had become. In 1972, Arminda chose to end her life prematurely at the age of sixty, seventeen years before our father died.

Arminda Aberastury had been born on September 24, 1910, began reading Freud in 1937, and Melanie Klein in 1942 (the year I was born) and by 1948 she was a member of the Argentine Psychoanalytic Association of which she was made director in 1958, the same year she was divorced from Enrique. Arminda lived to participate in the First Congress of Childhood Psychopathology in Argentina. Throughout Latin America, our mother is recognized as a pioneer of child analysis and its application in pediatrics and dentistry. Her work has recently been published in French. Thanks to this volume, Arminda Aberastury will also be appreciated in the English-speaking world. My brothers and I are grateful and proud to join in honoring her legacy and spreading her word for the benefit of children and their parents everywhere.

Author's preliminary note

Arminda Aberastury

This book, which begins with Freud's first attempt to cure a child's neurosis by applying psychoanalytic technique and concludes by providing new perspectives for therapy, brings together my experience and that of many analysts who worked with me.

It is testimony to my gratitude to Freud, who gave us the theoretical foundations of psychoanalytic technique; to Melanie Klein, whose ideas were my most valuable guides; to all those who contributed their efforts to the progress of child psychoanalysis and to those who collaborated in this book by generously offering me their clinical material.

The Argentine Psychoanalytic Association was recognized in 1944 by the International Psychoanalytical Association, the result of the tireless work that Ángel Garma had carried out in favor of the dissemination of the psychoanalytic method—with the group that initially accompanied him—since 1939. His interest in analysis was in children. The unconditional support that I received from both him and Enrique Pichon-Rivière—with whom I had worked since 1938 at the Hospicio de las Mercedes—allowed me to undertake the arduous task of taking the initial steps and creating the foundations of what we can call our technique of child psychoanalysis. In this same sense, I want to acknowledge here with deep gratitude what the frequent correspondence with Melanie Klein meant to me: I received valuable technical advice from her.

Although Flora Scolni also began her work as a child psychoanalyst at that time, I worked alone at first. My first collaborator was Elizabeth G. de Garma, who with great dedication and genuine talent for the analysis of children participated since 1947 in the training tasks, which even then were intense.

Interest in child psychoanalysis quickly grew, which made it possible and necessary for us to give technical and theoretical seminars at the Argentine Psychoanalytic Association since 1948. This progressive development began in 1948 and culminated in the holding of the First Symposium on Child Psychoanalysis in 1957.

From the beginning, I formed a group especially interested in these problems. As the years went by some abandoned the specialty, while others, once trained, continued their activities independently and created new groups.

Writing this book, in which I intend to convey my experience and that of my collaborators, was far from easy, and I would surely have abandoned the task without the unconditional help that Lidia Forti and Susana L. de Ferrer gave me. Luciana B. de Matte, Julio Aray, and Juan F. Rodriguez were valuable collaborators and their careful and intelligent revisions provided undeniable improvements in the text. José Alonso did not limit himself to copying the originals but sometimes interpreted them, suggesting subtle modifications.

Finally, I thank Decio de Souza for his dedication in discussing some aspects of this book with me, which gave me great encouragement.

Author's prologue

Arminda Aberastury

Freud's original works arose from the analysis of adults, but the nature of his discovery led him to investigate the years of childhood, as he discovered that the first causes of mental disorder had their source in factors active during the first phases of development. His conclusions about infantile sexuality were confirmed the first time psychoanalysis was applied to the treatment of a neurotic child. His ideas about development were enriched by subsequent findings in the treatment of neurotic adults, by direct observation of children, and by data communicated to him by psychoanalysts who worked with children. Their investigation into the mechanisms that drive children to play was fundamental to understanding child development.

Play had been studied by psychologists, philosophers, and pedagogues, many of whose findings maintain their validity today, but they pointed out only partial aspects of the problem or described the phenomenon without considering its unconscious meaning. In Freud's trauma theory of play, he does not exclude what had already been described in part, but goes further to explain the phenomenon in its entirety and in its essence. Already in his narrative of the five-year-old Little Hans Freud had interpreted games, dreams, and fantasies, but it was by observing and analyzing the play of an eighteen-month-old child that he discovered the psychological mechanisms of playful activity. Freud understood that the toddler not only replayed what was pleasurable but also repeated painful situations when playing, thus elaborating what had been overwhelming for his ego. The trauma theory of play developed by Freud has not been modified in its bases, and has been used for the creation of new techniques for approaching the child's unconscious in the treatment and diagnosis of childhood neuroses, which we will deal with throughout this prologue and the book.

In many of Freud's works I have found notes that were fundamental for the creation of the technique of child psychoanalysis. In the section "Symptomatic and chance actions" in *The Psychopathology of Everyday Life* (1901b), he recounts a symptomatic act in a thirteen-year-old boy and its interpretation, which could today be an example of the way in which a child can be analyzed; and in a small article "Association of ideas in a four-year-old girl," he points out the possibility of using early verbal expression for interpretation. In "Psychology of the schoolboy" he studied the reactions of children to teachers, as a repetition of the relationships with their parents—ideas that were later developed, allowing us to understand the reasons for learning difficulties, school maladjustment, and refusal instead of thirst for knowledge. In "Children's dreams" he analyzes children's dreams, highlighting that—as in those of adults—we must consider a manifest content and a latent one, which is reached through interpretation.

Based on Freud's findings, Hermine Hug-Hellmuth, Anna Freud, Sophie Morgenstern, and Melanie Klein sought a way to apply psychoanalysis to the treatment of children. Although they all contributed to my current technique, it was Melanie Klein's thinking that set the fundamental direction of my work.

Freud's discoveries about the dynamics of the unconscious, infantile sexuality, and the configuration and destiny of the Oedipus complex forced us to reconsider what a child was supposed to be.

Having pointed out that the death instinct acts together with the life instinct from the first moment, Freud showed that destructive tendencies exist together with the capacity for love, that the death instinct needs to destroy, and that this need must be respected—within certain limits. Above all, given that the conflicts caused by these competing tendencies are a continuous source of pain, we have been forced to modify our belief in the happiness of childhood.

When Freud described birth anxiety as the archetype of future anxiety situations—an idea that Rank would later develop brilliantly—he opened the way for all those psychoanalysts who dealt especially with intrauterine life, with the trauma of birth, and the early stages of development. All of them, by developing Freud's original ideas, contributed to the understanding of the infant's mind, laying the foundations for a proactive way to prevent childhood neuroses.

All of these findings provoked rejection and aroused resistance—especially those concerning infantile sexuality and the Oedipus complex. The adult's repudiation of the child's sexuality was expressed in the need to ignore it, in the desire to prohibit its flourishing by inventing legends that replaced the truth, and the wish to deny the child any clarification. Freud already showed in the history of Little Hans that when the adult lies in answer to the child's questions it drives the child to lie and creates serious conflicts in him.

When in 1900 Freud discovered the importance of the early relationship with parents for the development of future object relationships, he laid the foundations for a new technical discovery—decisive for the effectiveness of his method: the use of transference for healing in psychoanalysis. In "Delusions and dreams in Jensen's *Gradiva*" (1907a), Freud describes this discovery with special clarity:

> The process of cure is accomplished in a relapse into love, if we combine all the many components of the sexual instinct under the term "love"; and such a relapse is indispensable, for the symptoms on account of which the treatment has been undertaken are nothing other than precipitates of earlier struggles connected with repression or the return of the repressed, and they can only be resolved and washed away by a fresh high tide of the same passions. Every psycho-analytic treatment is an attempt at liberating repressed love which has found a meagre outlet in the compromise of a symptom. (p. 90)

Freud came to the discovery of the Oedipus complex through his self-analysis and then through the transference. He says in his

Autobiographical Study: "I had in fact stumbled for the first time upon the *Oedipus complex*, which was later to assume such an overwhelming importance" (Freud, 1925d, p. 34). He pointed out that this was the central issue of his self-analysis: "I have found, in my own case too, [the phenomenon of] being in love with my mother and jealous of my father, and I now consider it a universal event in early childhood" (Freud, 1897).

Appreciating the fundamental importance of Freud's findings for the creation of child psychoanalysis was what prompted me to begin this book with the story of the first history of a neurotic child treated by Freud, move on to present his clinical technique and how it evolved, and how I arrived at my current technique. I have tried—not without difficulty—to ensure that it was the clinical material that led to the theory and to transmit my conviction about the importance of child psychoanalysis for psychoanalytic research and methodology.

Part I

History of psychoanalytic technique

CHAPTER 1

Analysis of the phobia of a five-year-old boy

With the publication of the story of Little Hans, Freud (1909b) laid the foundation for the understanding of preverbal language and the use of interpretation in the analysis of children. His approach, however, did not account for the management of transference as a technical instrument. This was partly due to the epistolary way the treatment was carried out, and partly because, in regards to adult treatment, he had yet to appreciate the technical importance of the link with the therapist. In order to understand how child psychoanalysis was born, I would like us to travel back to Freud's first discoveries concerning the healing of adult neurosis.

Freud's invention of free association with adults

The first time he spoke of psychoanalysis as a therapeutic method of his own was in 1896 when, due to his discovery of the value of free association, he was able to become independent of hypnosis and suggestion, techniques that he had used for the exploration and healing of hysteria until that moment (Jones, 1959, p. 296). The fact that many of his patients continued to speak freely, without hypnosis or suggestion, and could, through associative chains, access the memory of childhood traumas, showed him the key role of free association, a technique he later used methodically in the exploration and healing of his patients.

When it comes to understanding this evolution of Freud's technique, there is no more illustrative example than his first histories. His great, new discovery was the evaluation and understanding of the bond between patient and therapist as a technical instrument. This, he called transference. He discovered that transference had its roots in the earliest stages of childhood and that in the therapeutic relationship the patients relived their first object relationships. Attending to these, the analyst could interpret the positive and negative transference reactions as repetitions of those past situations. Freud understood the therapeutic value of interpretation early on, when he found that, by communicating his discoveries to his patients at the right moment, he could make them aware of what had been repressed until then. Free association, transference, and interpretation were the three pillars of Freud's technique for making the unconscious conscious.

Freud's indirect treatment of Little Hans

In 1906 Freud attempted, for the first time, to apply this method to the cure of an infantile neurosis: the zoophobia of a five-year-old boy called Little Hans. Freud did not directly observe little Hans, except once, but collected material from Little Hans' father who presented Freud with his observations of his barely three-year-old child, sharing any manifestations of curiosity and sexual activities pertaining to his son that could confirm Freud's discoveries about infantile sexuality, and authorizing their later publication.

The history of this child, in effect, corroborated what Freud had affirmed until then about infantile sexuality and about the importance of the Oedipus complex. In addition, it paved the way for the interpretation of preverbal language and made a fundamental contribution to the understanding of phobias. Neither Freud nor his immediate successors could foresee the scope of his discovery, until the experiences of child psychoanalysts confirmed the impact that traumatic situations had on the child's development, how the child expressed himself during treatment, and how treatment evolved until he was cured.

Until the emergence of the phobia, Little Hans seems to have been a child who developed normally. His parents described him as a happy child, with good relationships with his environment, who often enjoyed playing. They did not refer to illnesses or difficulties during his development that would suggest an unresolved conflict.

The data that Freud gives us about the patient is incomplete today. We know nothing about the pregnancy, his birth, breastfeeding, and achievements of early language and walking. We can but deduce from the mother's subsequent attitude, in light of our current knowledge, that the toilet training must have been severe, because the child suffered from persistent constipation that was treated with the violent emptying of enemas and laxatives to which he objected by kicking. He was curious about animals urinating, and pointed out their "thingy." His interest is not exclusively theoretical but incites him to touching himself in masturbatory ways that distress his mother, who threatens that the doctor will cut off his genitals if he continues to touch them. This threat will be one of the triggering traumas of the infantile neurosis.

Freud considers that the birth of the sister was also traumatic for Little Hans. Rereading the history and studying it in the light of current knowledge, we understand that it was not so much the fact itself that disturbed Little Hans, but the obfuscations of the truth that surrounded this event and everything related to sexual life; the lies that contradicted everything he observed. Little Hans both notices and denies that his newborn sister is different from him, by stating that she has a very small thing.

The history indicates abundant genital trauma: 1) the patient's mother prohibited him from masturbation, and since this prohibition was useless, she threatened to take him to a doctor who would cut off his genitals; 2) she gave him an inaccurate description of the difference between the sexes, assuring him that female genitalia are identical to male genitalia; 3) when his mother conceived and bore a daughter, the parents supplied the patient with the well-known story of the stork, while simultaneously exposing him to his mother's room, where he saw the doctor's bag and a basin with blood, which he linked with delivery; and 4) the child was no longer allowed to sleep with his parents after his sister was born.

When studying the evolution of the symptom, Freud insistently points out that before the appearance of the phobia, Little Hans had an anxiety attack and that, at four years and eight months, he had an anxiety dream, in which he expressed the fear of being abandoned by his mother. The first symptoms of the phobia—which would go on to condemn Little Hans to self-isolation in his house for fear of seeing a horse—appeared shortly after. Two events appear from the beginning in connection with the phobia: 1) fear he felt when he saw a horse fall, gasp, and kick, and 2) fear that the horse would bite him. When the father interprets that there is a relationship between that fear and his sexual curiosity, there is an intensification of the anxiety, and a compulsion to look at the horses that scare him, which perpetuates the fear.

At this time Little Hans falls ill and has to stay in bed for fifteen days due to a severe flu. I think that this illness was a consequence of the anxiety mentioned above. The flu is followed by a tonsillectomy, after which the phobia intensifies markedly. Although Freud did not value tonsillectomy as one of the triggers of the disease, today we must, especially if we take into account that the mouth played an important role in this phobia and that Little Hans frequently points out that the white horse will bite his fingers, and later that it will enter his room.

Analyzing the details of the fear

I will address the kicking, being bitten, the fall, and the characteristics of the feared horse—and expose not only the motivations that Freud points out, but also those that we would value today.

Little Hans used to see his mother when she defecated, and this fact, according to Freud, contributed to insistently equating the process of childbirth with evacuation and representing it as the fall of fecal matter in the toilet. The kicking that he feared so much from the horses was similar to what, according to his parents, Little Hans did when they imposed toilet training.

Prior to his becoming afraid of it, Little Hans played at "being the horse" displaying its peeing, mostly with other children, and sometimes with his father. At that time, his mother's pregnancy increased his curiosity regarding everything sexual in nature, as well as the frequency of his masturbation, and the mother not only threatened to cut off his genitals, but later proposed to put him to bed with his hands tied, so as to prevent the act from taking place.

With all these antecedents, we understand that the tonsillectomy must have been experienced by him as the fulfillment of that maternal threat, intensifying the castration anxiety due to the displacement of the genital to the oral. If part of his throat could be amputated, it was possible that the doctor would do the same to his genitals. The consequent equating of the mouth with the vagina, in accordance with the above, made the patient focus his fear of horses on their potential to bite. The patient concentrated on the fingers, because masturbation could also be prevented by biting or cutting them off or tying up the hands.

A prime characteristic of the feared horse was its white color, and I think this detail could have originated in the white color of the doctor's apron during the operation. The traumatic significance of the tonsillectomy escaped Freud's understanding and perhaps this was the reason he was unable to explain some of the details of the phobia: the white color of the horse, the meaning of the mouth, and the significance of the muzzle.

Technical findings: Advances and limitations

When Little Hans begins to display the fear, the father, guided by Freud, intervenes as a therapist. He interprets for Little Hans that the anguish and fear he feels are a consequence of masturbation, prompting him to abandon it. The threat of castration is thus reinforced and determines new aspects of Little Hans' neurosis. The small improvement obtained with this newfound interpretation soon dissipates, and Little Hans instead develops a flu, after which he undergoes a tonsillectomy.

It is clear that, as a result of the interpretations, Little Hans became aware of the reasons for his fear, and memories that were repressed arose, which, in turn, made it possible to reconstruct the path from the anxiety crisis to the appearance of the phobia. Freud focused on the following: 1) the previous significance of the horse as an object of preference and interest, as can be deduced from the first accounts of games played with his friends and with his father, in which the horse played a very important role; 2) the memory of an incident in which his friend, Federico, who was somewhat older than Little Hans and strongly identified with his father, fell to the ground and injured himself while playing horses; 3) the prohibitions that were phrased in the same terms by both the parents, when referring to masturbation, and a friend's parents who referred to the dangers of a horse's mouth, and 4) the temporary union with everything related to pregnancy and the mother giving birth, since at three and a half years of age he simultaneously receives the mother's threat and witnesses the sister's birth. The horse phobia prevented Little Hans from leaving the house and made it easier for him to stay next to his mother, thus satisfying his possessive desires at the cost of an intense repression of his genital desires.

These conflicts were joined by the memory of anxieties related to the initiation of toilet training. Little Hans linked the horse's kicking with his own kicking when they forced him to stop playing in order to make him defecate. It was also evident that he identified childbirth with evacuation, explaining, through this identification, the fear of kicking the horse. The fear of being bitten by the horse had been linked to the fear of the mother's genitalia, and the memory of the threat of castration that she made.

We know that in phobia the displacements are multiple. In Little Hans, the fear of being bitten soon evolved to the fear that a horse might enter his room, a movement explained by the fact that his room was the scene of masturbation and prohibitions. Today, we cannot avoid the honest consideration that the mother's threats increased Little Hans' anguish to an extreme degree and that these threats, in turn, increased his curiosity to see the genitals, leading him to a cycle of compulsive masturbation as a means of confirming that the threat had not been carried out.

Adhering to criteria that the experience in children has amply corroborated nowadays, Freud believes that an adequate sexual clarification would have helped Little Hans to overcome the compulsion to see the mother's genitalia and thus avoid the intensification of anxiety. The mother's initial lie about the difference between the sexes, compounded with the threat of castration, reinforced the compulsion to see and touch the genitals; this increased anxiety being an adjunct to the somatization that kept him in bed with the flu for days. Presumably, being in bed and suffering from a fever increased his compulsion to masturbate, an activity that was not only prohibited, but was pointed out as a reason for his illness, thus reinforcing his castration anxiety. The tonsillectomy acted as a trigger.

Freud did not appreciate the meaning of the operation as castration, but today, through many similar experiences, it is very evident to us. In this, as in many other cases, tonsil surgery is experienced as a warning that the dreaded castration can also be fulfilled. It is important to note that it is at this moment that Freud points out for the first time that the feared horses were white.

We assume that this white horse represents the surgeon with the white apron performing the much-dreaded castration displaced to the throat, and the usage of "fingers" and not of "hand" is also a reference to the operative maneuver and the instrument of masturbation. In addition, another feature of the feared animal was the "black thing in its mouth," which turned out to be a leather muzzle. This is why he is afraid of being bitten by white horses, or those with muzzles, or of having his fingers removed.

Everything suggests that he experienced the operation as punishment for masturbatory practices performed with underlying oedipal fantasies. When Little Hans resists going to Freud's office, his parents lie to him, promising that if he accepts, he will see a very pretty girl at the teacher's house. This attitude allows us to deduce that he was also taken to the operation under this sort of deception.

In this first and only consultation, Freud understands that two details of the feared animal are related to the father's whiskers and glasses. He interprets that Little Hans' fear of the horse arises from his intense aggression to the father and the fear that he will take revenge. He surmises that these feelings are the consequence of his loving wishes towards the mother. After this visit, the important improvements begin, but Little Hans insists, exercising acute common sense, that his love and his fear towards his father are coexistent, a truth that Freud will only discover later, in his paper on inhibitions, symptoms, and anxiety (1926d). For now he recognizes paranoid and depressive anxieties and their origin.

In this part of the history, Freud interprets Little Hans' game of loading and unloading. He discovers that, due to a substitute symbolic relationship, it is possible that the game represents the process of childbirth and defecation. This interpretation is later confirmed when, in his games with a doll, Little Hans uses the same symbols to represent what the delivery and evacuation meant to him; symbols which condense and displace the figure of the horse, making specific the situations of greatest fear.

At this point in the treatment, Freud points out that Little Hans boldly seizes the direction of the analysis, and since his parents delay the explanations that they should have given him a long time ago, he communicates to them through his games with a doll representing birth. Through these same games, he elaborates the process of the evacuation and the loss of a part of himself; a fulfillment of the much-feared threat of losing the genital. The operation, a reality check signaling that part of his body is being taken away, transformed a previously fantasized fear into a real one, prompting him to associate the loss of fecal matter with the loss of the penis and linking this with birth as a product of genital union.

The greatest point of interest in the history, if we are to consider it the starting point of the child psychoanalysis technique, is the efficiency of the interpretations and their consequences.

Through the analysis of games, fantasies, and dreams, Freud studied the different symbolic forms with which a child represented the mother's body and its contents: a bathtub, a bus, a moving car. The common denominator was that the object be full of contents; that it be a carrier object capable of holding smaller and heavier things inside itself. This is much like a womb. He then extended this meaning to the evacuation process. One of the most exciting arguments in the history is his interpretation of the detailed description that Little Hans gives of his sister's life in the mother's womb. Freud points out the evidence that this knowledge is within the child.

The process of loading and unloading, that which symbolizes childbirth, appears to be equated with that of intestinal evacuation. The beginning of the phobia, which was the fear that a horse would kick and fall, was linked to Little Hans' own infantile kicking when forced to defecate, as well as the displacement of that fear to the birthing process. It is evident that the child had a knowledge of intrauterine life. He describes his sister traveling in a closed box, in which she ate and relieved herself, and from which she could not exit. He acknowledges this journey as taking place during a summer in which his mother was six months pregnant.

Today we know from numerous analyses of children that the mother's pregnancy is perceived from the first moment and it is expressed through games, thus confirming what Freud observed. When Little Hans tried to elaborate the problem of the difference between the sexes, the difference between adults and children, and the fear of his father as a rival in the mother's love, he expressed it in a fantasy in which a large giraffe and a girl symbolized the difference of sex. Little Hans took possession of the girl (the mother) by sitting on her and arousing the anger of the big giraffe (the father), prompting Freud to interpret that the difference in size of the two giraffes symbolized the difference of the sexes. Here we find, once more, that later experience in the analysis of children confirmed Freud's interpretation. In a series of fantasies in which Little Hans describes things that are forbidden and punished, such as jumping fences or breaking glass, Freud interprets incestuous desire and punishment for him.

In another of Little Hans' fantasies, a plumber with a screwdriver takes out "the little thing" and gives him a big one. In the first part of this fantasy, he repeats, almost without deformation, the traumatic situation of the threat of castration made by the mother. In the second, he mentions the modification achieved by the treatment, through which he receives the power from the father. According to Freud, this happy elaboration of the Oedipus complex was made possible by the interpretations above and explained the disappearance of the phobia. Since Freud was especially interested in studying the influence of sexual traumas on the etiology of neuroses, and since, within the arena of phobias, he granted special importance to traumas of the phallic phase, most of the data refer to that time of his life. If we were to write Little Hans' story today, we would focus on the many other details of his journey that would make this evolution understandable.

The treatment was not carried out using standard procedures of psychoanalysis. Freud saw the patient only once, and the treatment, while still administered under Freud's supervision, was carried out primarily by the boy's father, who was deeply involved with Freud's discoveries. Freud's traumatic theory of neuroses had led him to focus on the importance of infantile sexuality and to formulate this essay on its development, but it lacked the experience of the direct observation of a child, which would have allowed a confirmation of his discoveries about sexual evolution. The treatment of infantile hysteria would have amply permitted this corroboration. Freud had postulated the existence of the Oedipus complex, and the observation of a neurotic child would have also confirmed its importance in the emergence of neurosis, *while* it was happening. For this reason, the case cannot serve as technical teaching in regard to interpretation or handling of transference. However, many of Freud's findings, some barely outlined, paved the way for the discovery of a technique that would allow us to understand preverbal language and interpret it.

Experience showed that the child, though he could not express himself fully through words, was capable of understanding what the adult was saying. Thus, due to a firm grasp on the latent meaning of games, drawings, dreams, and associations, the interpretation would be as effective as it was in treating adults. It remained to be seen whether the child would be able to establish a transference link with a therapist, as an adult would do; and if so, whether the contribution of child analysts would be recognized.

Once free association was replaced by preverbal language and the child's ability to understand the interpretation and establish a transference with the therapist had been tested, then the necessary requirements to put forth a technique for the psychoanalysis of children similar to that of adult psychoanalysis were met.

The continuous evolution of this technique, the birth of which we will present in the next chapter, allowed for several developments:

1) The analysis of very young children, from fifteen months onwards;
2) The ever-increasing number of cases that were successfully treated, including psychosomatic conditions such as ulcers, ulcerative colitis, asthma, eczema, and acetonemia; and
3) Prophylaxis of future illnesses, through psychoanalytic counseling of the infant, as a consequence of progress in understanding development.

Commentary on Chapter 1

David E. Scharff (USA)

It is a pleasure to comment on the first chapter of Aberastury's book, in which she faithfully summarizes Freud's Little Hans paper, and comments in a penetrating way on the importance of several crucial elements of Freud's previously postulated theory and technique such as the Oedipus complex, the central role of interpretation, the functions of symbolization and displacement, the role of traumatic events in Hans' young life, and the quest for honesty and truth.

When Aberastury published this book of seminal work on child analysis in 1962, she was gathering elements that had helped her establish her own way of working with children, but also offering a kind of encyclopedia of then-current ideas for this relatively recent invention. By this, I mean that she presents child analysis, introduced and developed by Melanie Klein and Anna Freud, as a kind of second-generation development, when adult analysis was already well established.

Today, reading this chapter as a contribution on its own, I see a faithful rendering of Freud's ideas and activities in supervising and guiding Hans' father, in applying Freud's own ideas to both understanding the case, and in guiding the father's interventions—at a time when no one had ever treated a child. These represent a wonderful illustration of Freud's genius. Arminda Aberastury fully understood that, and her narrative establishes this case as the beginning point of child analysis. Controversies are to follow: Can children, even in analysis, develop a transference neurosis (if there even is such a thing as a transference neurosis)? Are children capable of something approximating free association? Is the analyst more of a "real object" than a transference object? And can something approximating analysis even be done when the analyst is a parent instead of an unrelated clinician?

Looking back now, more than sixty years after the publication of her book in Spanish, I am impressed by what Aberastury could see and summarize. Naturally, there is much we can now add concerning Little Hans' family dynamics in the light of new information concerning his mother's psychopathology, intense marital conflict, and multiple suicides in his mother's family (Wakefield, 2007). We bring to bear new perspectives from years of experience recorded in the literature since then. And we dare hope that sixty years from now, a new generation of colleagues will build on what we are thinking, while still appreciating what we brought to the table.

There is unquestioned value in rereading classics like this to acknowledge these authors and their insights, rather than to take them for granted. So, I note and appreciate that Aberastury recounts with due gratitude the way that Freud illustrates the Oedipus complex, the fear of castration that troubled Hans, the importance of his mother's threats of castration in the form of his phobia, the trauma of the birth of his sister, his quest for truth in the face of the parents' obfuscation of the story of pregnancy and birth, and the role of his tonsillectomy in the development of his castration anxiety.

The Little Hans case, and Arminda's discussion of it, reveal many discoveries and validations of theory. However, there are some things illustrated in this faithful record of Freud's work with Little Hans and his father that were neither noted by Freud nor by Aberastury, but that we can now see. I will cite two as most prominent in the advance of psychoanalysis generally and specifically of child analysis.

The first is the role of transference. By the time of Freud's reporting the Little Hans case, he had discovered transference and its role in analysis, having described it in a postscript at the end of the Dora case (Freud, 1905e, pp. 116–119). But there is no reference to transference in the case of Little Hans, and, indeed, since the treatment was carried out by Little Hans' father, the dynamics of transference would have been difficult to deduce and describe. In the Dora treatment, although Freud described a paternal transference that he thought he had not handled well, he never saw his own role in symbolically repeating aspects of the trauma that Dora's treatment by her family had visited on her. However, I would note parenthetically that just as Freud "invented" child analysis in the case of Little Hans, he had already "invented" analysis for adolescents in that very Dora case, a fact that has generally been overlooked in the haste to criticize Freud for what he missed about Dora!

Transference—and for that matter countertransference—should also be considered integral to this case. We have smatterings of observations to draw on, for example, Hans' fear of castration which according to Freud, would have been at the hands of father. So, Hans is giving his associations directly to father, with (presumably) a mixture of admiration and idealization on the one hand, and fear and doubt on the other. For instance, Freud makes it clear that Hans does not really believe the story of the stork, and that Hans has his own story of pregnancy to pit against it. Little Hans tells his own story with his own fantasies and elaborations to his father, about whom he must have a profound mixture of feelings. What is the role of possible fear of retaliation in their relationship, or, for that matter, of the identification and idealizations that must also be present? And to what extent do father's interpretations seem intrusive or traumatic to Hans?

Furthermore, father is reporting the whole matter to Freud, an authority figure who father also idealizes and with whom he identifies. What is the role of that transference, and of unspoken countertransferences both in father and in Freud? Father is concerned for his son, of course, but is blindly following Freud's instructions. And it seems to me that Freud is rather over-the-moon to hear of a case that confirms his theories. Freud's idealizing transference to the case and to father is also palpable! And in a way, Aberastury's recounting of the story echoes that idealization, even though she is about to go on to describe what were by then more modern ideas of child development and treatment.

We can add to this that there is no mention of countertransference, a locus of experience and information which, following developments of Heimann (1950), Racker (1967), Winnicott (1947), and others, is now widely seen as central to all analytic process, and is a mainstay of decoding experience with children.

Transference and countertransference develop within and enrich the analytic relationship, which is of overriding importance in providing the holding and containment that make analysis possible. This multidimensional bond, conscious and unconscious, established through words, actions, expectations, and fantasies, makes analytic process and growth possible. The analytic relationship was exemplified by Freud's clinical work but went unremarked. Fairbairn (1958) described its centrality, locating the fulcrum of analytic action in the relationship rather than on any specific element such as interpretation, genetic reconstruction, confrontation, or dream analysis. Enrique Pichon-Rivière spoke of the analytic relationship as a link that each new patient–analyst couple forms, draws from, and contributes to within a preexisting analytic matrix from which they benefit and to which they bring change, just as a child is born into a preexisting set of family relationships which shape that child's development while the child's presence has a reciprocal impact on the evolution of the family and the social culture (Losso et al., 2017; Scharff et al., 2017). Freud's case report, and Arminda Aberastury's faithful summary of it, are precursors of these further developments.

In this opening chapter, Aberastury gives us the story of the foundation on which all later developments in child analysis have been built. She credits Freud, as she should, and leaves us eager to read the rest of her chapters in which she goes on to document her own and other developments built on this foundation.

CHAPTER 2

Birth of a technique

When other analysts tried to apply Freud's method for the treatment of adults to young patients, they faced almost insurmountable difficulties, with the most important being the inability to elicit verbal associations from the child. Thus, the fundamental instrument of adult analysis was lacking and the different ways of adapting the analytical method to the child's mind gave rise to techniques in child psychoanalysis.

One of the first attempts was that of Hermine Hug-Hellmuth (1921) whose method was to observe the game her patients played and play along with them, within their own environment. Unfortunately, she did not leave a true systematization of this method. Sophie Morgenstern in France and Anna Freud and Melanie Klein in Vienna developed their own methods and published the first books on child psychoanalysis.

Morgenstern (1937) worked at Heuyer's clinic where she studiously pored over children's stories, dreams, daydreams, games, and drawings, constantly searching for the latent content hidden underneath the manifest content. More than anything else, the value of her work lies in the exposition of the method of child analysis through drawings; a method which emerged during the treatment of a case of a ten-year-old boy who had suffered from total silence for two years. At the beginning of the analysis, he suffered from acute anxiety that was not spoken of, but was clearly expressed in drawings. Indeed, the only interpretable material was the art work the child made at the request of the psychoanalyst.

These drawings depicted huge objects, animals, and people, always facing him aggressively. The symbols repeated at a frenetic pace: a werewolf, animals with their tongues sticking out, a tongue with a padlock on it. The wolf symbolized the father and his anxiety in front of him. By means of an upside-down displacement, his genitalia were represented by the padlocked tongue. Here is a series of his drawings with comments from the analyst (Figures 2.1a and 2.1b).

The boy's castration anxiety had been intensified by traumatic situations and the expression of this anxiety, a crucial symptom in the case, disappeared entirely once it was interpreted. The patient regained

Drawing from November 21, 1926. Of enormous psychoanalytic interest, Santiago's drawing clearly captures the different phases of the castration scene.

Figure 2.1a. Castration anxiety in a ten-year-old boy.

Drawing of December 17, 1926. In front of a church, and separated from it by a large house, a man with the beard-tongue makes his first appearance.

Lower part of the picture of December 17. You see here a scene of castration, and beneath that you see Santiago grieving for being separated from his mother.

Drawing of December 24, 1926. The man with the cap is cutting Santiago's tongue.

Figure 2.1b. Castration anxiety in a ten-year-old boy (continued).

his speech, and this success encouraged Morgenstern to apply her method to all children, with pictures standing in for the free associations given by the adults. Her method was a valuable contribution to the field of child analysis and the material for drawings is still one of the most important resources today in non-analytic psychology as well as in psychoanalysis.

In analytical treatment of children, drawings and the symbols used in the drawings led to interpretation of their unconscious meaning. They were later of use to those who engage in analytic research as stepping stones to expanding and confirming their own conceptions. In cases like the one Morgenstern analyzed, where there is an intense inhibition of play, the drawings can be very useful. It is not uncommon, however, that the child draws little, except during the period between six and twelve years. I think this is because those children express their conflicts in play, and, except in special cases, they do not need another outlet for expression.

When children draw during a session, it is preferable they do so freely, adding words or making gestures that have the value of associations. If we do not understand what a child is expressing, we may question some details of the drawings or what they represent. But we should not overuse this approach. If we observe the total situation well, we can understand the child's drawing without questioning the child.

Vignettes of interpretation of drawing in child analysis

Luis, a nine-year-old boy who was asthmatic, suffered from a marked inhibition towards play, hardly spoke, and only drew. Luis either created or copied characters, usually from comic books, and recounted their conflict in detail. When he began his analysis with me, he was subjected to a very severe diet, because certain foods triggered severe asthma attacks followed by acetonemia. His limitations and his feeling of drowning were expressed by his drawing of a castaway on a small island (Figure 2.2).

The character was forced to stay on the island, an area so small that it required him to avoid movement, leaving him cowering. His only food

Figure 2.2. Luis' castaway island.

was fish, of which he was already fed up. It is interesting to note that the gravest mistakes in the upbringing of this child were keeping him on a quiet regime, completely contrary to the normal social demands of his age, and restricting his room size so he could hardly move in it. In the drawing, he condensed all these situations: the restriction, the drowning, his small room, and the limitation of nourishment.

Amanda, ten years old, told us about her sexual games with her brother through a drawing. "I'm going to paint a room," she said, but drew only the bed and nothing else. When she finished, she wanted to paint the quilt, but she started to jumble the colors and the bedspread expanded, becoming an overlapping collage of hues that covered the frame. The symbolic meaning of the confusion and flooding of boundaries was quite clear.

Maria, age ten, expressed the same situation with additional symbolism. She drew a house and a tree intertwining (Figure 2.3). "They are papa and mama," she said. Then, she drew another house, along with another tree, this one smaller (Figure 2.4). "It's me and my brother," she added. In other words, she and her brother played the same sexual games as their father and mother.

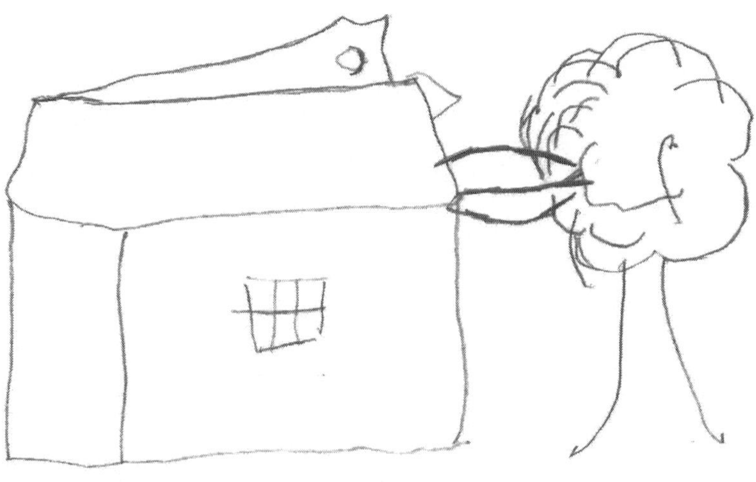

Figure 2.3. Maria's first house and tree.

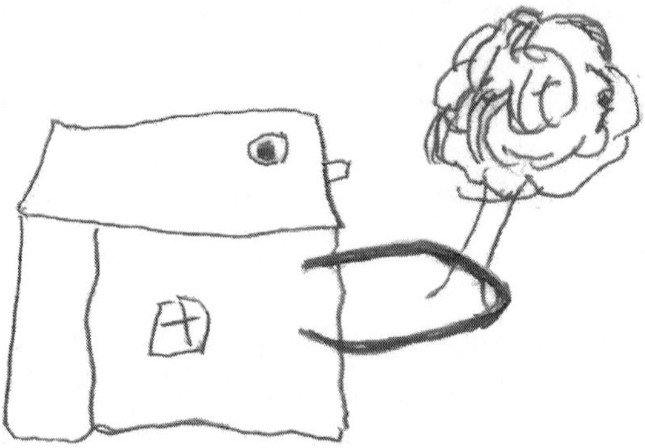

Figure 2.4. Maria's second house and tree.

Enrique, seven years old, who suffered from cryptorchidism, drew characters with two very marked characteristics: they had uniforms and their legs were always uneven, one shorter or skinnier than the other. The meaning of the uniform was to match, to be uniform with the others, and to unify his body. Its use was to iron out his defects in its cover of him. But his attempt failed, as represented by the maimed leg, which pointed to the abnormality of his testicles.

Paula, ten years old, an asthmatic girl, represented drowning by drawing children without a neck and with their arms emerging from the throat (Figure 2.5).

Figure 2.5. Paula's child.

Respiratory difficulty was also expressed through the drawing of houses with very small windows, which were placed very high, touching the ceiling (Figure 2.6). When her asthma attacks disappeared, she drew children with necks, as well as anatomically correct arms stemming from the shoulders. The house's windows were dropped to the correct height (Figure 2.7).

Figure 2.6. Paula's tall house.

Figure 2.7. Paula's windows.

Emilia, ten years old, represented her experience with analysis by drawing a little boat with two fishermen. "The fishermen are you and me," she said. She claimed the fishermen were taking out all their "macanas," a sort of truncheon. She then drew her "macanas." They were all illustrated representations of male genitalia. At that moment in her analysis, she was preoccupied by her concern for the difference between the sexes, as well her jealousy and envy of her brother, whom she imagined as her mother's favorite.

Theodore, eight years old, expressed his anguish over masturbation in a drawing (Figure 2.8).

The accusing hand was pointed to a chest, which he referred to as a "chest of secrets." The arrow that drove the hand started from the region of the genitals. The other accusing hand pointed to the bed and a spider bathed in light sitting on it, with which he tried to tell us that he masturbated in bed and at night. The character's face was that of a monster, thus expressing his fear of being caught, as well as his dread at the concept of transforming into a monster if he continued his masturbatory habits. The light also carried the meaning of a query in need of clarification.

Figure 2.8. Theodore's chest of secrets.

Estela, ten, expressed her guilt over the death of a little brother somewhat younger than her by drawing a house. Next to this, she drew a rope with washed men's clothes hanging on it. Through her analysis, it became clear that, due to special circumstances, she was believed to be guilty of her brother's death. She became ill as a result of the loss, and the parents sent her to a mountain retreat, separating her from them for two years. The house she drew was the one at the mountain retreat. It was clear that she thought her parents had thrown her out of the house as punishment for her brother's death.

In Switzerland, Madeleine Rambert (1938) published a work in which she presented a new technique for the analysis of children. It consisted of a game with puppets representing archetypal characters: father, mother, aunt, governess, teacher, doctor, lawyer, priest. The game included a variety of costumes meant to represent the gendarme, the devil, death, and other such concepts. According to Rambert, this method allows the child to express conflicts and situations that would be otherwise too difficult to verbalize and, in addition, it allows for the satisfaction of sadistic and masochistic fantasies that could not be released in daily life.

This method, although attractive, is only one way of focusing the problem, since there are many children whose inhibitions would prevent its use. Furthermore, it would not be practical to apply it to very young children. The characters can so clearly substitute the real parents, that this can make it difficult for a child to express their conflicts.

After these individual forays into finding a way to work clinically with children, two clinical researchers attempted to systematize a method of analysis for children: Anna Freud and Melanie Klein.

Anna Freud

In her research, Anna Freud recounts ten cases of children between the ages of six and twelve, all with severe neuroses, and through work with them she studies the scope, limits, and difficulties of analysis. She maintains that the situation of the child in the face of analytical treatment is different from that of the adult. The child is not aware of the disease and generally lacks a wish to be cured. In general, children do not suffer the consequences of their own disorders, do not come to the analysis of their own volition, and, lastly and most importantly, do not provide verbal associations, thus lacking a fundamental instrument for adult analysis. She searched for a method that would allow her to adapt the technique created by Freud for the treatment of adult patients to young patients.

For Anna Freud, part of the difficulty could be overcome by carrying out preparatory work to put the child in a position to face the analysis. This method is similar to that developed later for the analytical treatment of psychotics, in which prior non-analytic work puts the patient in a position to be analyzed. This preliminary phase intends to lead the child to understand the analytical effort and the therapeutic purpose, granting awareness of the disease as well as fostering a desire to modify the state.

Once the treatment has reached this point and the analytical work can begin, a problem arises: how to analyze the child? Anna Freud does not depend on the use of play as an element for analysis. She uses the interpretation of dreams, daydreams, and drawings. She reports that children dream and relate dreams easily; the clarity or incomprehensibility of these depend on the intensity of the resistance.

Children's dreams are generally easier to interpret than the dreams of adults, and are more direct expressions of wish fulfillment. The latent and manifest content are almost identical and the dream-craft is limited to the realization of satisfied wishes. Certain pleasant or painful situations can be elaborated as dreams, even in very young children. Milton Erickson (1941), for example, studied a dream in an eight-month-old boy whose father had to be absent for an extended period of time. The little boy used to play a game with his father that he found very pleasant. On the second night after the separation, he repeated all the movements of the game in his sleep, laughed as giddily as when he was playing, and then succumbed to a general relaxation, followed by a quiet, deep sleep.

In older children, dreams can also be interpreted without associations, because it is fairly common for a child to dream of simply repeating an event from the previous day. In the cited work, Milton Erickson recounts the case of a twenty-three-month-old boy who woke up screaming in anguish and expressed in his language, which was still rudimentary, that his sister had fallen and injured herself. This dream was the repetition of a real situation that had occurred a few days before. Indeed, his sister had fallen and hurt herself just as he'd dreamed it.

His mind was re-treading the traumatic situation and playing it out for him (Garma, 1948). When Sigmund Freud refers to childhood dreams, the cases often share wish fulfillment as a dominant theme. But in somewhat older children, those with a more structured ego and superego, dreams are already distorted by dream-craft. A ten-year-old boy, during an analysis focused on masturbation and its consequences, had a dream he described vividly.

"The maids burn matches on the table, the tablecloth is burned and not the blanket underneath. It seems strange to me that Mom said that the mattress can burn," he says.

The latent content of the dream is an attempt to reassure himself against the dangers of masturbation.

Anna Freud teaches the processes of performing the interpretation of dreams during the psychoanalytic treatment of children. She highlights the collaboration of the "little patient." She suggests that the dream does not come out of nowhere and that the child must help her find the reason for the dream. The child habitually recounts the events that have arisen on that or previous days, sometimes providing a certain type of association that can be used in the same way as the free association of the adult. The child accepts with pleasure the interpretation of the dreams and assists in the search for latent elements with the same interest with which they might complete a puzzle.

A case from Anna Freud

I will cite one of the cases Anna Freud (1927b) presented. The patient was a nine-year-old who, after just five months of analysis, began to refer to masturbation. The sensation of heat that she felt in her genitals was so intense that she could not tolerate warm clothes, was beginning to fear fire, and could not bear having a lit gas stove near her room. On the day before the dream, the housekeeper had asked for the girl's help lighting the stove, since she was unable to do so alone. The girl dreamed that she could help her housekeeper to light it easily but the stove exploded, and then, as punishment, the nanny put her in the fire to burn. The manipulation of the stove meant the manipulation of her genitals; the mistake that appears in the manifest content is the expression of her criticism of masturbation, with the explosion standing in for her type of orgasm.

Two months later, she related another dream that allowed the interpretation to be completed. In this dream, two bricks were on the furnace and she was afraid that the house was about to catch fire until someone took off the bricks. When the girl woke up, she had her hand on her genital organs, forming an association to the part of the dream that referred to bricks. She had been previously assured that if one puts bricks on one's head, the head will stop growing. With this association in mind, the interpretation becomes simple. The inability to "grow up" is one of the punishments for onanism. The meaning of the fire, in this dream as in the previous one, is sexual arousal. While she is masturbating, she remembers the prohibition to masturbate and feels fear. Finally, the stranger removing the bricks is possibly the analyst, with her reassuring statements.

Working with a dream

During the treatment of a twelve-year-old girl suffering from ulcerative colitis, the girl's therapist, Sara G. de Jarast (1958), pointed out to me that the analysis was developed mainly through dream interpretation. According to her, this increase in dream activity was due to the age and characteristics of the patient who had a conflict between destroying and being destroyed. During her analysis, which lasted eighteen months and consisted of five or six weekly sessions, she brought two or more dreams to each session. Her effort to understand them, as well as the co-elaboration she provided the therapist, made many of these dreams come through with exceptional clarity.

For example, at a decisive moment in the analysis, during which there was great concern about the outcome of her treatment, she had the following dream:

"I was in a canoe with other boys, headed down a river that ended in a muddy stream. I went down and walked there. There were rigid nuns on both sides who stared at me. I continued on foot and found some critters with Bambi faces, but they were ferocious dogs that bared their teeth and grinned."

The river that turns into a stream and then into mud mimics and symbolizes the transformation sequence of stool. She associated the animals with Bambi, a character in an animated movie where the mother dies, leaving her child abandoned and helpless in the middle of a storm. Ultimately, it is the father who saves him, and Bambi needs to lean on him to grow. The child felt intense guilt in the face of her fantasy of her mother's death and feared that her hatred might kill her.

The nuns were a part of her superego, rigid and inexorable; they symbolized the prohibition of becoming a woman, of growing up, of the demand for instinctual renunciation. The Bambi creatures with the mouths of ferocious dogs represented the ulcers that she experienced as caused by the mother biting her, as well as her *own* unfulfilled desires to bite.

Her growing difficulties and her fear of becoming a woman are clearly present in another dream, which she elaborated on when she had to enter high school. This transition meant, at least for her unconscious, a drastic and sudden journey from girl to teenager.

"I was in a subway station, where a train was moving slowly. I ran and stretched more and more, trying to reach it, because my schoolmates were in it."

Reaching the train symbolized the rate of growth of her sisters, who had developed quickly in reality. She felt that she was stuck in a certain stage of development—the oral incorporative stage—and that, due to not being able to stretch enough, her companions would keep moving forward, even as she diminished. In actuality, she simply appeared younger than she was because she was small and thin.

These difficulties were corroborated in another dream.

"Maria, who is the maid, buys me a pair of shoes with high heels. But the heels are made of cardboard and I fall." Maria was the mother who did not support her in her growth and, in the transfer, the therapist as well.

On another occasion she dreamt the following:

"I am going to the Zoological Garden. There, many cages are filled with good animals. But, suddenly, they all transform into beasts." In this case, the caged animals clearly represent the internalized conflicts in the intestine. She felt trapped and caged. At the time, she was dealing with bouts of diarrhea and experiencing the suddenness of fiercely eruptive fecal matter. These were behaviors she associated with wild animals.

Daytime dreams, images, and the positive transference

Along with the interpretation of subconscious dreams, Anna Freud (1947) also highlighted the importance of daytime dreams. She put forth the idea that the narration of these fantasies could be useful in the analysis of children whose unique psychic situation would make the fantasies, in the context of this approach, more relatable than in adults. Another technique she used in tandem with this was her interpretation of drawings. She clearly pointed out that, in general, the drawings repeat or complete the material of daydreams and dreams. She cites, for example, the case of a girl with obsessive neurosis, who would often pair accounts of her anal fantasies with drawings.

She considers that, at least for a limited time, a child kept in a positive transference situation will, out of love for the analyst, produce a certain type of association that, although isolated, is immensely helpful in analytic work. She cites the case of a girl who relied on her babysitter as a way of guarding against the analyst's attempt to free her of that dependency and of her masturbation habit. The resistance to analysis was resolved when Anna Freud asked the girl to see pictures in her mind. The child closed her eyes and, adopting a strange squatting position, continued to describe everything that happened within herself in great detail. She saw her nanny surrounded by dancing demons and flying over the sea. This meant to Anna Freud that she could pry her from her babysitter but then the girl would no longer have any protection against her temptation to masturbate and would be vulnerable to the analyst's efforts, which might make her mean.

Regarding the analysis of playful activity, Anna Freud does not give child's play the same value as verbal associations in the analytical treatment of adults, and maintains that it is only a technique assistant, even though Sigmund Freud, whose approach she valued highly, had laid the foundations for child analytic play technique. Sigmund Freud (1920g) closely observed a little boy who threw down a reel and got it back again, making it appear and disappear, thus trying to control his anguish in the face of the inconsistent presence of his mother. He showed how, by playing, the boy could part with her without any danger of losing her, since the reel came back whenever he desired. This game thus allowed the boy to unload aggressive love fantasies in front of his mother without any risk, since he was the absolute owner of the situation, allowing him to elaborate on his anxieties in the face of the unavoidable separations that reality imposed on him.

Melanie Klein

The technique created by Melanie Klein (1932) is based on the use of play and builds upon Freud's investigations. She proposes that a child at play can overcome painful realities and instinctive fears by projecting them to the outside and onto toys. This mechanism is possible because the child develops the capacity to symbolize early on. Displacement of the internal situation towards the external world increases the importance of the real objects. If, at first, these objects are suffused with hatred and loaded with destructive impulses, then, through transformative play, they become a refuge against anxiety arising from that hatred.

The toy allows the child to overcome the fear of objects as well as the fear of internal dangers. It is fantasy, tested and made possible by reality. In this way, the toy acts as a "bridge between fantasy and reality." What I have observed in children allows me to confidently affirm that, if given due time and sufficient play, they will progressively adapt to reality. Each stage of development requires certain games that must be understood and facilitated so as not to hinder their normal evolution.

Play technique applied to both treatment and diagnosis does not exclude the use and interpretation of dreams, daydreams, and drawings. However, I have observed that, if they are offered the possibility of expressing themselves through play, and the selected games are interpreted appropriately, children will report few dreams or no dreams, with a similarly low output in drawing. Of course, in special cases, like in some of the aforementioned analyses, inhibitions to play determine that children express themselves through dreams and drawings.

Games, like dreams, are meaningful activities. The function of the game is to elaborate traumatic situations that are excessive for the ego. Dreams fulfill a cathartic and slow assimilation function through the repetition of daily events and role changes. This process can, in short, make active what has been passively suffered. Play does not suppress tendencies. Rather, it channels them. This is why the child who plays represses less than the child who finds it difficult to dramatize their conflicts effectively. We saw this when Freud's young patient played with his reel, making it appear and disappear, as a means to try to overcome the anguish caused by his mother's absence.

Another child, Joaquín, was less than two years old when he was gifted a younger brother. In the days leading up to Christmas, he played for hours at drowning, destroying, and annihilating baby Jesus, only to later save and restore him, thus unloading his burdensome and contradictory affections for his new sibling as he tried to adapt to the situation. A child who has suffered the ordeal of an operation commonly creates a game out of the situation. This often consists of a doll suffering through a similar procedure, while the child takes on the role of the surgeon. Children who suffer from difficulties at school tend to play school-based games, taking on the role of harsh teachers who punish and reprimand underachievers.

Another apt example of the value of a game is hide-and-seek, which serves the purpose of reassurance when faced with the possible eradication of loved ones, and peek-a-boo is the first game observed in babies. During the analytical treatment of children, it is an unwritten rule that, during any transference phase, the fear of loss can be worked out by playing this game with the therapist, as described to me by Lidia S. de Forti. A common time for this game to appear is when the end of treatment is announced, or whenever any such loss is anticipated. Observation of infants has shown that hide-and-seek is one way for the baby to work through the depressive position (A. Pichon-Rivière, 1946).

Clinical examples of play

Six-year-old Julia, who was raped by an adult, constantly played at putting bigger things in small holes. "It's hard to put something big in something small," she would repeat monotonously as she played. Next, she drew a girl whose skirt had a demon ornament on it, saying at the end: "It is inside her."

Pedro, ten years old, who was being analyzed for presenting multiple neurotic symptoms, was struggling with learning difficulties, lacked a connection with the outside world, was plagued with fears of poisoning, and was riddled with homosexual aggression (A. Pichon-Rivière, 1946). He was known to burn cotton during his sessions. He understood that it reminded him of something that aroused great anxiety and irritation, but he felt powerless to try to ascertain what it was. During one of the sessions, while tediously burning the cotton, he related to me that his mother had dispensed an unjust punishment on him that day. He then had an intense anxiety attack and recalled an incident suffered when he was five years old: he was a boarding student in a school where he suffered severe and unjust punishments by one of the teachers and always hid, out of fear, his wishes for revenge against her. He waited with anticipation for August 19, a Swiss national holiday, in which, according to him, "everything was allowed." That day, he tried to burn her blouse, which was made of cotton. "That's the one I wanted to burn when I burned the cotton," he said. He did not succeed and this created a bitter sense of helplessness in the face of his teachers and their injustice. These first traumatic experiences in his relationship with the teachers, which repeated before him the overwhelming frustrations suffered in the first two years of his life, made it enormously difficult to stay in contact with the outside world and stay up to speed in his education.

Carlos, an enuretic boy who had suffered a homosexual aggression when he was four years old, was intensely afraid of being damaged and worried that his penis could no longer function normally. He would create fish (symbols of his penis) with a broken tail (symbol of homosexual aggression). This same child had strong feelings of guilt in front of his younger sister, who was also enuretic. He thought that the sexual games he performed with her, and the fact that they consisted specifically of forced oral sex, were the cause of her disorder.

He symbolized it during treatment in a game in which he prepared pudding cups for the sister, who would eat them and get sick. Other forms of sexual games were expressed through the exchange of objects with his sister, with Carlos gifting her phallic symbols like sticks, pencils, revolvers, and then demanding that she give him small bags, purses, or boxes, which symbolized the female genitalia. In this game, which was repeated with me during treatment, he was always afraid of harming both of us and of taking the most valuable thing, suffering obsessive doubts before deciding on each exchange (A. Pichon-Rivière, 1951).

Juan, ten years old, was working out his conception that the mother had inside her dangerous penises that he had stolen from his father. He played with a warship that lost all its guns and was transformed into an aircraft carrier, where he could land safely. In this way, he tried to elaborate his fear of the female genitalia, from which he removed all the dangerous cannons—which for him symbolized penises that could destroy him.

Eight-year-old José played for several sessions with figurines, and though I tried to join in and promised to play according to his rules, he would invent a new one every time, sometimes on cue, just so I could never win. If I tried to rebel against these modifications, he would yell, "Inconsiderate! Ungrateful!" and many similar reproaches. In this game, he elaborated his conflicts with his mother, whom he saw as a highly irritable woman. Her biggest mistake was clearly the inconsistency in her educational norms, which changed according to her mood. If she was happy, she would allow anything and everything. In a second, however, she could swing to a punishment or a limitation. When the boy protested as a result of these changes, she would reproach him by reminding him how tender she had been with him moments prior.

Fantasies, desires, and experiences shown in play

Oral experiences are expressed in terms of filling containers with content. There are children who only play to fill, but cannot decide to remove anything from the content. They are children who have lived through very painful experiences of oral frustration, who have suffered from strong envy and fear of abandonment, and whose play is an attempt to keep intact the source of gratification that is the mother, so as to not expose themselves to future deprivation. It is also a defense against an intense desire to destroy it all, caused by envy and frustration. Similarly deprived children may choose some food and proceed to sell it, give it to the dolls, or gift it to the analyst, but then demand immediate restitution.

Others play at buying and selling things, characteristically rotten or poisoned food, which corresponds with eating disorders. These children usually suffer from anorexia, and the reason for their fear of poisoning emerges in the first months of life. A child who sucks from an empty breast, or one with little milk, attributes the hunger pains and discomfort to the breast, seeing it as something that poisons and destroys. All subsequent meals maintain this meaning.

Others, when playing, suspect that the weight of items is purposefully inaccurate, and that when they buy, the fictitious store is giving them less than what they paid for. The interpretation of this situation is obvious.

Experiences with cleanliness also appear, specifically in games in which, suffering from anguish and a fear of dirtying, the children pass contents from one vessel to another. The details of the game are revealing of each individual experience.

A girl whose learning to be clean was too early and abrupt relived these experiences in the analysis. It led to her smearing paint on her hands and arms. She then asked me to remove her panties and take her to the bathroom. When I was on the way to the bathroom, she asked me for something to eat. Thus, she subjected me to a sort of test: whether or not I was capable of gratifying her, even if she got dirty.

All of these examples add validity to the claim that

> the child expresses his fantasies, desires and experiences in a symbolic way through toys and games. In doing so, he uses the same archaic-phylogenetic means of expression, the same language that is familiar to us in dreams, and we will only fully understand this language if we approach it as Freud has taught us to approach the language of dreams. Symbolism is only a part of that language. If we wish to correctly understand the child's play in relation to the totality of the behavior during the analysis, we must not restrict ourselves to a mere unspooling of meaning that deals with each symbol separately. However clear those symbols might be, we must also take into account the mechanisms and forms of representation used in dream work, being careful to not lose sight of the relationship of each factor to the overall situation. (Klein, 1932, p. 27)

During the analysis of children, it is common for a toy or a game to take on different meanings according to the overall situation. Therefore, a game is only understood and interpreted when the global analytical situation in which it has occurred is taken into account. A doll, for example, will sometimes represent a penis, sometimes a generic child, sometimes the specific child himself.

> The *material* that children produce during an analytic hour, as they pass from play with toys to dramatization in their own persons and, again, to playing with water, cutting out paper, or drawing; the *manner* in which they do this; the *reason* why they change from one to another; the *means* they choose for their representations—all this medley of factors, which so often seems confused and meaningless, is seen to be in perfect conformity with a plan and the underlying sources and thoughts are revealed to us if we interpret them just like dreams. (Klein, 1927, p. 32, fn. 6)

The game takes place in the consulting room, within certain temporal and spatial limitations. The distances and proportions with respect to the child and the therapist, as well as the child's mobility or immobility in the clinic, can teach us a lot about the relationship with space and body scheme. When the child plays, the most common drive is to try to represent something. We could say that the child is fighting *for* that something, and all these meanings must be interpreted to gain access to the deepest layers of the mind.

When interpreting a game, we must consider:

1) Its representation in the space
2) The traumatic situation involved
3) Why it is surfacing here and now, in our presence specifically
4) The role of the set dressing, costuming, grace, humor, or anger in the game. This, like the dream, is an activity full of meaning and is the basis of all subsequent learning or sublimation.

The understanding and interpretation of the preverbal expressions in the child have led us to the creation of diagnostic methods based on play and drawing. The observation of the first hour of play, as we will see in Chapter 7, allows us to know the unconscious fantasy of illness and cure. It enables us to evaluate the severity of the neurosis according to the level of play. This observation has become a standard method for diagnosis of infantile neuroses (A. Pichon-Rivière, 1950b, 1958c).

In children over five years of age, we add the interpretation and appreciation of the "House Building Game" (A. Pichon-Rivière, 1950a) and the drawing of the human figure. In the House Building Game, made with a special material that allows for the accurate reproduction of all the aspects of a real home, the child expresses many of their own fundamental conflicts. It can also be observed that the body scheme is modified and in what way it has been changed. Severe neurotic or psychotic children do not build houses according to a criterion of reality proportional to their chronological age. An eight-year-old child, for instance, would consciously know that a house has a floor, a roof, walls, doors, and windows. They would, however, forget to add some of these elements, or else use them incorrectly. When elements are missing or used improperly, construction becomes difficult or impossible. Although children consciously understand this, they nevertheless feel unable to find the solution. All these deformations are due to internal conflicts that have a meaning and can be interpreted, and they reveal to us the body scheme of their engineer.

According to Schilder (1958), the bodily self, scheme of the body, or image of the body is a creation, a construction, not a given. It is not concerned with a figure, but focuses on the *production* of a figure instead. The image of the body is not a static phenomenon. It is acquired, erected, and achieved in continuous contact with the world. As it is not a structure, but a structuring, it undergoes continuous changes in relation to external and internal events. Body image is mutable. It can retract, expand, connect part of the exterior world with the interior. It erects itself, rebuilding itself each time it falls. Emotional influences change the relative value and clarity of different parts of the body, according to libidinal tendencies, and this change, which can affect the total body surface area or can change certain strengths in the body, is most aptly expressed in the deformations of the construction. In line with the symbolic content of the house, all these deformations or changes of the body scheme determine which parts of the house correspond with which modifications suffered by the builder.

Each child values a part of the house they build, emphasizes something that another element will cancel out, adds something that does not exist, or eliminates fundamental parts in the construction. The language used in this game is spatial language, which expresses one's experience in space, as well as one's current situation in relation *to* space and one's own body.

Maribel and her house

We will now relate the case of Maribel, observed by Lidia S. de Forti, in which the emphasis was placed on the construction of the roof, which symbolically represents the mind. The roof (Figure 2.9) had the following characteristics: it had a double configuration marked A and A1, and the space between the two roofs was enclosed by bars so that "no one could escape."

The traumatic situation that caused Maribel's illness transformed repeated "secrets" and "lies" that her environment imposed on her into "truths," demanding that she share them. Maribel's mother, whose first marriage was unhappy, became pregnant with her while still finalizing her divorce, making it impossible to legalize the situation at the time. Maribel was unwanted and her parents married seven months after her birth, marking her, at that time, as a newborn. Her parents lived with

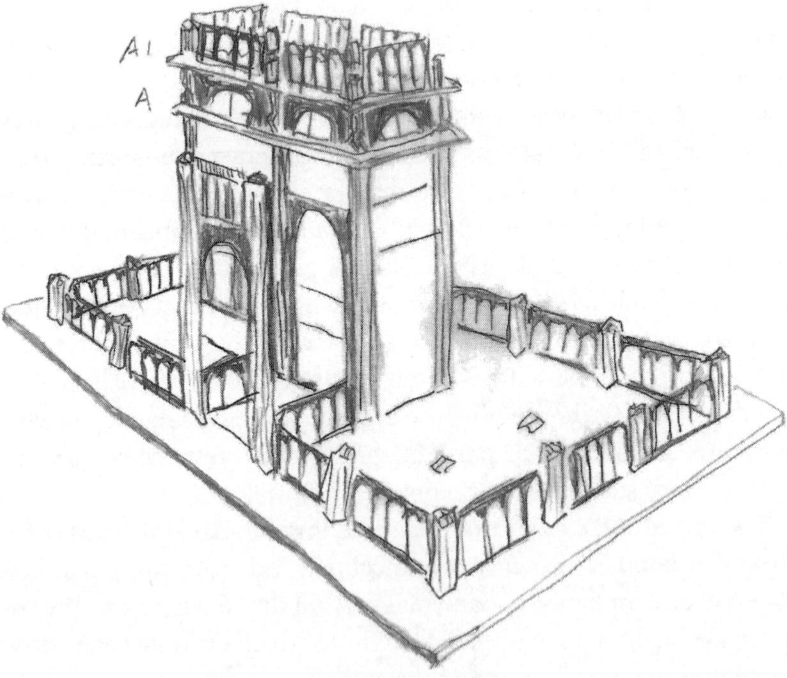

Figure 2.9. Maribel's roof design options.

her in relative harmony until she was two years old, at which point the father went abroad and married another woman.

Upon learning that the girl's mother was now living with a man with whom she'd had another daughter, the father decided that Maribel should live with him. As he could not achieve it amicably, he resorted to kidnapping. While she lived with her mother, Maribel was assured that her real father was not the one who had lived with them and whom she saw periodically, but that it was this other one who was living with them at that time. In turn, the father, when he kidnapped her and took her to live with him, told her that the real mother was not the one who had lived with her until then, but was the woman who was there with him now, and demanded that she call that woman mother.

The girl remembered her mother and asked about her, but in a feeble attempt to make her forget, her father and his woman friend told her that the actual mother was only a friend who took care of her at a time when her real mother was ill. The girl continued to interrogate them for a while and refused to use the term "mom" to refer to her stepmother. After the birth of her sister, the girl stopped asking questions and submitted to what was required of her. Then, a true obsession awoke in her. She longed to know all the details regarding sexual life. This curiosity, and the habit of talking about dirty things in a rude way at school, made her parents fear that the families of her friends and classmates would shun her. This was one of the reasons for the inquiry into her mental state. In addition, she suffered from terrible nightmares, from which she awoke with an intense need to urinate and a startling lack of memory regarding her dreams.

When they consulted us, the patient was eleven years old and in fifth grade. The father believed that the symptoms were related to the reported trauma and was willing to clarify the situation. The mother, on the other hand, was stubbornly opposed to any clarification, and maintained that the girl did not understand or remember anything regarding the story. She even considered it counterproductive to make her aware of the truth.

The first years of life were thus recounted by the father. Maribel was not the result of a planned pregnancy. The mother breastfed her until she was five months old and had a good relationship with the girl. Maribel reacted to weaning with intestinal disorders and always had restless sleep.

The parents did not remember any details regarding her first steps or the general process of walking, language acquisition, and toilet training. She excelled at school. While finishing the house (Figure 2.9), Maribel said "It will be boring." She drew the roof marked A. Then, she lengthened the poles by adding smaller poles. These she balanced in a rather unstable fashion, supporting them only by one point of contact. Between the poles she added, she placed thick, metal bars, and, on top of them, she placed another roof (marked as A1). I think it is impossible to find a better way of expressing how untenable the demand for secrecy was for Maribel. The fence that surrounds the building reveals her distrust of the outside world due to increased paranoid anxiety. I would like to emphasize, in particular, the symbolism of the double ceiling as an expression of the dual version of fused maternity and paternity, with the required secrecy looming large and putting up a concerted effort to restrict the truth. When asked who lives in her house, she slips up.

"Dad, mom, mom and the boys, a little one and a big one," she says. Through this mistake, she reveals that she already knows the truth.

In addition, the six rooms built are designated as a dining room, two bedrooms, a kitchen, and a room for the children to play. The key detail here is what is missing: the child forgets to note the fate of the bathroom, actively repressing the symbol of the sexual and the dirty. In this forgetfulness, she expresses the repression imposed on true knowledge. Additionally, the drawing of the human figure, with and without its clothes, revealed valuable insight into the diagram of the child's body. We agree with Enrique Pichon-Rivière that a child five years or older is able to reproduce the human figure accurately, and that each deformation in the representation corresponds, as they do in the construction of the house, to interpretable internal conflicts. When drawing the human body, children with asthma or serious breathing difficulties tend to suppress the neck and draw the arms in the neck region. This symbolizes the suffocation itself, as well as the posture that usually corresponds with shortness of breath.

Epileptic children draw slowly, holding the pencil with such force that it can pierce the paper. They tend to obsessively trace over the same line, or keep scratching at a cut they've already made. The arms usually show a marked inequality, both in length and thickness, thus symbolizing what is expressed in construction through the unevenness of the sticks.

In hypochondria, the intercostal spaces are marked, and in extreme cases, the gastrointestinal tract. Rodolfo, five years old, suffered from asthma, recurrent angina, sinusitis, and intestinal parasitosis. He was left-handed and wanted to become a woman. He had suffered repeated homosexual assaults by his older brother, and his parents did not seem to have effectively supported him through this situation. In his first analysis session, he showed, through drawing, his breathing difficulties, his feeling of collapse, and his feminization fantasies. He expressed an unconscious fantasy that showcased these symptoms by drawing a house with a single window that was almost attached to the ceiling. The imperfection and destruction of his body were externalized and concretized in the features cut from the walls and the base. His difficulty with concentration, later confirmed by the mother, was expressed by the hole in the ceiling (Figure 2.10).

Rodolfo's ideas regarding the differences between the sexes were very confusing. He was especially perplexed by the role that each of the sexes had in procreation. This was shown in Figure 2.11.

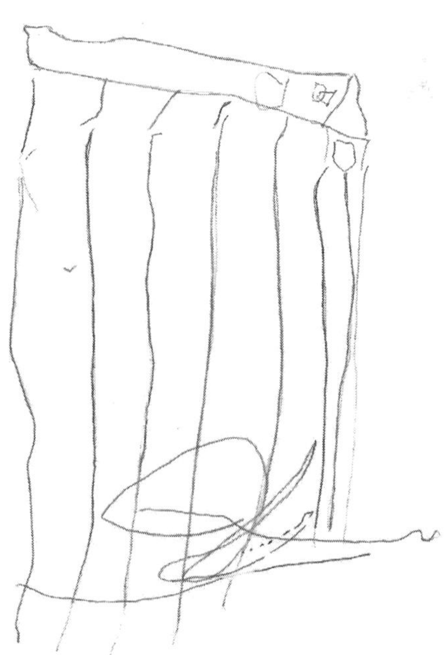

Figure 2.10. Rodolfo's imperfect house.

Figure 2.11. Rodolfo's gender confusion.

Indeed, if we were to draw a vertical line down the middle of the drawing and observe both sides comparatively, there would be obvious discrepancies in the length of the hair, the thickness of the arms, and the shape of the hands. His befuddlement is most apparent on the left side of the drawing, where he placed the invaginated penis with three tips, which, being the youngest of three siblings, he associated with the three seeds that fertilized the mother. We see that the two genders, the feminine and the masculine, are represented in the genitalia, pointing to a dichotomy inherent to the conflict.

In summary, playtime, house construction, and the representation of the body are useful methods of observation in order to diagnose the infantile neuroses of children over five years of age. In children below this age, we must resort to merely watching the play. Once the neurosis has been properly assessed, it organizes the case and indicates the treatment to be recommended, as we will point out in Chapter 8.

Commentary on Chapter 2

Lea Sofer de Setton (Panama)

Arminda Aberastury, pioneer in child and adolescent psychoanalysis in Latin America, started as an auto-didactic and became interested in creating a theory and a technique for work with children. Teaching herself, Arminda studied the writings of Freud and Anna Freud. Her interest in child analysis began in 1937 in Hospicio de las Mercedes where she worked with her husband, a renowned analyst, Enrique Pichon-Rivière. While he was attending a woman patient, her daughter was waiting outside in the hall. That eight-year-old girl couldn't read or write, and her diagnosis was oligophrenia. Arminda observed this girl and tried to teach her. Reading Anna Freud, Arminda came to believe that the diagnosis was wrong and the child couldn't learn because she didn't want to know about her mother's illness.

Arminda traced the history of child analysis beginning with Sigmund Freud and his case of Little Hans (1909b). Freud did not treat Hans himself except once, but he worked with the observations Hans' father brought him, figuring out the symbolic meaning of the child's play and surmising his fantasies of castration. From this early case, Freud built a base for comprehending the preverbal language of children and interpreting the meaning of their words for the child's benefit. This case introduced concepts concerning the power of infantile sexuality, castration anxiety, the Oedipus complex, and the understanding of phobias. The learning from that case was tremendous. Arminda recognized that Freud had laid the foundation for child's analytic play technique but she realized that he had not covered everything. He had not investigated details regarding the mother's experience of the pregnancy and birth, the infant's response to breastfeeding, the acquisition of early language and walking in relation to the emergence of teeth, or the severity of toilet training. His psychoanalytic method relying on free association in the verbal dimension was not adequate for the treatment of young children. Anna Freud followed her father in valuing the interpretation of dreams as the royal road to the unconscious, and she used this technique with children too She helped her child patients to analyze the manifest content of their dreams and reach the latent content, which she understood to be the oedipal material she had learned about from her father. Arminda learned from Anna Freud, but she regretted that Anna did not use play as freely for unconscious communication and analytic interpretation as Arminda herself would learn to do.

Arminda turned to the work of Hug-Hellmuth (1921) who began observing children's games in their own environment. She studied the work of Sophia Morgenstern (1937) in France whose interest was to understand the latent content of children's stories, dreams, daydreams, games, and drawings. Similarly, Anna Freud used dreams, daydreams, and drawings in her work with children. Arminda acknowledged the impact of all these women on contributing to an important aspect of child analysis, still in use today.

Arminda presents several vignettes on the interpretation of drawing in child analysis. She showed how children could present their life situation in their drawings. Luis, an asthmatic nine-year-old who felt afraid of drowning and who was kept on a severe diet, expressed his limitations in a character, cast away on an island, surrounded by water, and where he could eat only fish. Like Luis, Paula, was also asthmatic and shared Luis' fear of drowning. She represented her feelings in images of children without a neck.

The drawings of Luis and Paula reminded me of my case of Natan, a nine-year-old boy who drew a school in which the police came to force discipline on the children. From this drawing I learned that Natan used to punish himself every time he felt he misbehaved.

In 1938, Madeleine Rambert in Switzerland described her new technique for the analysis of children. She used a game with puppets of different archetypal characteristics such as father, mother, aunt, governess, teacher, and doctor through which children could show the conflicts that they couldn't put into words. Arminda added this to her interest in drawings as she built her own technique.

When Aberastury discovered Klein, she studied her work intensively to learn Klein's technique with very young children, building her understanding from the use of play as well as the interpretation of dreams and fantasies. Aberastury exchanged letters about technique with Klein from 1945 to 1958, met Klein, and was in supervision with her (Figures 2.12 and 2.13). For Klein the child creates the play to be able to elaborate on what is happening and process it with the analyst's help. The child has the capacity to symbolize and displaces his internal conflicts onto the external world. In the treatment session, the external world is represented in play; and the toys are the connection between fantasy and reality. Toys and games have different meaning according to the total situation, the psychoanalytic space, the trauma, and the affect expressed.

Arminda discovered the House Building Game, and developed it not only as an aid in the diagnosis of infantile neurosis but also as a treatment tool (A. Pichon-Rivière 1950a). The house is built with special material that fits together to create the shape of a real house of various designs. Deformations of the construction of the house are interpreted as expressions of various internal conflicts. She also used the drawing of the human figure in her work. Arminda presents examples of cases where fantasies, desires, and experiences are shown in play that includes drawings, puppet play, house construction, and dreams.

In work with dreams, Arminda found that the clarity of the dream narrative and the analyst's understanding of the dream depends on the intensity of the resistance to the emergence of the unconscious desires and their expression in the transference. In children, dreams may so directly reveal the desires that the latent and manifest content are almost identical. Children's dreams may simply repeat the events of the day before without symbolization and therefore need no interpretation. Or the dream content may be replayed in the play session and allow for interpretation of the resistance seen in the dream and the unconscious transference in the play.

In Arminda's view, an analysis cannot end until the patient has adequate language, which allows more adaptation to reality. The analysis must continue because child analysis is not only to cure the child, but to prevent future disorders.

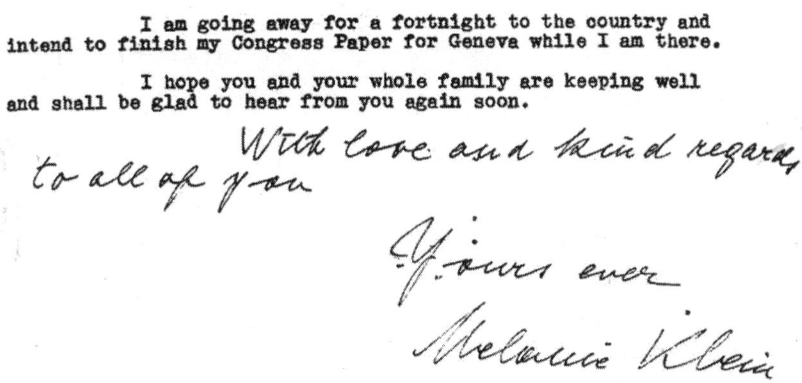
I am going away for a fortnight to the country and intend to finish my Congress Paper for Geneva while I am there.

I hope you and your whole family are keeping well and shall be glad to hear from you again soon.

With love and kind regards to all of you

Yours ever

Melanie Klein

Figure 2.12. Closing of a letter to Arminda from Melanie Klein.

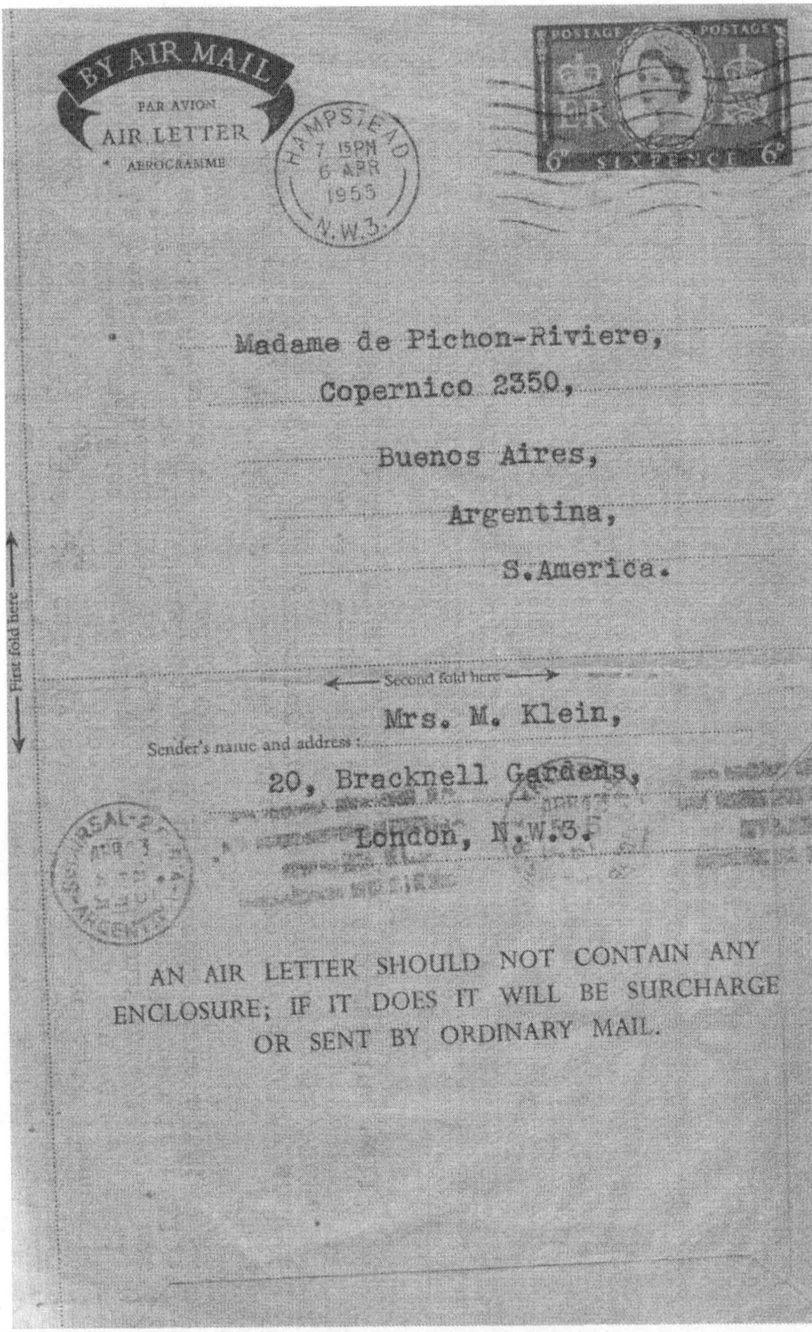

Figure 2.13. Letter from Klein to Aberastury, April 3, 1955.

CHAPTER 3

Two streams in child psychoanalysis: Anna Freud and Melanie Klein

When the first child analysts encountered the common hurdle of a four- or five-year-old patient being unable to freely associate as an adult does, they were disheartened. The dissatisfaction deepened when comparing the results with those obtained by Freud from Little Hans' case. The difficulties they encountered had not arisen in that case, mainly due to the fact that the child was talking to his father in his own house. Perhaps because of this, the first analysts thought that the solution was to analyze the children at home, instead of in the consulting room. They soon saw that, while this situation *seemed* simple, it actually added unnecessary complications to the relationship with the patient and the family. It started becoming clear that a therapy session needed to be carried out in the right setting, and it was necessary to find a technique that would make this possible.

It was only through the works of Anna Freud and Melanie Klein that child analysis techniques were under discussion. From the first moment, fundamental differences were raised between the two directions. The arguments were centered on the transference approach, specifically on differences that implied theoretical divergences on concepts such as the formation of the ego and the superego, the Oedipus complex, and the object relationship. From this divide, two schools in the psychoanalysis of children emerged.

According to Anna Freud, children have an immature infantile superego and they do not have the capacity for transference and, therefore, prior non-analytical work is necessary in order to prepare them for analytical work. This includes making them aware of the disease, instilling confidence in the analysis and in the analyst, and creating a positive transference through the external decision to internally analyze oneself. Anna Freud adapts her method to different cases. In some, she adapts to all the whims of the child. In others, her technique follows the ups and downs of the child's humor. In yet others, she will demonstrate her superiority or ability, transforming herself into an interesting, useful, and powerful person whose help the child can no longer do without. The therapist's only concern in each case is to create a sufficiently strong and positive bond, in order to ensure continuation of treatment. (In later works, she partially modifies, abbreviates, or eliminates the preparatory phase prior to introducing the child directly into the analytic situation.)

In Anna Freud's view, we cannot speak of a transference neurosis in children because children do not experience their analysts as new editions of their parents: They have not exhausted the old edition. She holds that the only way a child could develop a transference neurosis is to remove the child from the home, and that would bring difficulties in adjusting back to the family home and a likely return of symptoms. In the course of analytic treatment, the neurotic symptoms of adults transform gradually as they abandon the old objects to which their fantasies clung until then, concentrating their neuroses instead on their analysts, transforming the old neurosis into a transference neurosis. For Anna Freud, none of this happens in the analysis of children, and there is no easily interpretable transference.

We see a limitation here. By avoiding analyzing the destructive fantasies of the child in the analysis, dissolving the negative transference by non-analytical means, and forcing the patient to experience a sort of transference idyll, the little patients had to act out all the destructive fantasies that arose, because they were not interpreted in the transference situation and in its relationship with the original objects. Empathy transforms the analyst, for the moment, into a good object but at the cost of a future dissociation between good and bad objects, and a reinforcement of the patient's pathological defenses, and makes the negative transference more difficult to handle. Even if this "good" phase leads to the progress of the analysis, it is interfered with by the repression of fantasies about the "bad" analyst. Furthermore, when the analyst is kept artificially "good", the patient will choose someone else as the persecutor; this figure being generally a family member that is far less prepared than the analyst to deal with the hostility of the patient.

The need to confer an educational role on the psychoanalyst, as well as the conception of transference that we have exposed, are both based on what A. Freud considers the fundamental difference between the analysis of children and that of adults; one which arises from the immaturity of the infantile superego. To justify the analyst's educational mission, she says, the analyst must teach the child to master instinctual life. Furthermore, the analyst's opinion will determine which part of the infantile impulses is to be suppressed or condemned, which part is to be satisfied, and which must be driven to sublimation. The analyst will analyze and educate at the same time, and will occupy the place of the child's ideal ego.

According to her, the child superego's dependence on original objects is maintained during the period of latency and prepuberty. The weakness of the ego, as well as the dependence on the demands imposed *by* the ego, ideally explain for Freud the double standards children have when faced with two worlds: that of adults, and that of children their own age. This is why certain things disgust them when they are with adults and not when they are with other children.

The analysis of children requires, according to Anna Freud, a more intense positive bond than that of the adult. This is due to the fact that, in addition to the analytical purpose, a pedagogical objective is being pursued, and pedagogical success will always depend on the affective bond of the student with the educator. Therefore, when negative transference appears, it might be a useful way of knowing the child's conflicts, but it must be dissolved immediately, even when not through analytical means, so that the child can be reconquered. Freud maintains that it is not possible to access the unconscious because of the barrier imposed by imperfect language and because play is not a valid tool analogous to the free association of the adult. She does not agree with Melanie Klein's play technique, in which children's playful activity is equated with the free association of the adult, nor with Klein's interpretation of play.

The study of defense mechanisms marks this second epoch of Anna Freud's work and I consider it a valuable contribution.

For Anna Freud, the game is merely a complementary technique that helps clarify the impulses of the id, but does not allow us to see how the ego works. She proposes to resort to substitute methods capable of informing us about the functioning of the ego and its defenses against affects, for instance, by conversion into the opposite, displacement, or repression. Although the symptoms and defenses against affect are transferred to the analytic situation, the neurosis remains centered on the original objects and only extends to the analysis to defend against danger, and does not need to transfer the affections to the analyst because the original objects still exist. Freud finds that acting out is frequent, and can be dangerous, in the analytic situation as it is in the family environment. Even though Marianne Kris (1959) presented the development of a transference neurosis in a four-year-old, the general opinion was that the child, though showing obvious signs of transference, did not make a transference neurosis.

Melanie Klein

For Melanie Klein, on the other hand, the capacity for transference develops spontaneously in the child, The positive and negative transferences occur from the first moment and the analyst should *not* take on the role of educator. She notes that the child's anxiety is intense and that it is the very pressure of these early anxieties that sets in motion the repetition compulsion (a mechanism studied by Sigmund Freud in the dynamism of transference and in the impulse to play). This leads to symbolizations and personifications of the first object relationships, superego formation, and adaptation to reality expressed through interpretable games. In her early work, Klein argued that, through the symbolization process, the child managed to distribute love to new objects and find fresh sources of gratification. Later, she affirmed that children also repeat their anxieties and displace them onto objects in the analytic setting. Through the mechanism of displacement and repetition, children diminish and dominate their anxieties, moving away from their dangerous original objects.

The replacement of the original object, whose loss is feared and regretted, by others more numerous and replaceable, the distribution of feelings across multiple objects, and the elaboration of emotions through the experience of loss and recovery—as seen by Sigmund Freud when he analyzed the game of the reel—together form the basis for playful activity and the capacity for transference. Through the mechanism of projective identification, children make positive or negative transferences determined by whether these objects excite or alleviate their anxiety. This mechanism is the basis for the transference situation, in which the relationship with the original objects is repeated.

The first defenses in the child's relationship with objects arise from aggressive tendencies. They are projected from the subject and destroyed in relation to the object. From the first moment, the child projects his destructive tendencies, as well as those of love, onto the analyst and onto the toys, with an intensity that will vary according to the degree of fusion that the life and death instincts have achieved. In play, the child assigns to the analyst such varied roles that the child is able to personify the id and, in this projection, allow expression of fantasies without arousing too much anxiety. With anxiety diminished, the child will be able to take on the role that was previously only assigned to the analyst.

Regarding the roles within the play, we observe that the object can very quickly change from good to bad, from ally to enemy, and, as the analyst assumes and interprets the hostile *and* positive roles required by the game, constant progress can be made towards more realistic identifications. One of the purposes of the analysis is the gradual modification of the excessive severity of the superego. This is achieved, in part, by role play interpretation, especially of roles that display the negative transference and idealizing transferences that defend against persecutory anxieties. Analysis of the positive and negative transferences reduces persecutory anxiety, thus diminishing the idealization and the resistance it represents.

In the course of treatment, the analyst will represent a variety of figures that correspond to those that the child introjected in early development. The analyst will be introjected as a persecutor and as an idealized figure of various degrees and nuances. Since the young child has left behind a large part of his Oedipus complex and, due to repression and guilt, is far removed from the objects that he originally desired, the analyst's relationship with them will undergo distortions and transformations so that the present objects of love are imagos of the original ones. Hence, this process may very well produce a "new edition" of the originally desired objects. The symptoms will change, increasing or decreasing according to the transference situations. It may be that, at home, the patient relapses into habits, symptoms, and patterns of behavior that had disappeared.

Unlike in adults, in children the unconscious is in closer and more permeable contact with the conscious and they are more profoundly dominated by the unconscious, which is why symbolic representation prevails in their analyses. As in work with adults, we find resistance, which in children manifests as panic attacks, frequent interruptions and changes in the game, boredom, or distrust. The symptoms vary by age, with anxiety attacks and crises of fear being more frequent in young children in whom the negative transference produces fear, while in older children—especially those in latency—it takes the form of distrust, reserve, or outright disgust. When the child manifests shyness, distrust, boredom, anxiety—signs of negative transference—the interpretation reduces it by moving negative affects back towards original objects or situations.

When studying anxiety in relation to the material offered, one always stumbles upon the feeling of guilt. By interpreting guilt in relation to original and transference fantasies, it is possible to reduce the negative transference in favor of the positive one. The most intense transference anxiety is that of the revival of first object relationships, with paranoid and depressive anxieties being the most predominant.

In the fight against the fear of the closest objects, the child tends to refer that fear to more distant objects—since displacement is one of the child's ways of coping with anxiety—and thus sees in them the "bad" mother and father. The child who feels threatened always expects to meet the "bad" parent and will react anxiously to all strangers. In the relationship with the therapist, the negative transference will be highlighted and, through this mechanism, the child will maintain a good imago of their real parents.

Summary of the Anna Freud approach to child analysis

1) There is no spontaneous transference in child analysis.
2) Although the child might show positive and negative transference reactions, this is not necessarily equal to a true transference neurosis, partly because of the immature mental structure, imperfect language development, and dependency on the parents, and partly because these conditions force the analyst to carry out educational work.
3) The child cannot make a second edition before having exhausted the first, so the analyst must be an educator because the child's superego is not yet mature and still depends on the external objects that originated it.
4) The negative transference should not be interpreted, but must instead be dissolved through non-analytical means.
5) Only with positive transference can useful work be done with the child.

Summary of the Melanie Klein approach to child analysis

1) The same anxiety that leads to the division of imagos—good and bad—in early childhood is revived in analysis; depressive and paranoid anxieties are experienced in analysis, expressed in play, and reduced by interpretation.
2) When in normal development, the division between idealized and persecutory objects and the hatred that stems from this division are mitigated by love, good objects are established in the internal world, and relations with the outside world improve. In treatment, this achievement leads to healing.
3) Progress in the ability to synthesize proves that the dissociation process originating in early childhood has decreased.
4) The performance of imagos with fantastically good or bad characteristics that predominate in mental life is a general mechanism in children and adults. Its variations are only of degree, frequency, or intensity.
5) These imagos correspond to intermediate states between the terrifying superego, totally separated from reality, and simpler identifications that are closer to reality.

6) To the extent that these intermediate figures appear in the child's play through the mechanism of symbolization and personification, we can come to understand the formation of the superego and dampen the severity of its effects.
7) Transference is the most useful instrument when discerning the mind of the child, as well as when discovering and reconstructing the child's early history.
8) The discovery of the transference fantasy, as well as the establishment of its relationship with the first experiences and current situations, constitute the main means of healing.
9) The repetition of early situations in the transference takes us back to situations in the first months of life.
10) In the fantasies with the analyst, the child goes back to their early days and, by studying these fantasies in context and understanding them in detail, the child gains a profound understanding of what actually happened in the mind during those early stages. At the conclusion of the analysis, the patient relives emotions from their time of weaning and the mourning of the transference is achieved through the analysis of paranoid and depressive situations.

Commentary on Chapter 3

Judith Edwards (UK)

Aberastury aims to show how psychoanalytic ideas continue to develop from their originator, Sigmund Freud, onwards. Classical psychoanalysis has taught us much about the passions which reign ungoverned within our minds. Sigmund Freud began the project with his ideas about sexuality and jealousy, Melanie Klein followed on by teaching her followers about envy, guilt, loss, and reparative love, and Donald Winnicott took up the cudgels with his assertions about the vital need for play. The great psychoanalyst Wilfred Bion (1970) reminded us of our need to think, our need to communicate our thoughts and our desire to get to know. As Bion said, "a Freud can discover and establish psychoanalysis, but it must be maintained by a continued supply of 'genius'" (Bion, 1970, p. 74). This is essential to the continued existence and vitality of psychoanalytic thinking. The various contributors to this book, working in cooperative thinking, demonstrate the fascinating variety of perspectives that clinicians bring to a project. As Bion advised, using what one receives, digests, and creatively evaluates to generate something new, as Aberastury did, and as contributors to this volume are doing now, shows the power of independent thinking. It is, and of necessity must be, a continuous process. The natural history of ideas evolves through links both between disciplines and between theoreticians and practitioners, as the chain of psychoanalytic knowledge lengthens over the generations from Sigmund Freud onwards. The process of theory building in psychoanalytic cultures continues to be exciting and generative.

This book with its clinical examples from Argentina and commentaries from English-speaking analysts aims to offer a free association of thoughts between those working in the psychoanalytic discipline, from theories about birth onwards. It is a slow art, necessarily slow. Would most discoveries have been made sooner or later? Bernard of Chartres (1904) said that we (the moderns) are like dwarves perched on the shoulders of giants (the ancients) and thus we are able to see more and farther than they did. This is not at all because of the acuteness of our sight, but because we are carried aloft and elevated by the magnitude of giants (as the infant is carried on the parents' shoulders). So we are all grateful to Sigmund Freud, who wished to make a science of the ideas which underpin the psyche.

My own training started with Freud, then moved on to Melanie Klein, Anna Freud, and Donald Winnicott. Anna Freud became an analyst in Vienna when she was twenty-five years old, having been in analysis with her father for three years, which is something that we would now consider very inappropriate. She was a careful, cautious, and rigorous woman, rather shy, and after the First World War was involved in setting up nurseries for traumatised and displaced children in Vienna. Then during the Second World War when she and her father had fled to London, she established the Hampstead War Nurseries that then became the Hampstead Clinic, a privately funded clinic originally for disturbed and blind children, and later a training center for child psychotherapy, renamed the Anna Freud Clinic after her death. Anna Freud had spent thirty years at the Hampstead Clinic. At the War Nurseries she received children from poor parts of London, disturbed and traumatised by the bombing. She put great emphasis on the continuity of psychic processes from infancy to old age, and also the connection between pathogenic roots in childhood and neurotic and psychotic illnesses later. She emphasized the importance of environmental factors, and the primary significance of parents who she thought were central in supporting a child's therapy.

From the beginning of their careers, Anna Freud and Melanie Klein battled, along with their respective followers, about both theory and technique. In 1927 Anna Freud fired as it were "the first shot" with her book *Einführung in die Technik der Kinderanalyse* (published as *Introduction to the Technic of Child Analysis*, 1928). In this she openly criticised both Klein's technique and her theoretical framework. Ernest Jones organised and published "A symposium on child-analysis" later that year, which led on to the Controversial Discussions of 1941–1945 (King & Steiner, 1991). Was Klein deviating from or extending Freud's ideas? In effect, who was his rightful daughter—Anna or Melanie?

How do you engage a child? Anna Freud didn't believe in an immediate transference to the therapist. Again, this was in opposition to Klein's view of early object relations. Putting greater emphasis on the internal world, Klein thought that we are socially wired to relate to others from the beginning, splitting experiences into "good" or "bad." Anna Freud focused on the real parents. She talked of a new *developmental object* rather than a direct transference to the therapist as being like a parent. There has been a growing appreciation of systemic forces, and since 1960 working with parents has been the accepted norm at both Kleinian and Anna Freudian training centers for child psychoanalysis and psychotherapy.

Great differences emerged about the role and meaning of play. Klein considered play to be the equivalent of free association—a road to the dynamic unconscious and the pathway to interpretation. But Anna Freud did not think all play was driven by phantasies. According to her, play could be regarded as repetition to master a skill, for instance when catching a ball, and was not necessarily about holding and throwing away an object, which was what her father had opined in the *fort-da* observation (Freud, 1920g, pp. 14–17). Anna Freud majored on the idea of managing the drives rather than releasing them, later defining the management activities as defenses of the ego. But both practitioners felt, in opposition to Winnicott, that the secondary processing of feelings was not possible without words.

The Ego and the Mechanisms of Defense (1936) was Anna Freud's first comprehensive work on psychoanalytic theory, towards an elaboration of psychoanalytic developmental psychology. The structural theory places the ego at the center as a psychic agency: an ego which has to serve three masters and therefore adopt compromise solutions along the way. Anna Freud saw that "the investigation of the id and of its mode of operation was always only a means to an end. And the end was invariably the same: the correction of these abnormalities and the restoration of the ego to its integrity," and she concluded that "the proper field for our observation is always the ego" (Sandler & Freud, 1980, p. 200): It is, so to speak, the medium through which we try to get a picture of the id and superego.

It was early in the second decade of the twentieth century that the psychoanalytic method began to be adapted to therapeutic work with children: Klein and Anna Freud together through their sterling efforts led to the establishment of this new profession of child analysis and the establishment of psychoanalytic child psychotherapy which is now the prevalent method of treating children in the UK. But they became lifelong professional antagonists, and this resulted in the Controversial Discussions from 1941–1945. Klein's (1952) view that the human infant is object related from birth has been completely and fully validated. But Anna Freud thought such differentiating capacities were hardly credible; and they threatened her father's notion of primary narcissism. Following on from her own ideas Klein developed the notion of the rudimentary psychical activity she called *phantasy*, a complex internal edifice used for defensive purposes, and she linked this with adult mental illness. Anna Freud could not accept this idea of early onset of complex process and pathologies, but felt they started much later.

The discussions could not be resolved and resulted in the creation of three schools of thought within the British Psychoanalytical Society—Freudian, Kleinian, and Independent.

It is the contribution of both women, Anna Freud and Melanie Klein, that adds up to a rounded definition of infant development and child mental health needs.

CHAPTER 4

The development of psychoanalysis for children in Argentina

An early interest in the mental life of the child led me, many years ago, to nursery work. In 1937, by way of this work, I first came into contact with the case of an eight-year-old girl. I saw her often in the waiting room while her mother was undergoing psychiatric treatment. Her intelligent and anguished expression made me doubt the diagnosis that had been placed on her. I gathered that, despite renewed attempts to interest her in knowledge, she had not been able to learn reading or writing. The professionals her father consulted claimed she was an oligophrenic. My first approach to her mind was pedagogical. I wanted to know if the girl could learn or not.

During the long interviews I held with her while her mother was in treatment, she peppered our lesson on reading and numbers with stories about her life. I concluded that the resistance against acquiring knowledge stemmed from severe pain the child felt upon learning of the mother's illness and recalling all that she had suffered during her psychotic episodes. Her mind had been paralyzed by this conflict, and I was communicating this to her. I also understood that the lies that adults told her in order to comfort and reassure had actually created great confusion within her, causing a loss of confidence in the possibility of ever acquiring the truth. After this enlightenment, she was able to begin learning. So, yes, the girl could learn.

Since my interviews with her were successful and the girl was acquiring knowledge daily, I took to reading a treatise on child psychoanalysis in order to find more ways to help her. At the same time, encouraged by the results I was getting, I cared for an eleven-year-old boy who also had learning difficulties. He was subjected to intense corporal punishment and it was apparent that this had played a huge role in his intellectual inhibition.

In the office of the League of Mental Hygiene at Las Mercedes Hospice, I conducted the first psychoanalytic treatments of children, adhering to the technique described by Anna Freud in her book. I worked only with children over six years old and tried to get them to share their conflicts and dreams. Small toys, pencils, and paper were always made available to them. At the time, I read a small technical book in which a psychogenic muteness had been described in an eight-year-old boy. I remember being amazed at the world that arose from the interpretation of the drawings, the only way this child had of communicating with the therapist. That same year, I joined the newly created Education Sciences Department in the Faculty of Philosophy and Letters.

The first stage in the development of child analysis in Argentina

The year 1942 was crucial to my career as a psychoanalyst. In April, I began a didactic analysis with Ángel Garma. That same year, I discovered Melanie Klein's play technique, which she had based on Freud's discoveries about the meaning of playful activity. As there was no one among us who could advise me on the application of the technique that I had studied only in treatises, my findings could only be compared with the discoveries I'd made in my own analysis, the observations I'd made in previous years, and the research on the observation and treatment of psychotics conducted by Enrique Pichon-Rivière. It was around this time that a frequent correspondence with Melanie Klein allowed me, due to her generous instructions, to solve many of the technical difficulties presented to me daily.

The first history that I published corresponds to that time, and it was during that treatment that I first understood the symbolic meaning of the deformations in the design of a house that a child builds. In the context of "the House Building Game," the patient showed me difficulties with breathing, struggles with connecting, and disorders in sublimation. The comparison of this case with others, as well as the elaboration of what I was discovering, constituted my first original contribution to the psychoanalysis of children. Reading the works of Homburger and Schilder was very useful in preparing for this book.

In those years, certain members of the Institute of Psychoanalysis were already interested in working with children. In my preliminary note, I have referred at length to the importance of the work of Elizabeth G. de Garma, specifically in terms of the development of the psychoanalysis of children in Argentina in those years. I shared training tasks with her, but, fundamentally, it was the exchange of ideas and the discussion of cases that constituted a source of mutual enrichment. In 1948, she presented fragments of the analysis of a twenty-one-month-old boy to Melanie Klein and a group of children's psychoanalysts in England, and I presented the first hour of play. Discussing technical problems with them enriched our knowledge of the psychoanalysis of children.

In that year of 1948, the first course on psychoanalysis of children was given in the Argentine Psychoanalytic Association, which since then has been part of the required education for everyone who follows the career of child analysis. Concurrently with teaching at the Institute, I continued to hold study groups and technical courses to improve the education of those wanting to specialize in child psychoanalysis. In our Association, as in all analytical groups, few are dedicated to this specialty. But when, in 1951, I was appointed reporter to a panel in Paris on the topic of "Transference in the Analysis of Children," I was already able to point to a group of child psychoanalysts working in Argentina that was not of insignificant size and whose members had all received their training at the Institute.

At the Pichon Rivière Institute, the training was eventually extended from 1948 to 1954. Anyone who was interested in the analysis of children could, in this Institute and under my supervision, achieve the hours of observation of play necessary to begin their journey as a children's therapist. Trainees were also taught various techniques, such as interviewing parents as well as presenting, discussing, and analyzing weekly cases.

Many who were trained during this early period ended up publishing work and participating in study groups. Later, some of them chose not to follow my technical evolution, or else continued their activities independently, while new people came forward to collaborate.

The Symposium on Child Psychoanalysis held at the Psychoanalytic Association of Argentina in 1957 was an example of how much work had been done in those years. It marked the end of the first stage in the development of child psychoanalysis in Argentina and ushered in a new era.

The second stage

In 1957, I read my work on teething at the Paris Congress, which was considered a fundamental contribution to the understanding of the first year of life. By pointing out the existence of a genital phase prior to the anal phase, and by observing that it existed as an attempt to elaborate the loss of the oral bond that must be renounced after teething, I modified the pattern of libidinal development, facilitating the understanding of some early childhood disorders that accompany this process and that occur in the second half of the first year.

This period of the child's life is characterized by varied learning and converges with the acquisition of achievements, which, in turn, leads to a fundamental change in the face of the external world. This change is as significant as that of being born: the child stands, walks, talks, and weaning occurs. When a child is born, the oral sucking phase is structured, which is essential for the survival of the human being. This is not only due to the necessary food supply, but also occurs because it allows the child to bond with the mother, thus overcoming the trauma of birth.

In the oral-sadistic phase, the appearance of teeth as instruments that make possible the fulfillment of destructive fantasies determines the nature of the oral bond and the need to redo it through another area of the body. In this period of life, the discovery of the vagina in the female and the need for penetration in the male both initiate the genital stage that we have mentioned, in which the penis–vagina union replaces the mouth's connection with the breast. At this stage desires can be satisfied only with fantasies and masturbatory acts, which are included in the infant's play activity. The impossibility of the total fulfillment of this union forces a regression to the moment of birth, in which there were oral, anal, and genital tendencies that united the child with the mother. From there, the psychosexual evolution of the child continues with the successive structuring of the ensuing phases: anal and genital. The repeated failure to maintain the unique union with the mother prompts the child to work through this loss by searching for the father, as well as for new objects in the external world.

In this sense, standing and walking arise as an urgent need for the child to separate from the mother, so as to not destroy her. Simultaneously, these same achievements also serve the child's need to get her back. The same happens with language, which allows for the magical reconstruction of objects and serves to elaborate the depressive anxiety increased by teething. Pronouncing the first word means, for the child, a repairing of the loved and hated object, which the child rebuilds within and launches out into the outside world. After this, the child begins to understand that the word puts him in contact with the world, that it is a means of communication. In this way, walking and language have the same meaning as birth: to separate and then, through other means, regain contact with the lost object.

I consider this approach essential to understanding many of the common symptoms present in the infant within the second half of the first year: symptoms which, for years, were placed under the label "teething disorders." It also aids us in the understanding of the zoophobias so frequently found within this period of development, which are aptly explained by the existence of the early genital phase.

Some years ago, I published a case in which I was studying a phobia in an eleven-month-old girl. The defense mechanisms that determined this symptom do not differ from those of a phobia such as that of Little Hans, which Freud described as corresponding to the phallic stage. Taking into account the existence of the previous genital phase, we understand that the contradiction with Freud's work is in appearance only. The phallic phase that he indicated corresponds to the end of the Oedipus complex, whereas the phase that we study is the one that marks its initiation. The fixation point for phobia is still, for us, the genital phase, but it is also a phase that is prior to the anal organization. If, in addition, we understand that, within development, the obsessive symptoms appear in the child *after* the phobia and are their attempt to elaborate, we must also understand the anal phase as structured *after* the oral and genital phase, as both consequence *and* solution to the conflicts created during this phase. Although I have discussed and exposed this concept in seminars and study groups, Jorge Rovatti was the first to present a case in which he illustrated these ideas. This publication marked the beginning of what I consider to be the second stage in the history of the psychoanalysis of children in Argentina.

In November 1959, Susana L. de Ferrer, someone who, in this second stage of the analysis of children, was as crucial to me as Elizabeth G. de Garma was in the first, organized a round table of psychoanalysts, pediatricians, and pediatric dentists focused on the psychoanalysis of children during the Congress of Pediatrics in Mar del Plata. In May 1960, the analysts and candidates who were members of this roundtable formed a study group with me. Its purpose was to discuss cases and raise technical problems, all in the name of creating unifying criteria and, thus, differentiating our technique from others that, while originating from the same sources, did not meet our current requirements. The group's task was, and still is, the presentation and discussion of cases, the selection of those most helpful to understanding the appearance and dynamics of the previous genital phase, and the curating of various clinical materials deemed sufficient for publication.

The technique used by this group is the same one we describe in this book. In the course of it, fragments of the work of each of my collaborators will be presented. I would be remiss to end this chapter without mentioning the influence that psychoanalysis, specifically that of children, has had on some pediatricians and child dentists.

The influence of child analysis on pediatrics and dentistry

Arnaldo Rascovsky devoted himself to pediatrics until 1939, and his later work was already being influenced by psychoanalysis. Having started his training as a psychoanalyst alongside Ángel Garma, Rascovsky organized a service in which the treatments were psychoanalytically focused, though it is worth noting that the children were not treated with psychoanalysis. The result of those years of work were a host of articles on childhood epilepsy and obesity. He was also intensively studying the fetal psyche.

Following a different trajectory, Julio Tahier also found himself intertwined with the psychoanalysis of children. He was interested in my findings on infant insomnia, disorders that accompanied teething, and febrile episodes in older children. Driven by these interests, and having begun analysis himself, he did not abandon his career as a pediatrician, but rather oriented it towards a psychosomatic approach to the disease. At the British Hospital, at the request of Dr. Bruer, he organized a service for psychodiagnosis and orientation to psychoanalytic treatment, subsequently adding group analytical treatments for children and mothers.

At the time of writing this book in 1962, I want to acknowledge that the Children's Hospital works under the analytical guidance of Professor F. Escardó, the chair of the Department of Psychiatry and Psychology, Pediatrics and Childcare, as well as with the Childhood Psychiatry Group, Professor Carrea's Room XVIII, and Room I of the Pediatric Clinic. Diagnoses and treatments for children will soon be carried out at the Dr. Enrique Racker Psychoanalytic Clinic, dependent on the Argentine Psychoanalytic Association's approval.

An article on teething, which I wrote at the request of José Porter, encouraged a group of children's dentists, who well understood the deep meaning of the mouth and teeth in children, to be analyzed. They subsequently organized and followed their own child psychoanalysis courses, on which I've collaborated since 1955 with Julio Tahier and Ángel Garma. When Gerald Pearson was among us, he found this collaboration between dentists, pediatricians, and psychoanalysts of children very remarkable. This makes sense, considering every psychoanalyst knows the decisive importance of the oral area in the development of the individual, as well as the sheer anguish that any and all dental treatment arouses. José Porter, María Inés Egozcue, and Samuel Leyt all share the credit for this revolution in dentistry. Susana Lustig de Ferrer began her 1960 dental sessions with a story about the meaning of the mouth and teeth in the later life of the human being. This is indicative of the degree to which the psychoanalysis of children has influenced this branch of dentistry.

This chapter was merely an effort to describe the origins of the psychoanalysis of children in Argentina in preparation for the presentation of my current technique, which is the fundamental goal of the book. If I have omitted someone's work, it is because my approach, in keeping with this goal, is to refer only to the origin and development of those techniques that are inextricably linked to my first steps and further development.

Commentary on Chapter 4

Virginia Ungar (Argentina)

I am very grateful for the editors' invitation to comment on Chapter 4 of their English version of Arminda Aberastury's classic. It led me to reread her volume on the theory and technique of child psychoanalysis which, in my opinion, has not been surpassed more than fifty years after its publication in Buenos Aires.

It is very moving to accompany the author in her journey through the history of analysis with children in Argentina. The practice of child analysis was born with Arminda herself, from her encounter with an eight-year-old girl whom she saw in the "Hospicio de las Mercedes," a psychiatric facility. The girl was then waiting for her mother who was in treatment with Enrique Pichon-Rivière, Arminda's husband, for help with a chronic psychotic disorder.

As she recounts it, Arminda noticed an intelligent and anxious look in the child's eyes which did not fit the diagnosis of oligophrenia that had been given to the child. Coming from a pedagogical background, Arminda set out to see whether the girl could start learning. She began by teaching her the alphabet and numbers. As they tried to read together, she and the girl had long conversations. Aberastury then turned to Anna Freud's book on child psychoanalysis to help her understand the child's learning delays and came to the conclusion that the pain of recognizing her mother's illness, coupled with the lies told by adults to reassure her, paralyzed her ability to learn. According to Arminda, after she made some psychoanalytic interpretations based on her reading of Anna Freud, the child began to learn. We can safely say that this act of deciding to apply the psychoanalytic approach in the treatment of the little patient who had been labeled (and written off) as oligophrenic, was an act of tremendous courage and a daring bet on the possibility of the girl's development. The story allows us to witness the foundational moment of child psychoanalysis in Argentina. It is well known that Aberastury was the pioneer in this field, the one who opened the way for many analysts to take up the torch, allowing child analysis to develop in a way that is still remarkable today in the global world of psychoanalysis.

We can associate Aberastury's moments of discovery with the creation of the play technique by Melanie Klein who first saw little Rita in 1923 in her own home. Klein (1955) mentions how in the same year, this time in her clinical practice setting, when trying to help a seven-year-old patient with a severe inhibition of play, she resorted to looking for toys in her children's room and offering them to the little patient. Klein points to this moment as the birth of the play technique which is the central basis of psychoanalytic practice with children.

Both in Melanie Klein's account and Arminda Aberastury's chapter about the beginnings of child analysis in Argentina, the two pioneering women analysts of children let us accompany them in what in classical epistemology is known as the "context of discovery." According to Reichenbach (1938), the *context of discovery* refers to questions related to how new ideas or hypotheses are generated in science. The *context of justification* is related to the criteria that such hypotheses must satisfy to be accepted into the theoretical body. As clinicians, we can extend this perspective to another dimension that could be called the *context of application*, which is the field that these ideas are taken up and put to work in practice. From this point of view, we not only detect where and when an idea has emerged, but also how it has developed and, in this case, expanded.

In the account of this initial moment, we can notice something that can be applied to all transcendental discoveries. In psychoanalysis, they do not emerge from "revelatory ideas" but appear in the confrontation with "obstacles" that emerge in practice. These obstacles or impasses expose the insufficiency of the theoretical body and/or the method available up to that moment to account for the problem. In this chapter, the author recounts the path she has followed in the development of child psychoanalysis from her early papers and introduction of the House Building Game (A. Pichon-Rivière, 1950a) up to the date of publication of her book in Spanish (Aberastury, 1962). She describes her encounters with the work of Sophie Morgenstern, Anna Freud, and Melanie Klein. She exchanged letters with Melanie Klein and became a disseminator of her ideas, which she then developed in the light of her own clinical experience and that of contributions from her colleagues in Argentina.

The author gives an account of the expansion of child analysis and its impact on other disciplines such as pediatrics, dentistry, psychiatry, as well as education and law (A. de Pichon-Rivière, 1958b). In short, this chapter takes the reader on a journey through the origins and development of the contributions of Arminda Aberastury and her disciples in clinical practice and beyond.

For my part, I think it is important to highlight an aspect of the text that is related to the transmission of psychoanalysis. I think that where child analysis has developed considerably, it is not only because of socio-historical-cultural circumstances that called for psychoanalytic insight, but also because of the strong conviction, enormous enthusiasm, admirable courage, great observational skills, and, above all, unusually great creativity of the first child analysts. Psychoanalysis of children and young people is still relevant today. Facing the challenges of the times forces us and them into the psychoanalytic realm to question ourselves. Therein lies the vitality of our practice and our contact with young people who are in the process of development, as are we.

Arminda's ability and devotion to passing on her knowledge and pioneering passion for the task to those who followed her indicate her genuine generosity. We can observe this in the way she credits her colleagues in this chapter. A whole generation of analysts followed her impulse, and transformed it into its contemporary form in clinical practice, teaching, and publications that have transcended the borders of Argentina and have, in turn, opened up new developments in clinical technique and theory.

Part II

Technique in child analytic practice

CHAPTER 5

Initial interview with the parents

When parents decide to consult us about a child's problem or illness, I immediately request an interview, advising them that the child should not be present, but should be told of the consultation. Although we suggest that both of the parents participate, it is common for the mother to attend the meeting without the father, and it is very rare for both of them to show up. In some special cases, relatives, friends of the family, or governesses have come to represent the parents. Any of these possible situations is, in itself, revealing of the functioning of the family group in relation to the child. When the interview is with both parents, we must be careful not to show favoritism, although there will inevitably arise a greater understanding with one parent over the other. This understanding should serve to comprehend the problem and not to create new conflict.

To evaluate the nature of relationships in the family group, specifically in regards to the couple, we will rely on our impression of the data recorded in the interview. This should not resemble an interrogation, in which the patients feel judged. On the contrary, the interview must serve to alleviate the anguish and guilt that a child's illness or conflict arouses. In order to achieve that goal, we must assume the role of therapists of the child from the first moment, taking charge of the problem or the symptom.

The data that parents give us is often inaccurate, distorted, or very superficial, because they do not usually have a complete knowledge of the situation. During the interview, they may forget part of what they know due to the anguish it causes them. They tend to experience the initial questioning as a prosecution. Furthermore, they cannot, in such a limited time, establish a relationship with the therapist, a hitherto unknown person, that is complex enough to allow them to delve into their problems.

It is necessary that limits be placed on this interview; that it be directed according to a previous plan. Otherwise, the parents, though conscious of the need to talk about the child, will tend to avoid the subject by instead sharing confidences about themselves. The interview structure agreed upon by the parents and the therapist must focus on the child and his or her relationship with the parents, and this focus must not be abandoned throughout the course of treatment. As previously stated, the goal is to obtain the data of greatest interest in a limited time frame, which fluctuates between one and three hours.

We do not consider it advisable to end the interview without having obtained basic information:

a) The reason for the consultation
b) The child's history
c) What a normal day looks like, how the child spends a Sunday or a holiday, how the child's birthday unfolds; and
d) The nature of the parents' relationship with each other, with their children, and with other members of the immediate family environment.

I chose these guidelines after researching and testing several alternatives, and will attempt to substantiate these choices in the following sections.

a) Reason for the consultation

The decision to inquire firstly about the reason for the consultation stems from the most difficult initial obstacle for parents: talking about what is not going well with their child. The resistance to doing so is not conscious; the parent has already surpassed any conscious barrier by making the decision to consult us. To alleviate any subconscious resistance to the topic, we must try to reduce the amount of initial anxiety. This is precisely the effect achieved when the therapist takes charge of the disease or conflict directly and from the first moment. In doing so, the therapist safely and effectively secures the role of analyst of the child.

The parents should feel that every detail they can recall about the reason for the consultation is important to us. Whenever possible, we must carefully record the dates of initiation, development, aggravation, or improvement of the symptom. We must then compare them with those that we record over the course of the interview.

When they feel safe and understood, the parents are more likely to accurately recall the events when we inquire about them later. We must accept, however, that complete or partial forgetfulness of key events occurs frequently, and that any inaccuracy may not be apparent until months later, when the child communicates it to us during their own treatment. If the child improves and the anxiety that caused the forgetfulness decreases sufficiently, the parents might also be able to recall the triggering circumstances repressed in the initial interview.

Despite this inevitable limitation, the data obtained is valuable not only for the study of the case, but also because it can help us understand the etiology of infantile neuroses, and build knowledge about prevention.

If we are to conduct an in-depth assessment of the relationship with the child, the comparison between the data obtained during the child's analysis and the information provided by the parents in the initial interview is of utmost importance.

b) History of the child

During a parent session, I am primarily interested in knowing the emotional response, specifically that of the mother, to the announcement of the pregnancy. I inquire as to whether it was wanted or accidental, if there was a desire to abort or any such attempt at rejection, or if they accepted the child with joy. Then, I ask them how their feelings evolved. Was there excitement upon conception? Has that changed? This is all important because, from the moment a child is conceived, everything that happens is crucial to their subsequent evolution.

All current studies place their emphasis on the mother's relationship with her child. Furthermore, it is a proven fact that the mother's emotional rejection, both of the sex of her child and of the idea of having the child at all, leaves deep traces on the child's psyche. For example, a child born with the mission to unite a couple in the process of separating will bear the stamp of this effort. Failure will determine in that child a great distrust in themselves and in their ability to feel fulfilled.

The mother's response to how she coped with her pregnancy is indicative of the quality of the beginning of the child's life. I do not expect the reaction to reflect truth. Instead, the expectation is that the parents' reactions when confronted with the material offered by the child be used to further the investigation.

In some cases, I found a trend: the concealment of important facts. However, most of the time, the problem was rooted in forgetfulness, omission, or distortion of memories due to unconscious conflicts. Sometimes this forgetfulness was so striking and incomprehensible that, in my experience and that of other analysts, only a staggering frequency of similar events proved a lack of conscious deception or voluntary concealment. I am referring, of course, to cases in which abortions were not mentioned, before and after the birth of the patient, as well as circumstances where family life was completely abandoned *during* the pregnancy.

Although, in reality, many children are not wanted by their parents—at least at the moment of conception—the answer we receive from parents in most cases is that their child *was* wanted. If the idea of accepting the rejection is even entertained, it is often a feeling attributed to the other spouse. Similar difficulties arise when we question the parents about pregnancy and delivery. It has become all but the norm that the antecedents recorded in the first interview read as follows: "Desired child, pregnancy, and normal delivery." Naturally, this information rarely remains in the reconstructed history.

Clinical example

For example, we took on the case of a two-and-a-half-year-old girl who had first been diagnosed with epilepsy and then with oligophrenia. In the antecedents, she appeared to be the desired daughter of a well-matched marriage. She had a three-month-old sister and her mother did not remember any difficulties before or during the pregnancy.

Apparently, the girl was born via normal delivery and had a smooth development. At nine months, however, she fainted while the mother bathed her. The mother told her to lean her head back and, at that moment, the girl lost consciousness. At thirteen months, she had her first seizure. On one occasion, the mother was carrying the daughter in her arms while also carrying several packages. When one of them fell, she placed the daughter on the ground in order to pick it up. The daughter suddenly collapsed and lost consciousness once more. She had to be hospitalized due to the incident.

Let us now look at the real conditions under which she was conceived, the accurate details pertaining to pregnancy and childbirth, as well as the way by which we arrived at this data. At the behest of the analyst we initially consulted, the mother entered my mothers' counseling group. At the same time, her daughter began an individual analysis.

Little by little, we arrived at a surprisingly ample flow of memories that modified the initial data. In effect, the mother now recalled a previous three-month abortion. She also remembered that, during her third month of pregnancy with the patient, she had suffered losses, as she had in her first pregnancy. The doctor had advised a scraping, noting that even when the pregnancy came to term, there would be a risk of giving birth to a sick child. Despite this medical suggestion, the mother insisted on continuing the pregnancy, staying in bed until the moment of delivery.

During this same group session, she told us a moving anecdote. As a child, she pretended that her dolls were "morons" and that only she could heal them. When the doctor warned her about the possibility of having a sick child, she recalled that old childhood fantasy and resolved to take care of herself, in order to keep the child healthy. This memory gave her the strength to immobilize herself in bed for such a long stretch of time.

At the time of delivery, there was a complication. When the forceps were about to be applied, the mother made "a supreme effort" to avoid them. Indeed, it was not even necessary to resort to the forceps at all. The girl was born with a congenital hip dislocation, and in the third month after her birth—the same month of the pregnancy in which the losses appeared and immobilization began—the mother decided to consult doctors for the dislocation. They immobilized the girl until she was nine months old, an end-date that coincided with the end of the pregnancy and the end of immobilization of her mother. This clarification was the result of interpretations made to her within the group, as well as the improvement of the daughter in treatment. The child's improvement alleviated her anguish and guilt, allowing her to more easily access and recall the events that triggered the girl's serious illness.

The birth experience and breastfeeding

Mothers hardly remember or consciously value the importance of the facts related to pregnancy and childbirth. Unconsciously, however, everything is recorded. Thus, we should not be puzzled if questions about the birthing process lead to simple, reductive answers like "short," or "long," with no further elaboration. It is convenient to ask whether the pregnancy was carried to term, whether the birth was induced, whether anesthesia was given, how the relationship between the mother and the midwife functioned, whether, at the time of delivery, the mother understood the process well, whether they were asleep or awake, accompanied or alone. These questions sometimes open new avenues to remembering, so long as the therapist maintains the spirit we have indicated during the interview and helps, above all, in assessing the importance of the relationship with the child.

When we have enough information about the delivery, we ask whether the mother breastfed the child. If so, it is crucial to inquire whether the child had a sucking reflex, whether they latched on well to the breast, how many hours after birth the child fed, and the condition of the nipple. Then, we must ask about the feeding rhythm. We must inquire not only about the number of hours that the child was left free between feedings, but also how long the baby fed from each breast. Feeding on time and at a pace predetermined by the mother is rare. The most common situation consists of the mother not limiting the suction time, not respecting the intervals between meals, and not setting a fixed time to start feeding.

This leaves the mother overwhelmed by the obligation to feed her child. If she does not have a set time to start or a regular interval between meals, her entire life is limited by the child's needs. This robs her of time for herself. For this reason, the way in which the relationship with the child is established provides us with important information, not only about the patient's history, but also about the mother and her conceptualization of motherhood. The way in which the first post-natal relationship is established is of utmost importance in the later development of the child. We are well aware of the significance of birth trauma throughout the life of the subject. The observation of infants and the analysis of young children have taught us a great deal about how to help them work through this trauma. One of the essential elements in the pursuit of this goal is to provide the baby with sufficient physical contact with the mother after birth.

This contact should be as close as possible to intrauterine contact, should be established as soon as possible, and can be mutually beneficial. For the child, the moment is an opportunity to partially recover what was lost without excessive delay, which would, by nature of intensifying the child's frustration and feelings of helplessness, increase their destructive tendencies and make it difficult to establish a relationship with the mother. For the mother, on the other hand, this situation presents a parallel; the birth of the child is a detachment that repeats her own loss of *her* mother. The act of giving is, for her, a constant renewal of what she herself received as a daughter. For this reason, the more she gives, and the better the conditions of this giving, the more her bond with the internal mother will be enriched.

The common suggestion that the baby be taken away from the mother so she may rest is counterproductive in this context, because neither parent nor child will rest well while suffering from frustration. Another common piece of advice is to establish breastfeeding at a regular rate. At the beginning, breastfeeding is subject to the needs expressed by the child, and it is common for the intervals to fluctuate between two and a half and three and a half hours. Gradually a more regular interval stabilizes. This is helpful and advised, as it offers the child a way to control anxiety, one of the most arduous tasks to which the self is subjected after birth. Feeding on schedule offers stability in the supply. This stability arises from consistency. The object is the same, has been presented under similar conditions, is static, and, if possible, in the same room. The mother is in the same chair, the posture is similar, and the intervals are equal. We all know how easy it is for the child to adopt a rhythm when we have found one that works. For this reason, after the first attempts, the most appropriate rhythm is chosen and respected.

Knowing the free hours of the day is useful not only for the working mother, but also for the mother whose only requirement—apart from the baby—is to care for herself. When a mother tells us about the details of breastfeeding, we must insist on learning as much as possible about how these basic requirements have been met for both her and the child. A healthy mother does not need advice in raising her child. She instinctively grasps the child's needs; an organic understanding that leads her to provide unprompted touch, love, and nourishment. Only when there are inhibitions or deficits do these basic human urges ever need to be taught. Or rather, re-taught. No need that arises within the child—be it hunger, cold, thirst, a need for contact, or a need for suitable clothing—will escape the understanding of a mother who feels linked to her child by a connection as subtle and secure as the umbilical cord that conjoined them in intrauterine life.

Any mother, however, may often become alarmed when the child cries. Her first reaction is, most often, to feed him. She then tends to despair if the child doesn't accept the offer, but it is common for a baby to cry because of reliving a bad experience that produces a hallucination. The mother's voice and a dispensing of new affectionate signals, whether a smiling look, physical contact, rocking or singing, are often enough confirmation to counteract the bad internal imago that produced the hallucination with a current pleasant experience. On the other hand, it is likely that a child who is reliving a bad experience with the breast—perhaps due to momentary pain or colic—will see this new offer of food as a danger, and will reject it with fear.

If the act is forced and the child cannot defend against the intrusion, they must ingest the food, which further reinforces the terrifying imago. This highlights the importance of understanding the mother–child relationship, specifically by inquiring about the way the mother used to calm the crying baby and how she reacted when the child refused food. This elucidates the child's first experiences.

In comparison, the response usually recorded in the history does not tell us much: "Breastfeeding up to five (or eight, or nine) months."

Again, this route does not provide a formula for truth, but, through it, we do achieve a framework under which we can further investigate.

These details regarding the relationship with the child, which we do not often receive from the mother, gradually emerge from the child's material as it is analyzed. The child does not expect merely food from the world, and food is not all a mother can give. Today we know of mothers who have not breastfed their children, but who have had very effective contact with them, and have thus determined a better maternal imago than in the breastfeeding situation that is not loving. In fact, some mothers who breastfeed consistently have, in later stages of the child's life, failed to achieve affective contact and have not offered the child any gratification, which, in turn, stunted the possibility of a good connection. For these reasons, we must always remember that any information we learn about the breastfeeding of a child during that first interview constitutes only a beginning. It is merely a small piece of the whole we hope to appreciate more fully through analysis of the child, as well as through new interviews with the parents, which are especially useful for the confirmation of research and the acquiring of new data.

When we ask mothers how many hours after delivery they saw and put the newborn to the breast, they are often amazed that they can't remember. Such intense emotions are usually totally suppressed by conflict. Experience shows that the more established that first relationship is, the easier and more detailed the mother's memory of the event can be.

If the mother has not been able to feed her child, or has done so for a very short time, it is advisable to ask for a detailed account of the following elements: the administration of the bottle to the child, whether the mother held the bottle in close contact with the body, whether she gave it to the child while in the crib, what the size of the nipple hole was on the bottle, as well as how long it took the baby to eat.

When a child relives lactation during treatment, they show us significant details in their play. A two-year-old patient was almost exclusively concerned with weighing food on a scale and trying to keep the two dishes at an even height. When the therapist asked the mother—who was very obsessive—about the characteristics of breastfeeding, she reported that she weighed the child after each feeding and made sure to keep the child on each breast for an equal amount of time.

Weaning and the move to solids

Continuing with our examination, we must ask how the baby accepted the change of food from the breast to bottle and from milk to other foods. We must inquire as to how the child reacted to the change from liquids to solids such as porridge or meat, which requires chewing. This way, we can come to know a lot about the child, the mother, and both of their potentials for the disposal of old objects. The passage from the breast to another source of oral gratification requires a work of psychological elaboration. Melanie Klein found it similar to the exertion to which the adult is subjected when they experience the loss of a loved one. The way in which the child accepts this loss will determine their behavioral pattern moving forward, influencing how the child will cope with the successive losses of later life, which require adaptation to reality.

A mother who has solved this problem during her own childhood, or through psychoanalytic treatment, will deal with her child's oral phase difficulties by transitioning to new foods slowly, sometimes reinforcing, or even temporarily forsaking the attempt. If a patient informs us that the baby rejected the change of food, we must ask the details pertaining to that very process; namely, whether the attempts were made with patience or irritation. This helps us rebuild an accurate picture.

It is important to note the date of weaning and its conditions. Sometimes we discover that the child has held on to the pacifier or bottle for five or six years, even though the parents initially claimed that weaning occurred at nine months.

Increasing independence after six months

The degree of dependence and independence in a mother–child relationship is also reflected in the interplay that occurs when a baby begins to move by themselves and expresses the need to do so. The mother may or may not note this need, which inevitably leads to her either satisfying or frustrating it. Between the third and fourth month of life, the child enters a period during which the psyche is subjected to new and definitive demands. These are specified in the second half of the first year of life, with the initiation of crawling and language.

Beginning to talk

When children pronounce their first word, they experience an instant connection to the world. They identify language as a way of making themselves understood. The appearance of the object the child names, as well as the emotional reaction to this communicative achievement, will solidify the child's beliefs in the magical capacity of the word. Initially, this is a relationship with internal objects. But through gradual learning and reality tests, language becomes a communication system. These conclusions, which are the result of the observation of infants and the analytical treatment of children suffering from speech disorders, make our research into language initiation and development one of utmost importance. This is especially true if we are to assess the degree to which a child has adapted to reality, as well as the bond that has been established between the child and the parents.

Characteristics like language delay and linguistic developmental inhibition are indicative of a serious difficulty in adaptation.

Very often, we find that parents do not remember the age at which their children spoke their first word, or can't seem to provide an accurate time frame for when disorders began. In this period of life, the figure of the father takes on a role of great importance, and the real or psychological absence of that role can severely impede the development of the child, even *with* an understanding mother who attempts to satisfy the need.

Beginning to walk

We sometimes meet ten- or eleven-month-old children whose mothers forcefully adhere them to a daily regimen more fitting for a three year old. Therefore, when we ask the mother at what age her son walked, we are really asking whether, when he wanted to walk, she allowed it. Was he freely permitted? Was he encouraged? Was he blocked? Was he rushed? Were the parents limited to observing the activity? Were they involved? These are all crucial questions. Few are the times when this development occurs normally.

The walking aid, or walker, is a good example of a substitute for the mother. However, though it is better than immobility, it will never replace the safe arms of the mother for offering continuing support to the child as he or she reaches out to experiences in the world confidently and without haste. Children who can thus identify with their mother's ambulation incorporate the ability to walk into their way of being. The child's development will consist of a search for opportunities to eat, sleep, talk, and walk like the parents. According to what the child, within the context of their unconscious fantasy, is receiving from them, the parental teachings will be incorporated as an achievement of the ego, or else become part of a healing superego that will block the action, causing the child to fall.

When we question parents about this, the mother's answers often shed light on her ability to detach well from her child. These questions can tell us, for example, whether the parents still indulge their nostalgia for when the child was a new, clean baby, or might result in comments regarding how much work the baby was at the time, and how the mother is glad to see the child making progress every day.

For the child, walking has the meaning—among myriad others—of the separation from the mother, already begun through birth. Therefore, the understanding mother allows her child to walk without haste or hindrance, in order for the detachment to be peaceful and joyful, as well as to offer the child a pattern of behavior that will serve them in the world.

We often ask if the baby tended to fall when they started to walk and if, at a later point, the child would bump into any obstacles, because the answers help us clarify the degree of guilt involved, as well as the specifics of the development of the Oedipus complex. The tendency to hit oneself or to incur accidents is indicative of a bad relationship with parents and is equivalent to a partial suicide, due to an unhealthy channeling of destructive impulses.

Expulsive tendencies manifest in the body and mind of the child in the second half of the first year. Projection and expulsion are ways to relieve tension and, if these mechanisms are blocked, the emotional charges accumulate; a process which, in turn, produces symptoms.

Sleeping

One of the most frequent situations in this period of life is insomnia. This symptom, among many others, is apparent in the usual pathological pictures of the child, taken during the teething period. This, therefore, deserves our special attention. We are interested in knowing whether the appearance of the teeth was accompanied by disorders, or whether it occurred normally and at the appropriate time. We then ask about sleep, because the two are closely related. If there are sleep disorders, we ask about the behavior toward the child and inquire as to the feelings that the symptom stirs in the parents. The description of the room where the baby sleeps is important. So is whether the child is alone, whether they need the presence of someone, or whether some other special condition must be met for the child to fall asleep. During teething, transitory sleep disorders may appear, which may worsen or disappear depending on the environment.

This problem is one of the most disturbing in the emotional life of the mother, and is one that truly tests her motherhood.

The use of the pacifier as a crutch for falling asleep is one of many factors that promote insomnia. Parents often say that the baby does not sleep if they take the pacifier away. In our experience with mothers' counseling groups, as we analyzed their reactions to this problem, we found that the difficulty did not come from the child, but the parents, who either postponed the decision or created situations that made it difficult to solve the problem.

The weaning that usually occurs at the end of the first year of life means much more than the giving of new food to the child. It is the elaboration of a definitive loss. It is up to the parents to achieve this with the least pain possible. But this will only occur if they themselves have worked it out well.

Toilet training

When we learn details about toilet training—what age it first started and what form the toilet training took—our knowledge of the mother is expanded. We have found that, if toilet training is learned excessively early, under severe and strenuous circumstances, or if it is linked to other traumatic events, it can lead to serious disorders like enuresis. That is why the therapist should inquire about the age at which the learning began, the way it was carried out, and the mother's attitude towards cleanliness and dirt.

A baby of a few months does not have the motor development necessary to remain seated on the toilet or get up at will. This is one of the reasons why it is advisable to start toilet training when the child is ready to walk. From another point of view, premature control is not advisable when we consider that fecal matter and urine are substances that have, for the unconscious mind, the meaning of products that leave the body. In this role, they fulfill the function of reassuring the child of emptying their anxieties, which is normal at that age. After the first year, due to the symbolization process and the play activity that the child is already capable of carrying out, the positive and negative charges placed on these substances are displaced to objects and people in the outside world. This enables the child to dispose of them without excessive anguish.

Early toilet training imposes detachment from bodily products on children before they've had the chance to acquire the substitutes through increasing elaboration and the acquisition of achievements related to walking and language. If the demands for learning control, in addition to being premature, are severe, the resulting detachment is experienced as an attack by the mother on the child's interior, as retaliation for the child's fantasies, which, in that period, are centered on the parental couple in intercourse. This will result in an inhibition of these fantasies, and subsequent disorders in the development of ego functions.

The information the mother gives us at this point will not only guide us to evaluate the child's neurosis, but also help us understand the bond she has with her child. Few mothers recall these events accurately. Fortunately, the material from the analysis of children, especially that of young children, has allowed us to later reconstruct these experiences, comparing them with what the parents remembered.

Clinical example: An enuretic girl

One of the first cases that guided me in designing the parent interview method was that of an enuretic girl. The mother had reported in the initial interview that toilet training had begun with great patience and when the girl was more than one year old. This was strange, as we knew that, in theory, a child with this disorder had always been subjected to early and severe toilet training. However, through analyzing the girl's material, we learned that this had indeed been the case for her as well. In a subsequent interview, after months of successful treatment, the mother was amazed to recall that the daughter had been toilet trained at two separate points and that she had only remembered the second training in the initial interview. She had forgotten that her mother-in-law, who was living with them at the time, had attempted to start toilet training the child at fifteen days of age, against the mother's will, but with the consent of the child's father (her son). This situation was one of many in which the conflict between the couple was expressed. The circumstances in which this first control began, as well as the underlying marital conflict, successfully explain the forgetfulness of the mother.

When we question the parents about diseases, operations, or trauma, we record not only the severity of the impact, but also their emotional reactions to the events. The dates and circumstances of family life that accompanied these events are frequently forgotten. At this juncture, I would like to point out a very striking case of forgetfulness; one where the intensity of the selective memory loss can be linked directly to the severity of the conflict.

Clinical example of forgetting

I was consulted by a shy seven-year-old boy called Raúl who had learning inhibitions. There was nothing in the history to justify the severity of the symptom. When I questioned Raúl's mother about traumatic situations in the first years of his life, the mother replied that she did not remember any. During the analysis of the child, a dream emerged with characteristics and patterns suggestive of a traumatic situation. Raúl dreamt that he was in bed, surrounded by canines that sometimes took the form of threatening wolves.

Months after the first interview, and after the child's marked improvement in his school performance, the mother called me to tell me that she had remembered something important. She claimed she did not understand how she could have possibly forgotten to mention it in the first interview. When Raúl was two years old, she claimed, he had been mauled by a dog.

The dog lived with them and, due to its ferocity, was always tied up. One day, it got loose and viciously attacked the child. Raúl had to be hospitalized and the mother made it a condition that the dog be expelled before the child return home. The husband, who was very fond of the animal, ensured that he would never untie it again. The mother agreed to return home with Raúl, but the father failed to keep his word and, two years later, the dog attacked again. The mother, in an effort to defend the child, suffered serious bites on the chest and neck.

In less extreme, but similarly traumatic situations, such as illnesses, operations, or falls, similar forgetfulness occurs. For this reason, the data that we obtain in this part of the interrogation is often poor. Complications in common childhood diseases are themselves indicative of neurosis, and, for this reason, it is important to record them in the history.

Sexuality of childhood

When we ask parents about their child's sexuality, they are usually flabbergasted by the question. However, generally speaking, we are easily informed on this point, save for the all-too-common denial that any sexual activity has ever taken place in the child's life. In regards to this, we must find out what specifically they have observed about the child's sexuality. It is usually this moment in the interrogation that brings us the biggest surprises, not only about the adults' concepts regarding the child's sexuality, but also by the way the parents answer the child's questions. In mothers' counseling groups, we see many examples of the serious difficulty parents encounter when answering sex-based questions with the truth.

The conscious and unconscious attitude of parents towards the sexual life of their children has a decisive influence on the child's acceptance or rejection of their instinctual needs. What we know today about the instinctual life of the child and its early manifestations amazes adults. Freud also caused astonishment and rejection when he discovered that the suckling child not only feeds, but enjoys the stimulation of sucking. To affirm today that a one-year-old boy masturbates, that he has erections, that young girls know their vaginas, and that both feel the desire for genital union, opposes everything that, until now, has been accepted about the life of a baby. In fact, to speak of it is often to elicit immediate rejection.

When we ask whether the child engages in such sexual activities openly and what those activities consist of, the parents tend to answer that they have "discovered" or "spied on" the child during sexual activity. It is much less frequent that the parents relate the events as normal or common, as opposed to clandestine. There are parents who, due to a poor knowledge of what sexual freedom entails, favor or encourage their children to such activities, or openly comment on them as evidence of precociousness. There are others who believe that showing off naked, or favoring activities such as bathing with siblings, is positive for development. This type of parent usually anticipates sexual enlightenment and does not wait for the moment when the child requires it. The baby's yearning for genital union—which is expressed but barely satisfied through masturbation—is the engine that drives and sets play activity. Klein was able to discover that, behind all playful activities, there are masturbation fantasies. Parents are usually surprised at this notion and generally do not find a way to answer our questions regarding the child's favorite play. We do not know if they are simply astonished that we'd give importance to play, or if their reaction is driven by a sudden awareness of how little they "see" their child, even though the child is with them all day.

The detailed description of a child's play activities helps us have a vision of the neurosis and its normality. Freud discovered that play is the repetition of traumatic situations in order to elaborate them. The research shows that, by actively doing what was suffered passively, the child manages to adapt to reality. That is why we value inhibition to play as such a serious sign of neurosis. A child who does not play does not know how to deal with difficult situations in daily life, and so channels them pathologically into symptoms or inhibitions.

Going to preschool

In the modern age, it is favorable and it is in fashion to send children to preschool from an early age. In many cases, when the home is extremely small or the mother works, this can be a positive influence on the development of the child. When the child, however, feels disposed of, and believes that they are only being sent to school so the adults may be rid of them, this decision can be negative to their emotional health. When we ask mothers at what age they have sent their child to preschool as well as the reasons that led them to do so, we find that, in most cases, the decision was not driven by a need or desire in the child, but instead stemmed from the mother's own difficulties. It is common, then, for the entry into preschool to coincide with the birth of a sibling. This is far from favorable to the child's development, as it constitutes a new element of disturbance. Indeed, the child in these circumstances experiences more painfully the fact that the place that they habitually occupied in the house has been taken away.

Going to school means, for the child, not only letting go of the mother, but also facing a massive wealth of learning that, in the early days, arouses anxieties analogous to those seen in adults with test anxiety. I have observed that children who go to school too early tend to be at a disadvantage from those who go at four or five years of age. Staying at home, participating in daily activities, and having an adequate space to play freely should be the prioritized conditions for the development of a child up to four or five years of age. Activities at home and at friends' houses sufficiently satisfy the need for contact with other children.

During the analysis of children, it has been found that inhibitions and difficulties with attending school have their roots in the early years. It is also known that a child who has not played well does not learn well either. We cannot assess the severity of learning difficulties based solely on what parents tell us. It is common for an apparently well-behaved child to be secretly neurotic or have partial inhibitions that are not even perceived by the parents. In other cases, the parents might paint a very grim picture, only for the therapist to ascertain that the issue is only a matter of momentary or self-determined difficulty, triggered by events such as sending the child to the first grade at five years of age. This is why it is important to always ask about the age at which a child entered school, as well as their ease or difficulty with learning to read and write, whether the learning itself caused pleasure or feelings of rejection, and whether the child shows exaggerated anxiety or a deep concern to fulfill their duties.

c) A day in the life

The reconstruction of a day in the child's life must be achieved through the use of concrete questions that elucidate the basic tenets of dependence and independence, external freedom and coercion, stability and instability of educational norms, and ease of giving and receiving.

This way, we can come to know several factors: whether the demands are appropriate for the age, whether there is precociousness or delay in development, the exact forms of punishment and reward used on the child, the child's capacity for joy, their sources of enjoyment, and their reactions to prohibitions. This wealth of knowledge will allow us an unexpectedly comprehensive view of family life. What we record will be a valuable help when cross-referenced with the child's history. Based on it, we can unearth misleading inaccuracies and omissions, as well as their causes. It is common, for example, for the parents to omit a sleeping disorder from the history, which then manifests during the "day in the life" description as an evident and complicated nocturnal event, even if the parents have not given it value.

The description of Sundays, holidays, and anniversaries illustrates the type and degree of family neurosis: an insight which allows us to better estimate the child's own neurosis and guide us in the diagnosis and prognosis of the case.

When we ask about a day in the child's life, we must learn who wakes him up and at what time. In the case of children over five years of age, it is important to know if he dresses himself and how long this has been the case. If not, it is crucial to find out who dresses him and why. It is useful to know about this early moment in the child's day in order to assess his dependence or independence when compared to others his age, as well as the attitude of the parents towards the precociousness or delay in their learning. All this is of undeniable value because it gives us an accurate vision of the child's life. The parents may believe that their child is independent because he exudes a certain rebellious spirit, and, in an apparent attempt to counteract this, they feed him by hand, dress him, or bathe him as late as seven or eight years of age. The conflict is greater when, in opposition to this pathological dependence, they let the child go out alone or encourage him to participate in activities above his age group.

d) Family relationships

By the time we reach the end of the interview, the parents tend to feel less reluctant to confide than they did at the beginning, and are instead eager to provide an idea of their affective relationship with the child, as well as what it means to them.

We must accept that we will be privy to very little information about the true relationship between the members of the family unit, and therefore we must limit ourselves to merely recording the age, the location within the family dynamic, whether the parents are both alive, their profession, the number of hours they are away from the house, the general conditions of the family's life, and the sociability of every member. It might be necessary to take up more than an hour in order to effectively complete the story, especially for beginners. It is recommended that the necessary time be committed to the task, since the most fundamental aspect of this research is the accurate recording of all the data that we can obtain from the parents, prior to starting our diagnostic work or treatment with the child. I have pointed out that we should strive to understand the symptom in maximum detail: initiation, development, improvement, and aggravation. I will now demonstrate, by way of describing a case, the process through which I generally conduct an interview.

Clinical example: Parents of a two-and-a-half-year-old girl

I was consulted about a two-and-a-half-year-old girl called Elena. The reason for the consultation was the clear evidence of a marked delay in her walking and language abilities, as well as her restless appearance, which had caused increasing concern in the family for the past year. She had suffered a seizure at eleven months and another one at eighteen months.

Although both parents attended the interview, the mother spoke the most. The father only intervened when prompted, either by my questions or by the mother's requests for clarification. Otherwise, he was silent. When I insisted that the nature of the delay be explained, the mother slipped into a tendency to be vague. I asked her how the child walked today. She replied that her daughter did not like walking at all and that, when they went on walks together, she would end up taking the child into her arms because she was tired. She remembered that her daughter took her first steps around year one, but admitted that, since then, the child had not been very active, did not show pleasure in walking, and, though capable of standing, had grown used to being carried. In addition, she tended to bump against objects that she encountered on her path, often stumbling and falling as a result.

When I asked if she had crawled, they answered that she had not, partly because she did not express the desire to do so, and partly because the mother did not want the child to get dirty. I followed the same criteria and questioned her language, asking her how the child currently speaks. The parents pointed out that the disorder was mainly in the articulation of words and that, although she knew the names of all the relatives, objects, and actions that surrounded her, it was difficult to understand the child. When I asked at what age she had uttered her first word, the mother hesitated and questioned the father. They argued candidly over the precise date, which made me realize that, at that moment in development, there existed more pressing conflicts than language itself.

I asked them some questions, intending to help them orient themselves in time and accurately reflect on the girl's growth. Was it summer? Winter? Was she already walking? All this was meant to elicit answers that, when compared with the date of birth, should have guided me well. In this case, however, they did not offer clarification. The parents repeated that she was a slow child and always too calm, that she did not do any work, and, according to the father, they often felt that they had "no child at all." Although we did not know when she'd said her first word and what it had been, thanks to this data, we at least knew more about her emotional reactions. As in the story, the first seizure was recorded at eleven months, during a feverish episode. I oriented the questioning towards this symptom. The doctor they consulted did not give the event much importance. Since the mother had informed the doctor that the child also suffered from nocturnal terror, she was prescribed two epamines daily. They also recalled that, during that period, the child used to have frequent angina and it was during one episode that the seizure manifested itself. I asked if that period of nocturnal terror and febrile episodes had coincided with teething and they answered that perhaps that was so, but they could not be sure. They also failed to recall the date of the emergence of the first tooth. I asked how long they continued with the epamine and whether the seizures had repeated. From this question we obtained an interesting piece of information.

The second seizure occurred at eighteen months and was accompanied by a doctor's recommendation to increase the dose of epamine. The mother observed that after this seizure, the girl tended toward distraction and listlessness during the day. She also recalled that she suffered from intestinal disorders and that her appetite decreased. In considering all these elements, we can partially reconstruct a picture of the girl's life up to that moment.

In the second half of the first year, her basic needs for movement and discharge were not satisfied. On top of that, the blockage caused by the increase in the dose of epamine further slowed her development. Internal and external blockage appeared to have been the reason for her difficulties in walking and talking, as well as sleeping. We now needed to find out if there was anything in particular that explained her seizure at eighteen-months old.

The parents had told us that the second daughter was now three months old. By comparing the data, we realized that the seizure coincided with her mother's pregnancy. We inquired as to the age at which the sleep disorder started, since it had appeared before the seizure. We were told that the first instances of dread occurred when she was seven or eight months old. We asked if she slept alone at that time. They answered that she shared the bedroom with them until the second daughter was born.

We already had a panorama that confirmed for us the common characteristics of sleep disorders at that age: inadequate stimulation, lack of movement, and overstimulation from sleeping in the parents' room. Once more, I would like to point out that, even when verifying child-rearing behaviors as unhealthy as the one I am describing, our attitude must never be one of censorship or judgment. It should always be remembered that the purpose of this interview is to relieve parental tensions. We are, from the very first moment, the child's therapists. We are not parental censors. We are there to understand and improve the situation, not to exacerbate and aggravate it by increasing guilt.

Once this interview is finished, and if the parents have decided to only conduct a diagnosis, they will be informed of the day and time of the interview with the child, as well as its duration. If, instead, they accept treatment for their child, they will be given the general indications regarding how the treatment will be administered. We will detail these at a later point.

Commentary on Chapter 5

Nydia Lisman Pieczanski (Argentina and USA)

The world of child psychoanalysis must greatly welcome this overdue translation of Arminda Aberastury's pioneering work in child analysis. It is especially important to me because it brings back many memories of my experience as a young clinician in Buenos Aires, Argentina, in the late 1960s. Psychoanalysis was a cultural and medical hot topic at the time. Some of the most brilliant minds were part of the Argentine Psychoanalytic Association. This critical mass of psychoanalysts including practitioners who arrived from other South American countries and Europe found a home in Buenos Aires and developed many of the pioneering psychoanalytic concepts (Lisman-Pieczanski & Pieczanski, 2014).

Arminda Aberastury, "*La Negra*" as we called her, a term of endearment in Latin America, was one of the brightest in the pioneering group. In collaboration with Elizabeth Goode de Garma, she almost single-handedly created the Argentinean school of child psychoanalysis and trained the first generations of child analysts in South America. Inspired by Kleinian theory and technique, she frequently asked Mrs. Klein to review her papers and supervise some cases. Over the years, they had an impressive epistolary interchange.

Arminda's empathic and generous approach towards the younger generations was unique. I feel privileged to have worked with her for a few years when I transitioned from pediatrics to psychoanalysis. The group I was part of consisted of pediatricians and psychoanalysts, and its uniqueness was its diversity of ideas, social background, and cultural belongings. Even if you were young and ignorant, she created a safe and inclusive atmosphere that made you comfortable sharing questions and anxieties about your clinical work.

Arminda Aberastury had several pioneering ideas. One of these was around recognizing children as unique individuals with their own thoughts, feelings, and needs. Another critical idea concerned understanding a child's environment and how it may influence his or her behavior and development. Additionally, Aberastury emphasized the value of active listening skills to better connect with children and communicate effectively with them. Her approach focused on building solid relationships with children based on trust and empathy to help support their healthy growth and development. In terms of the setting, she initiated the idea of an individual box for each child's treatment because, according to her, it represents the inner world of each child. She insisted that even a little torn-off paper should be kept in the box. Her idea was that the contents of the box and its treatment by the child replicated the child's inner world (see Chapter 6). We see the way she set about developing a new technique.

As seen in the first interview in Chapter 5, Aberastury's approach to parents requires a nonjudgmental mindset from the clinician. The initial interview with the parents demonstrates how detail-oriented she was, establishing many items of inquiry that were not considered necessary until then. She follows the material very closely, understanding that many distortions at the very beginning slowly change, and that memories can be rescued and brought to the interview. She insists parents must understand that the focus is on their child and that this initial interview should not resemble an interrogation. She believed the treatment or assessment had already begun when the parents arrived. She was attentive as to whether both parents or another household member came to the meeting. She insists that the clinician try to be as neutral as possible not to give the impression that one is on the side of one parent.

The assessment interview with the parents lasted at least an hour, during which she inquired about the reason for the consultation, the child's development, and medical history. She asked them how their child spends a weekday, weekend, or holiday from waking up to going to sleep, and how birthdays unfold. She explored the nature of the parents' relationship with each other, their children, and other members of the immediate family environment. She paid close attention to the manifest content of their story and what they were concerned about. As the interview progressed, more information and memories entered the room. She considered that the narrative was the external expression of multiple unconscious phantasies about their child's problem and their connection to it.

In one of the seminars that I attended, Arminda gave an example of parents bringing a small child for a consultation because of bad behavior and difficulties in following orders. The parents described their child as very happy, curious, and easygoing. As the interview evolved, the parents started arguing about other symptoms they had just remembered. The mother recalled that during her pregnancy, she tripped on a step and fell down the stairs. She started crying, feeling entirely responsible for their child's behavior. The couple worked together to explore with Aberastury the mother's fear that their child had been badly damaged during her fall. Reliving this memory did not resolve the child's behavior. However, the example shows that information may have been entirely forgotten at first, and only later as the analyst listens do the parents gradually remember. It is an excellent example of how unconscious understanding of memories affects our relationships and perceptions of the people we care about.

Arminda describes how painful it is for parents to talk about their child's difficulties and how sometimes they unconsciously move away from the child's story to talk about their own stories. She pays attention to every detail, from the idea of having a baby to the mother's relationship with her pregnancy at different times until the birth. She considered every detail during the delivery process important, such as the use of anesthetics, the presence or absence of a partner, or the availability of a friendly network of family and friends.

Feeding was central in Aberastury's works in terms of the physical and emotional closeness of the mother with her infant. For her this is fundamental to the understanding of relatively early moments in a baby's life. She also believed dentition was closely related to overall physical and emotional development in infants and children. She suggested that the eruption of primary teeth could be an essential milestone in a child's growth, leading to increased mobility or enhancing cognitive ability. Additionally, she argued that dental problems often had psychological roots and were linked to unresolved conflicts or anxiety in a child's life. She was the first psychoanalyst to have study groups with pediatric dentists, where she inspired them to pioneer a new way of working with child dental patients.

Aberastury's theory links dentition and early oedipal configuration in psychic development. She outlines how the dentition process participates in the early turmoil related to the sexual developmental phases. She suggests that as children go through their dental stages, they become increasingly aware of the differences between genders, which excites them on an unconscious level. This excitement leads to feelings of anxiety and fear, which can then lead to various neuroses or fixations throughout the individual's adult life.

Aberastury introduced and developed working groups with parents and, based on her experiences with those groups, made significant contributions to theory and clinical practice. In these groups, the focus was on the children and how to protect them from unnecessary early trauma. For instance, the parents' group members had conversations about the benefits and negative aspects of circumcision in the life of a newborn. Most parents understood that circumcision could be a trauma to the vulnerable body of a newborn and that they could choose to avoid this traumatic experience. At a seminar I attended, I remember Arminda telling us the story of a mother-to-be in a parents' group. The mother in this story was a religious Jewish member of the group. She had a good delivery of a lovely baby boy, and did not arrange for circumcision. The father called Aberastury a week later, saying his wife could not connect with this beautiful baby. Aberastury called for an emergency session with the whole group in which the mother, crying, told the group that the baby felt alien to her. He was not her Jewish baby. After that intense, moving session, the mother decided to circumcise her baby. Two weeks later, she returned to the group very invigorated and delighted with her happy baby. She noted that intellectual information, instead of preventing damage, could impinge on a child's life.

This example from the parents' group clearly shows how Aberastury was both firm and flexible in her clinical work and open to acknowledging cultural differences. She understood how culture can impose specific behaviors that developed over thousands of years and how these behaviors influence the emotional bonding between parents and children. Any psychoanalyst interested in treating children should find the technical and clinical concepts described in this book as inspiring, relevant, and indispensable today as they were half a century ago.

CHAPTER 6

The office, the play material, the individual drawer, and technical problems arising from daily management

The setting

The room where a child is psychoanalyzed need not be large because the playing technique does not require much space. The walls must be washable and the floor should be covered with linoleum or Flexiplast. An asbestos sheet should be available to fit the table or floor, as it may be necessary for the child to play with fire. The optimal situation includes a bathroom attached to the work room, designated for the exclusive use of the patient. It must have a sink with running water, a toilet, a towel, toilet paper, a glass, and one or two chairs. If this bathroom is used outside working hours, it is necessary to ensure that no objects are visible or likely to be found by the child. The door that connects to the office must not be closed off from the bathroom, in order to avoid any unnecessary difficulty. The front office doors leading outside must be locked from the inside. They must be double doors or be made of soundproof materials. If possible, a climate of peaceful isolation should be maintained at all times, and only for exceptional reasons should the session be interrupted or someone else allowed to enter the office. A bell is useful in this regard, so that any necessary objects can be ferried in and out of the room at a moment's notice and without causing a distraction. A small and comfortable couch on which the child can lie down and talk is useful; even very young children come to need this, and those approaching puberty often directly ask for it. The table and chairs should be simple, comfortable, and strong enough to withstand wear and tear. There exists a standard list of materials required for meeting the needs of a child up to four or five years of age. With few modifications, this same group of objects is also suitable for the treatment of older children: buckets, plasticine, pencil, paper, colored pencils, rubber, glue, small dolls, cloth, toy cars, cups, saucers, cutlery, and scissors.

The personal drawer

A cabinet with drawers is necessary, within which the play material dedicated to each patient is stored. Each drawer must be locked at the end of the session and opened only at the beginning of the next session. Material stored in the drawer will include items of the sort the child chooses to play with at home. During the first parent interview, the therapist can have asked what the child tends to play with at home, and, whenever possible, can include that in the material provided in the diagnostic drawer. When observing a child for diagnosis, the therapist should offer the child play material kept in a diagnostic drawer. The drawer, though part of the office, must be kept under lock and key at all times it is not being used. It must be opened only when a child comes for an hour of observation. If it has already been decided that the child is coming for treatment, an individual drawer with suitable play material is prepared ahead of time. Throughout treatment, only the patient and the therapist have access to the drawer.

The situation may arise wherein a child comes for an hour of observation, and upon later deliberation, the therapist decides to analyze the patient. In that case, the material used in the first hour is usually included in the patient's individual drawer. This is later complemented and completed with objects the analyst decides are more appropriate for the child's age. The nature of the child's first action, and the length of time in session before the child makes that action, inform the analyst of the patient's attitude towards the world. The degree of inhibition of playing is also an index of the severity of the child's neurosis. The first session is of very special importance. In it, the child shows what their unconscious fantasy of illness and healing consists of and how they accept or reject the role of the therapist. When the patient and the therapist part, the patient must be reminded of the day and time of the next session.

From this moment on, the therapist, the private therapy room, and the individual drawer are receptively offered to the child. The prearranged drawer is a symbol of this situation, and should always be kept that way. The individual drawer progressively acquires enormous importance, though this is not always expressed openly. There are children who do not touch anything in the drawer for months (see the case of Verónica in Chapter 9). Others insist on leaving everything out of the drawer, as if to appear unbothered by ownership or a lack thereof. A practical problem that will inevitably arise is the restocking and replacement of the original drawer contents. Papers, glue, plasticine, and water should always be available to the child.

It often happens that a child wants to take home some of the material from the drawer. This should be avoided with proper interpretation. If the attempt to convince the child is unsuccessful, the analyst must try to make the child leave the object without violence. The analyst must refuse the request, pointing out that the material is for treatment and should be left in the office. If, according to the context of the analysis, the child taking the object home is considered useful, it can be allowed, but only as an exception to the rule. The analyst must also indicate why it is being allowed. If the child steals the object, this can be an element to interpret and analyze during the next session.

It is also common for the child to bring a toy or object from home, such as Elizabeth Garma's patient who brought a parrot. Bringing the object is usually a way of demonstrating to the analyst an aspect of their family dynamic at that moment. In that case, the patient is free to either leave it in the drawer (not if it is a parrot!) or take it back, and each decision can be interpreted by the analyst differently. Patients tend to leave the toy for a while, sometimes permanently. They incorporate it into the material that we have initially offered. This, in and of itself, is incredibly revealing. Children who react this way often live in a state of great helplessness and are thus fulfilling their desire to transform the office into their home.

Regulation of supplies: paper, pencil, glue, plasticine, water

All materials should be regulated in supply and application. In the same way, allowing the patient to play with water should not lead to the patient flooding the office. This is, of course, in addition to interpreting the reasons that drove the patient to flood or destroy in the first place. It is important to differentiate toys from materials that, like water, must always be available to the patient. Their use must be controlled by the analyst and, in general, they should always be within reach, but not if the child uses them for uncontrollable destruction. For example, if a child burns a block of paper, the analyst must, after sufficiently observing the characteristics of the game, prevent the act and interpret an expressive and constructive meaning to designate the remains as useless and destroyed matter. Children without major conflicts in learning will ask for journal sheets or junk if they feel the need to burn paper. The inappropriate use of this material has the meaning of mistreating parts of themselves, the therapist, and the bond between both. A child may try to flush sheets from their block into the toilet, soak them, shred them, squeeze them into a pulp, and throw them into the drawer or on the floor. All these behaviors should be timely, limited, and interpreted as petty suicides.

Paper, pencils, and colored pencils are the most effective means of communication for a child between the ages of six and twelve. Therefore, they must always be at their disposal for this purpose. The same can be said of plasticine. If the child, however, merely throws it on the ground and tramples it, the analyst must observe the action until it is understood in relation to the previous games—sometimes in connection with events during the beginning of the session—and then interpret it. If the same activity is repeated compulsively, the analyst must stop it, in addition to interpreting. For example, if the preceding game consisted of modeling a face, and the child decided that their final product was subpar, throwing and trampling the clay could be construed as the patient expressing to the analyst the feelings of helplessness and grief elicited by their perceived inability to create.

It is common for a behavior to change after it is interpreted. If, on the other hand, it continues, the analyst tries another interpretation because leaving the patient to their own destructive tendencies would merely increase their anguish and guilt. It would also be a mistake to interpret this behavior as aggressive. While apparently sadistic in nature, this type of attitude conceals, in truth, deep-seated masochism and guilt that drive the child to be stripped and destroyed with an urgent fervor. If a child verbalizes suicidal ideation or attempts suicide, the effective analyst will take immediate precautionary measures while vigorously interpreting the act. The analyst must give the same importance to the patient's possessions and to the bond that is established between the patient and the therapist through these possessions.

Example of play

A six-year-old girl used glue to smear the walls (see the case of Verónica, Chapter 9). The material that followed the performance showed that, for her, the emptying of the rubber bottle of glue was not a masochistic act, but rather a rehearsal for the possibility that something could serve to unite what she was destroying. She was trying to fix broken words within herself and the glue was a valuable substance that she could dispose of unconditionally. The right thing to do, then, was to fill her bottle every time the material was exhausted. If her intention had been to spread and smear it in a masochistic way, she would not have replenished it in such nurturing fashion.

Dealing with broken toys and used-up supplies

In summary, certain elements that are offered to the child to facilitate preverbal communication are basic and must be renewed whenever they become useful to express new ideas. The analyst should avoid the annihilation of those substances that symbolize contents of the patient or the therapist, as well as the link between them, and by this token the patient's integrity is preserved. The replacement of other materials, including toy cars, toy planes, and dishes, should occur whenever the child requests it and the circumstances allow for it. From this point forward, the material the analyst offers should be simple, of good quality, and, if possible, sturdy.

Suppose that a child organizes car races in which he competes with his brothers and destroys one of them during the game. If the patient asks us to fix the damage, the analyst, in addition to interpreting, must agree. A negative response might indicate to the patient that the analyst, and by extension, the external world, considers the destruction irreparable. Generally, it is wisest not to simply remove the broken car, even if the child asks us to do so. In addition to interpreting why the child cannot bear the sight of the wrecked car, which is usually interpreted as an accusation or a persecution, it is useful to point out the wisdom of keeping it. In spite of everything, the child sometimes does not accept this measure for fear of contamination. In this case, it is best to separate the toy from the rest or keep it apart, thus taking charge of the child's conflict. Invariably, the patient will later claim the toy in order to fix it themselves, or with the therapist's help. If this same child breaks a car in each session of their treatment, his analyst must not continue to replace it and must, instead, dedicate herself to interpreting the child's reactions to this frustration and the reasons that led to the destruction.

Example of play: Esteban age eight

During the analysis of eight-year-old Esteban, I was presented with this problem acutely, which provided me an in-depth education on this subject. Everything he placed inside the drawer, he would immediately smash on his first attempt at using it for a game. For weeks, I would replace the material according to his requests. Eventually, I understood that this was the wrong approach. I needed to face the consequences of his destructive tendencies and analyze what he was signaling about himself and his relationship with me. That drawer, full of broken toys, discarded scraps, and objects in disarray, lacking an attractive appearance or the spirit of play, was exactly how he felt about himself. Accepting the drawer in those conditions meant, for him, accepting himself as he was, without putting forward a happy, healthy version of himself. Adding attractive things signified a demand that he portray himself as equally attractive, as well as the consequent anguish at his inability to do so due to his illness.

In this case, I was able to analyze in detail the meaning of preserving, breaking, replacing, and reassembling the broken toys. I applied what I learned from that experience to similar cases and concluded that, in a technical sense, it is generally counterproductive to replace broken pieces, unless doing so can aid the expression of conflict and lead to understanding. In most cases, the object must be kept, even if the child pretends not to see it in the drawer. This rejection of a toy is due to a need similar to that of the adult who resorts to denying their own destructive tendencies and symptoms. To remove the destroyed objects from the drawer means to remove from the child's mind the knowledge that there is something destroyed and sick within *them*, because they will not feel capable of fixing it. The presence of the destroyed object is of great technical utility, since, when genuine repair tendencies arise, the patient will look for it and manage to fix it. In this sense, it is interesting to observe how the child progressively uses a hierarchy of substances to improve their repair, ranging from plasticine which joins weakly, to glue and cement which join definitively. The tendencies to repair imply the presence of underlying destructive tendencies towards the object and the self. The decrease in sadism to preserve the object—loved or in need—provides us with an index of the patient's greater adaptation to reality, as well as their capacity for enjoyment in life.

When the hour is over, the toys should be returned to the drawer, with or without the child's help. It is important to verbalize the following to the patient:

1) That material belongs to you.
2) The drawer will remain locked.
3) No one will have access to it in your absence and I will only open it as we start the next session.
4) Everything that happened during the session will be kept absolutely private.
5) This is our agreed weekly schedule. (Make the schedule available to the patient.)
6) Any changes in treatment or interviews with relatives will be discussed with you and then communicated to your parents.

Example of the process with Susana, a sixteen month old

Here is a summary of the first hour of the analysis of a sixteen-month-old girl who suffered a seizure. Since her parents told me she used to play for hours with picture books, I included a few in her drawer. In this case and others, the patient's ability to quickly find the objects best suited for her personal expression caught my attention.

Susana entered the office with her mother. She looked at the toys but did not touch them. She leafed through the books like an adult consulting a dictionary, and, when she found what she was looking for, she showed me. It was a picture of a little girl older than her, holding an apple in her hand. At the same time, she spoke the name of one of her sisters, a somewhat older girl. Then, she showed me another girl. This one was holding a balloon. All the figures she selected had elements in common: They always consisted of a visual representation of girl or woman who owned something. She named them all after her sister. She then returned to the first picture. She cupped her left hand, as if she were asking for something. With her right, she held out the book, and with her left, she tapped the page as if trying to make the objects fall into it. After repeating this several times, she showed me her empty left hand and motioned to the figure that represented her rival, holding the apple. She would do this while looking at me in a questioning way, as if asking for a solution. She repeated the same routine with all the images she showed me, exhibiting signs of growing impatience following each failure.

Through this first action, she expressed to me her rivalry with her sister, whom she saw as possessing something valuable, while she felt empty-handed. Her unconscious fantasy regarding her illness resulted in a cumulative sort of frustration. As a result of this, she *needed* the seizure to release the rage. It is possible that, without the picture books provided to her, she would have found another way to express herself, but their presence undoubtedly facilitated communication. The child's remarkable capacity to express her conflicts in a preverbal language has led us to the realization that there is no core difference between the analysis of children and adults.

In our analysis, we combed through hours of play, attempting to verbalize, in much the same way an adult does during analysis, the conflicts the child expressed in preverbal language. The experience was surprising, because it gradually confirmed our conviction regarding the similarity between the basic internal conflicts of adults and children.

Example of the process: Alba, a two year old

Two-year-old Alba's central conflict at the time was a fear that stemmed from a potential separation from her male analyst (Moisés Tractenberg). She reacted to his upcoming trip by crafting games in which she decided to follow him, or enacting scenarios in which she prevented him from traveling by holding him back with seductions or threats. In one of these games, she fashioned "travel tickets" out of small scraps of paper and placed them in the therapist's jacket pocket. This was aptly interpreted as a reassurance: If the analyst had a return ticket, the separation would only be temporary. The anguish of losing him and her refusal to separate from him were expressed through a game in which she turned herself into an airplane. With outstretched arms, she gave herself wings, then proceeded to act as if she were flying. In the language of an adult, this could very well be saying, "I'm staying with you."

This game expressed an attempt at manically denying a separation and, when this maneuver failed, it expressed the anguish of being small and unable to follow or reach the object being taken away. The patient then pretended that the therapist was flying and that she was a boat. The different speeds and altitudes of these means of transport made any meeting impossible. Thus, the rage, jealousy, and helplessness evoked by her therapist's journey and her inability to join him on it were successfully interpreted. Alba reacted to the performance with a series of seductive games, with which she tried to retain him; she danced, sang, removed her underwear, urinated, and defecated.

When, through interpretations, Alba was able to diminish her manic mechanisms and allow herself to feel the sorrow and pain of the separation, she played at climbing on a piece of furniture. From there, she jumped so that the therapist would catch her in his arms. This way, she elaborated the departure and the hope of the return as the therapist welcoming her with open arms. Climbing and then jumping off the furniture symbolized the landing of the plane and the arrival, return, and reconciliation with the therapist. Confirming this interpretation, the game that followed was hide-and-seek. The patient hid from the therapist and had him look for her, and vice versa. Every absence was followed by an encounter, thus elaborating her anguish at losing him and her longing for his return.

During the moments when the manic attempts to deny the painful reality reappeared, Alba would again initiate games of seduction or enact scenarios focused on following the therapist. This time, however, they led to more depressive games focused on separation. This process ultimately resulted in a game in which she checked her drawer, then listed her toys and family members, as if weighing and balancing her external and internal possessions, in order to more easily endure that painful separation.

This girl had very precocious genital development, which is why her seduction fantasies included such detail regarding genital union. The success of her analysis, which led her to cure the symptom—asthmatic bronchitis—was due to the fact that, within the transferential relationship, she was able to elaborate the loss of her original objects, and then her defenses against depression arose, decreasing her sadism and bolstering her ability to repair.

At the time, it was common for the girl to come to the session chewing candy or eating ice cream. She would offer to share these foods with her analyst. It is often more technically sound to interpret, rather than participate, in such activities, because these "childish things" find their equivalents in adult attitudes of great significance. If the analyst is lovingly understanding of what the child's frustration means, and interprets it effectively, the child will develop it, accept it, and feel understood.

We are forced to accept that adaptation to reality occurs earlier and more firmly in the child than we had previously supposed. Furthermore, from a very young age, the child has a healthy enough understanding of the demands of reality. Therefore, if the analyst is consistent from day to day and fulfills the role of therapist well the child will adapt to the analytic situation and deal with its frustrations.

Contact with the analyst

Many behaviors, such as those related to children consuming food during the session or seeking physical contact with the therapist, usually represent an attempted destruction of the treatment. In these attempts, children are trying to transform the analysis into a familial or social situation, thereby attacking the bond with the therapist and denying their own illness. It also frequently occurs that, at some point in the analysis, a child will seek out intimate contact with the therapist. It is advisable to react the same way as when the patient attacks or assails the therapist, interpreting the behavior, setting limits, and understanding the action as a comment on our relationship. In some very rare situations, I have found it helpful to more actively meet these needs. It is not uncommon for a child to try to attack us with hands, feet, and fecal matter, and it is extremely useful that we understand how to use interpretation or action to deal with an intention that, if carried out, can create an uncomfortable situation for us. This is especially true because, if these behaviors are allowed, they can be repeated in the future out of guilt and hatred. For example, in the case of a three-year-old boy who launched a physically violent attack, his analyst (Elizabeth Garma) chose to hold his arms tightly to keep him safe, acting like a vest and continuing to interpret the situation for him. During my analysis of a two-and-a-half-year-old boy, the patient suffered from an acute outbreak of anxiety and became possessed with the desire to hurt himself and jump out of the window. I had to resort to physical force to stop him. There are many other situations in which a child analyst might wonder what to do, especially when the instruments of work and interpretation prove insufficient. I believe that the limited scope of our influence is obvious whenever the physical integrity of the child, the analyst, or the office space is at risk.

Playing with fire

It is common for children between six and eleven years old, and especially those who suffer from enuresis, to feel the draw of playing with fire. The analyst must satisfy that need, but only under conditions which absolutely guarantee its safe fulfillment, in order to not spoil the work room. It may be necessary to include matches, a heater, or flammable material during a child's test. If the child is young, the analyst must choose wooden matches that can be handled safely. If the child is older, wax tapers can be used. If a heater or an alcohol lamp is placed in the drawer, a model must be chosen that works without danger of explosion. Alcohol must only be burned under the analyst's supervision and custody from this point forward, and far from the place where the child is playing. Any game with fire must be carried out on an asbestos sheet covering either the floor or the work table, so as to avoid irreparable damage. Sometimes the child will burn paper, cotton, plasticine, and even sulfur. Due to the fumes, the window must be kept open so that neither the patient nor the therapist should experience such discomfort that the session cannot continue. This extreme should never be reached and, if possible, the therapist should anticipate the situation rather than prohibit it.

Playing with paint

Suppose a five-year-old boy has brought paint from his house. In addition to painting on the sheets, he wants to paint on the analyst's clothes, face, or hands. This should not be allowed under any circumstance, because it is unpleasant and unnecessary. As a rule, I never include watercolor, tempera, or oil-based paints in the child's material. Instead, I offer finger paints or watercolor pencils, which fulfill the same function without the secondary difficulties of permanent staining. It is advisable for the analyst to wear clothes that do not limit performance and to avoid bringing in fragile, valuable articles like jewelry. As for the child's clothing during the session, this is to be left to the mother's discretion. For instance, Verónica's mother provided a rubber apron for playing with water (Chapter 9).

Concerns of male child analysts

Certain male analysts have raised concerns regarding what to do if a patient asks them to sew or knit something. In this, as in any problems that arise during a session, the analyst must consider the formal and manifest content in tandem with the latent content hidden behind it. In the foreground, the male analyst must assure the patient that it is common for a man not to know how to perform certain tasks. On a deeper plane, the analyst must grasp that the problem is not the child being ignorant of the task, but the feeling that the task is somehow forbidden.

To analyze a child, an analyst must have a wealth of knowledge that is not required in adult analysis. This knowledge must include, at the very least, rudimentary skills at making doll clothes, or wrappings to replace a ripped dress, which may represent fetal membranes (Garma, 1949). If the analyst manages to work out the castration anxiety and admits to the female yearnings for a child, the ability to do what the patient asks will spontaneously emerge. The male analyst can also acquire a certain manual dexterity, even when the anxiety of playing such an obviously feminine role is still intense. This anxiety may never be overcome and the analyst may feel unable to thread a needle or put a doll in a diaper. In that case, it is not wise that this person should continue to be a child analyst. This is not due to some arbitrary importance assigned to crafting doll clothes that might enable the analysis to proceed in a satisfactory manner, but because this limitation represents, within the analyst, an unresolved conflict.

Play skills of the child analyst

To be a child analyst, it is necessary to know and play a vast number of games proficiently. These include, but are not limited to, chess, checkers, basketball, and tic-tac-toe, among others. In-depth knowledge of the most popular characters and comic books is required. This can only be gained from reading the best-known children's magazines, remembering classic children's stories in detail, and reflecting on their meaning beforehand. In addition, the game itself must remain sufficiently enjoyable for the analyst. A good analyst must retain an agility that allows them to effortlessly face the repetitive physical demands of child analysis. This does not mean that if, on occasion, the analyst is tired or does not feel like moving much, the session is somehow ineffective. It is, however, unacceptable for an analyst to believe that they can provide a comprehensive analysis of a child while remaining in their chair, as is the case with adults. My interest in research, specifically when analyzing very young children, has meant that I have had to cope, more than once, with the fatigue and discomfort of a game. A notable example was the case of an eighteen-month-old boy who did not walk. I was forced to analyze the patient while sitting on the floor, and resorted to following him at a steady crawl when he decided to move. But physical strain is not always the problem. At times, it can seem tedious to devote entire play sessions to preparing and distributing imaginary meals to dolls, but as our understanding of preverbal language progresses, we begin to translate and break down the actions of the game into their smallest details, understanding them in the process. This makes for a much more exciting experience than listening to an adult's story. It is, however, common for the analyst to lack an immediate understanding of the activity. The anguish produced by this situation often propels the analyst to just engage in play, which is tantamount to simply joining the game, instead of assuming the role of therapist and reaching for lucidity.

Often, a child might ask that the material they have played with that day be kept out of the drawer, without anyone touching it, until the next session. In each case, this request will have a different meaning that must be interpreted. But the therapist must not acquiesce to the request because, although the underlying anxiety is usually tied to a fear of a change, exposure to that material cannot be imposed on other children. This might arouse their curiosity, as well as feelings of jealousy and anger, which would unnecessarily complicate the relationship with the therapist. It is also worth noting that, in exposing a patient's possessions, the bond of trust might be endangered, because the reactions the objects would elicit would be impossible to predict or control. Instead, the therapist must interpret the child's need to test them, the child's desire to know if the therapist will defend them from their compulsion to deprive and attack, or else from their need to expose themselves in an effort to arouse jealousy or envy for their possessions. Sometimes this request hides the desire that other patients might do the same, leaving their objects out so that the child might then be able to see what the other patients possess. In that case, when the analyst refuses, the patient will often insist that another child's drawer be opened so that they may see its contents. This is another request we must deny, as it would bring with it a chain of complications that would prove too difficult to handle and would fundamentally remove the assurance that a patient's materials be kept absolutely private. This mistake would be equal in severity to responding to an adult patient's queries about another patient by divulging personal details.

It is advisable to always note the factors that may have motivated this request, especially in children who, until that point, were handling their individual drawers well. It may be that, on the same day as the session, the child saw another patient, perceived a detail about the office, or noticed something new about the analyst themselves, and this element disturbed them because they did not understand its meaning. Sometimes an old bruise or scratch is discovered that day, and the child wants to ascertain the identity of the person who harmed or mistreated the analyst. In any case, the priority is to search for the source of the request within the child and *not* in the external world.

Many times, a child who has taken to drawing during the sessions will ask the analyst to hang the pictures on the wall as an exhibition of sorts. If we entertain, just for a moment, the results of agreeing to this request, we find ourselves faced with an army of negative consequences: Another patient might want to destroy all the drawings, angry and jealous that they have occupied a place that, at that moment, should be reserved only for them—they may want to remove them and take them home or they may draw on top of the originals and thus obscure them. Of course, any of these requests may be interpreted, prohibited, or allowed, without it becoming a fundamental obstacle to the continuation of the treatment. However, this would always result in the tendency to repeat similar situations, unnecessarily complicating and interfering with the treatment of that patient and others. If it is considered technically necessary to access orders like this, it makes sense for the therapist to offer the child an individual drawer and reserve its contents for that child alone, in keeping with the motto that "access to the drawer is only allowed to the child and their therapist." If it is considered technically sound to offer each child a box that belongs only to them, it is to respect their need to heal themselves and give them total possession, without interference, of elements that, for the child, will come to represent the primitive relationship with the mother. Due to this, the child's material must be available to nobody but the child; for, sometimes a piece of cloth, a small object, or a piece of wood can have enormous emotional value for the child, who feels terribly deprived and deceived if the object is touched, changed, or discarded.

Sometimes a child does not want to leave after the session is over. In this situation, it is convenient to close the individual drawer, say goodbye to its contents, and ask the person who accompanied the child to come in and fetch them. In the case of older children, it suffices to simply close the drawer. In any case, the drawer should not be left open. If the child escapes the room without closing it, it falls to the therapist to close the drawer before another child enters the room.

When the analysis must be interrupted due to vacation, or for any other reason, the therapist must remind the child well in advance and be attentive to their facial reactions when the child is faced with the imminent separation. These reactions can be telling of the child's comfort level when detaching themselves from objects.

When a child is ready to terminate the analysis, it is useful to remind her of the agreed-upon date of the final session. Do not assume that she knows or that her parents have told her. The decision must be discussed directly with the child, and must then be communicated to, and confirmed with, the parents. The arrangements for the treatment—its external, formal details—are terms that have been agreed with the parents. But, deep down, it is with the patient that we have entered an analytical pact. To decide to end an analysis, we must first assess the degree to which it has succeeded. An analysis can be considered complete if the child's symptoms have disappeared, if her interests have expanded, if she has a greater capacity for lasting enjoyment, and if she has struck a balance between dependence and independence with her environment.

As for the longevity of the results, to believe that undergoing a psychological evaluation equates assured, lifelong, mental and physical health is to be subject to a silly hoax or a utopian fantasy. The tensions and mistreatment that a child faces from the outside world can exceed his ego's capacity to elaborate them without becoming ill, and this can happen even if the analysis has been successful. On the other hand, analysis in childhood will allow the child a healthier development. One of the great benefits will be an improvement in his ability to play and learn, easily and with pleasure, as well as to face problems more effectively.

The analyst's role in the play

Analysts need to clarify their place in the play, determining how and when they should perform their duties. When a child asks to play, the analyst must know the role they are playing before engaging in the activity. If the child, for example, is playing at food preparation and wants the analyst to participate, the analyst should ask how to prepare the food, how it should be handled and served, and when it should be plated and ingested. This should be the case even when the child does not understand words very well and uses preverbal language to communicate. When it comes to an older child, the patient can often explain every detail of the role assigned to the analyst. For example, if the patient is a boy playing school and his male analyst is assigned the role of the student, the analyst must interpret the role reversal, and, additionally, ask the child to illustrate what kind of student the analyst should be, what he should do, what he wants from the child as a teacher, and what the child (as teacher) wants in return from his student. If the boy refuses or resists the suggestion to do so, it is necessary to formulate an interpretation that gives him an awareness of his disease again, reasserting the idea that this person playing the part of the student is their therapist and is not only playing, but psychoanalyzing. Only then can he understand and help the child.

Child patients are relieved when these limits are placed, as we affirm our role as therapist every time it is diluted and they affirm it too.

There is no doubt that a cold knowledge of technique and theory is not sufficient to analyze a child. It is necessary to find some of the joy that the child feels in playing, to maintain some of the naiveté, fantasy, and wonder that are inherent in childhood. Just as a writer has innate gifts of expression but also has to hone his craft, an analyst must not only absorb the theory and technique of psychoanalysis, but also possess that gift of analytic sensibility that cannot be taught, but can be remarkably developed with the individual analysis of the psychoanalyst. This can be understood in light of the importance of an analyst's work; work that requires a great capacity for connection and expression, both of which are developed through effective analysis.

On another educational level, there is a lot to be gained by learning to formulate interpretations. I advise all those who work in analysis, and especially those involved in the analysis of children, to practise interpretation outside of sessions. Get into the habit of repeatedly reviewing the material and formulating the interpretation in writing, reformulating it as many times as is necessary to produce the one considered appropriate. This does not mean studying template interpretations in order to simply hand them out, but finding the way to effortlessly achieve the distillation and expression of our understanding, and then formulating it with a language appropriate to the case and the age of the patient. This learning is comparable to the learning of music students, who must repeatedly transpose the same musical sequence to different major and minor keys, or undergo tedious composition exercises that will not transform them into creators, but will instead give them the possibility to effectively shape their dreams.

This study of the formulation need not be strictly written and should also be oral, because analysts must get used to hearing their own interpretations and be able to criticize themselves. Analysts who have spent years analyzing adults, and then begin to treat children, find that it is easier, after this experience, to formulate interpretations for adults. I believe this is due to the effort required to adapt knowledge, which until recently had been fixed exclusively on an adult perspective, to the language of a young child.

Feelings of annoyance and grief are often experienced when starting to work with children. At this point, it is necessary to accept that the child perceives, understands, expresses, and judges at a level that is very close to our own. One of the strongest frustrations we suffer as children is not finding an answer to our curiosity. Even more so, we struggle with not being understood when our communication is pre- or rudimentarily verbal. When interpreting the case of a sixteen- or eighteen-month-old child and observing the ease with which the child understands words, as well as the relief they experience at being understood, a common adult error becomes evident: saying anything and everything in front of a child due to the false assumption that they do not yet understand. Worse still is the parent who, when the child shows signs of understanding, silences them, expresses irritation, or considers the behavior exceptional. I have analyzed children as young as fourteen months of age and I believe that improvement of these techniques will lead to their application on even younger children.

The child's relation to the fee

In the technical treatises published to this date, the problem of fees in the analysis of children is not mentioned. With this issue, as with those raised previously, everything leads back to the conclusion that there is no difference between the analysis of children and adults. It is obvious that the child cannot afford to pay for treatment, but this does not differ from what happens in daily life and the child is clearly aware of this. No child, even a very young one, thinks or expects that a shopkeeper will simply give away a product, but will instead ask the parents to buy it. In this, as in all aspects of life, the child knows that parents or surrogates pay for their things, and treatment is included in this concept (Klein, 1945). For the child, as for the adult, it can become an issue that the sessions are paid for by someone else, but the patient's age does not factor into those problems.

It is convenient that the child should know the sessions are paid for within the first days of the month. It is preferable that, if knowledge allows, the child calculate the hours themselves. If possible, the child should deliver the money to the therapist. In the case of very young or very sick children, the necessary precautions must be taken so as to not risk the child losing the money. It is remarkable how even very young children remind their parents to pay for the sessions, walk in loudly claiming that they have the money, or assure the analyst that they have already requested it. In their games, they express their unconscious fantasies regarding payment, in the same way an adult directly or indirectly verbalizes their fantasies during their sessions. It is usually practical to suggest to the mother, during the initial interview, that she hand over the money to the child when they enter the office. It has been observed that, though the child allows the parent to take responsibility on other levels, they claim this act as their right to greater independence.

Example: Mario, seven and a half, and the fee

The case I will present in the following section showcases the insight the child has about the relationship between the number of sessions and the amount of the fees, as well as the difficulty or ease with which the parents face this expense.

Mario suffered from multiple phobias, nocturnal terrors, and uncontrollable aggressiveness, all of which made it difficult for him to get in touch with his environment. He was seven-and-a-half years old when he began his psychoanalytic treatment with Manuel Kizzer. The following session corresponds to the return of the holidays, after a year of treatment consisting of four weekly sessions.

Mario took Play-Doh and said he would make a ball with many feet, so that it would not fall. After reflecting a while, he claimed that it was very difficult to add so many feet, and that, instead, he would make a cannon he could fire. That day, upon entering the session, the parents had commented that they'd decided to reduce the analysis by one session because Mario had been improving and they'd been having financial difficulties. The therapist interpreted the multiple legs as a representation of Mario's need to ensure that he would not roll away, due to the insecurity that decreasing the sessions evoked. In addition, the decision had angered him quite a bit, effectively explaining the bombastic cannon.

He then said he would create a ball with thorns all over it, so he couldn't touch it. Then, he said:

"Do you know how much a quarter is?" This was interpreted by his analyst as an inquiry: how would he fare with a quarter fewer sessions? Would this make him relapse into his most feared symptom, which was symbolized by the uncontrollable aggression of the spiny ball?

He took money out of his pocket and said:

"It's a lot, isn't it? At my house, I'm going to do the following: I'm going to tie a string to the ceiling and I'm going to go up and up. But don't you think it's going to be difficult?" It is evident that, in the face of economic difficulty, a maniacal attempt arose within him—an urge to deny his impotence and offer his money. But the judgment of reality led him to express that he needed to grow suddenly in order to face that payment, and that this was as impossible as rappelling to the ceiling on a small, weak string.

I find the elements of the process through which this material is expressed very interesting and applicable to other cases:

1) The fear of relapsing into the symptom that caused him to suffer the most
2) The perception of the need for money to solve the problem
3) The acceptance of his own impotence; and
4) The insecurity and anger caused by the reduction in the hours of treatment.

The child who knows what a session costs tries not to miss it, claims minutes if he has missed his time, and manages not to be brought late to the sessions. If any situation arises where the problems are not clearly stated, there exists a deception that is unfavorable for the consolidation of the transference relationship and the continuity of the analysis.

Commentary on Chapter 6

Jill Savege Scharff (USA)

Reading Aberastury's theory and practice of child analytic assessment and treatment evoked in me the reassuring feeling of sharing principles, admiring her work, and the less comfortable feelings of envy, shock, and awe. There's envy of the luxury of having a playroom solely suited to work with children. Some analysts today do still have that. Virginia Ungar has a playroom with water and a linoleum floor and skirting like the setting that Arminda recommends. My own American analyst had a room with a couch, and a bare playroom with a linoleum floor which I could see off the waiting room. But for practical reasons, like many analysts today, I have one room with a couch that the adult analysand can use to facilitate free association, and the child can use it to sit or lie on or hide objects under it. There are two chairs for parents, and folding chairs in case a family has many children; and a bathroom. I like the lack of separation of adult from child in my setting, and I don't hide the signs of play from the adults. In fact, provision of play media may stimulate memories of childhood or offer the challenged adult patient a nonverbal way of representing the unrepresentable.

I use the low table that Aberastury recommends, and I like to play on the floor with younger children, as she did. We see Arminda in a photo of the House Building Game (this volume, p. xxix) in which she could explore the building's correspondence to the child's body image (A. Pichon-Rivière, 1950a, 1958a). For older children, I like a desk as well, allowing for work at various levels. Arminda recommends simple indestructible furniture and personal clothing, as essential now as when she was in practice. Her patient Alba who defecated in objection to her analyst leaving, reminded me of my child patient who had to climb and jump and smear his feces on my couch before his vacation. I was glad that, in addition to stopping the behavior and interpreting how desperately he wanted to show me that he could not leave me to go on vacation, I could wash and disinfect the tough fabric without angst—all of which Arminda would have validated (Scharff, 2017). Indoor/outdoor carpeting is warmer to sit on than linoleum, but it has the same feature of surviving spills. Where shock comes in is at the thought of floods and fire. I envy the child whose analyst can cope with that anxiety, but I could not offer matches or an oil burner to a child. We would have to find a different way of reaching emotions that flare up.

Also recommended is the chest of drawers, each drawer containing toys as personal possessions for the child's sole use. Arminda explains that the opening of the drawer symbolizes the analyst's receptive attitude and the drawer represents the child's inner world. The child opens the private drawer, and thus enters the world of the mind and the heart. It is a great idea, and many child analysts use the private drawer in this way, maintaining continuity and replenishing the items as the child uses them up. But I like more freedom, more room, more choice. I do not have a chest of drawers, and no drawer or box for each child. I conceive of the space of the mind and heart as my very private, soundproofed office, occupied by one child for the special time of the session. Each child has a folder for their work, but all child patients have access to all the toys, games, and blocks for building with animal figures to inhabit them, scissors for cutting and glue for linking objects, clay, and art media—including watercolors, which Arminda recommends against. But I find that some children like the dipping in water, the diluted colors, and the less bold outlines they produce in echo of their tentative exploration of their emotions. Unlike Arminda, I do provide a display board for drawings as an expression of the bond between us and as a record of the continuity in the play. Arminda warns that I would be "faced with an army of negative consequences." I counter with, "Then we deal with them." If a child pins their picture over another child's space on the board, we work to acknowledge wishes to exclude or annihilate the other, and understand those feelings and where they come from—often, but not only, from sibling rivalry.

Arminda asks all child analysts to be competent in a variety of games, pop culture icons, puppets, role play, repairs, sewing, and knitting. She ask us to be competent in skills usually left to the other gender, an important point of expression of the analyst's ability to represent male and female elements and their coupling in the self in order to evoke a complex transference and analyze it. As a woman of her time, she did not face the challenge of technology-mediated sessions and the demands of competence in videogames, as we do today. But her request for us to be comfortable with pop culture suggests that she would have got on board. She would have found the transference meaning in the gender-fluid patient's switching my head onto his body and vice versa, in the angry boy's encasing his father in flames on the image on his cellphone, in the use of killing games to express rage at brothers who replaced a firstborn in their mother's embrace. In our times, Esteban, who smashed the toys until Arminda made him face the consequences, might be smashing them symbolically, as Arminda joined him in a videogame. She might have felt some resistance to videogames as a distraction from analysis, but she would soon realize that virtual reality games for building houses and creating communities give the analyst a way to join the child's inner world, just as her patients (and her sons) used her House Building Game.

If I were able to be in supervision with Arminda, she might not like my office setup. She might caution me against arousing curiosity, jealousy, anger, deprivation, and betrayal, against creating a chaotic, rivalrous situation for the children, but I feel sure that she would not insist that I copy her exactly, just as she has taken what she valued from Klein and applied it in her own way. As I consider her point of view, I admit that child patients have been upset when their fabulous block constructions could not be kept intact; however, these would not fit in a drawer either. With no fuss, I can use my cellphone to take photos of the constructions which can be referred to the next day. I would explain to Arminda that I like the children to have free access to all the stuff in their treatment time, we work on the loss at the end, and we clean up together. Within that freedom, I agree with the need for limits, for asking for role induction before playing a part in a child's story, and above all for entering into the play with pleasure.

CHAPTER 7

The meaning of the first hour of play

By analyzing a five-year-old boy and describing his play activity, drawings, dreams, and daydreams, Freud laid the foundations for the technique of child psychoanalysis. He later discovered that, if a child plays, it is always indicative of a need to work out traumatic situations. The analysis of children confirmed these conclusions. However, as evident as it was that the fundamental problems of a child are expressed in this preverbal language, the treatises on the subject continued to affirm that the child, unlike the adult, lacked awareness of the disease or the will to cure it.

In applying play technique, I came to different conclusions. I found that, as early as the first session of an analysis or a diagnostic observation, the unconscious fantasy of illness and cure emerged. I then decided to investigate whether the child's material during treatment confirmed what I had seen during that first hour. I concluded that this was the case in all instances, corroborating the initial idea that the child knows that they are sick, understanding and open to accepting treatment. Through the play technique, individualized to suit each child, I verified that the child communicates to us their unconscious fantasy about the disease or conflict from the very first hour, immediately revealing to us the reason they have been brought to treatment and, in most cases, the unconscious fantasy of healing. In the healing fantasy, the child expresses the desire for change in the real outer world, as well as the desire to heal the compulsion to repeat such experiences.

I think the reason the fantasies arise so immediately is simply the fear that the therapist will repeat the negative behavior of the original objects that caused the disease or the conflict in the patient. The fear of the repetition of experiences with the original objects is due both to what has occurred with the parents, and to the child's own compulsion to repeat situations that harm him- or herself. Yet, the child shows a desire that the therapist *not* be like those objects, and, instead, assume a new role providing the patient with what is needed to help. This process is experienced by the patient as a new birth. The initial separation from the parents and entry into the analyst's office are often accompanied by anxieties similar to those experienced *at* birth.

The fear of repeating the relationship with the original object is what transforms the therapist into someone to be mistrusted. The original object, loaded with frustration and fear, is projected onto the therapist who thereby becomes transformed into someone feared by the child, someone expected to adopt the same negative behavior as the parents, and attack. In its beloved aspects this original object has also satisfied the patient's needs, and so its projection also confers on the therapist the attributes necessary to heal the patient. This double source of transference must be interpreted from the first moment, but since the two aspects are always present during treatment, the interpretation of their meaning must also evolve in successive sessions.

It is essential that, from the first moment, we assume the role of therapists. This helps the child position themselves as a patient and become conscious of the unconscious fantasy revealed in interpretation. I want to emphasize that we must interpret the double image and its meanings. In front of the parents, we must clarify our role as the child's therapist, very different from their role. We confirm this idea by asking them to make no changes to their family life, and by anticipating the confidentiality we will need to uphold during the child's sessions.

In the description of the office, I referred to the meaning of the individual drawer. I described the material that the therapist offers the child and the technical problems that arise from handling it. This individual drawer that we offer when we begin treatment is constituted from the first moment as a symbol of professional confidentiality. This secure drawer acts the same way as the promise of confidentiality we give the adult when they begin a psychoanalytic treatment in which they can have trust.

The cases that I am about to narrate refer to the first hours of diagnostical play and the treatment of children of different ages. Within them, I will specifically highlight those aspects that make up the opening moves. Their importance becomes evident in the subsequent course of treatment.

Case 1, Roberto, age two

Roberto is a two-year-old boy who has suffered from nocturnal terrors and has had a tendency toward insomnia since he was eighteen months old. His development seems to have been normal up to that point. After the first interview with the mother, we decided to observe him for an hour of play before deciding on his treatment. He was informed he was coming to see me, that it was not a pediatric visit, and that I would not check him or give him medicine. Instead, he was told that I would spend an hour with him and give him things to play with. He knew we would talk, and that we would try to understand the reason for his difficulties with sleep, as well as how to relieve them.

Roberto entered the playroom with his mother. She took a seat and the boy proceeded directly to the toys on the low table. He immediately began to play. He used saucers, cups, and cutlery, beginning a game session that lasted about ten minutes. During the session, he presented to us a pleasant, unhurried, adequate diet, fueled by affection and stability, as deduced from the details of the eating process. He interrupted the play to ask me to turn on the light. He then took a saucer, sucking and biting on it desperately, exhibiting increasing levels of anxiety. We will stop at this juncture in order to analyze his behavior up to that point.

The turning on of the light and the desperate biting and sucking taking place after a game of adequate feeding and satisfaction allowed us to discern when his nighttime symptoms manifested, and gave us a clue as to the reason for his sleep disorder. Desperately biting and sucking the saucer and the immediate anxiety crisis that followed expressed his potential feelings at night, if such desires ever arose. We know that the sucked and bitten plate exists as a real object in the external world. However, it also represents an internal object, a symbol of the introjected breast that was once external. At that moment, when playing, the boy not only bites and sucks the plate, but also the internal object that attacks him; in this case, his forbidding mother. As a therapist, I was experienced at repeating the internal prohibition, which is why he gave up the play and underwent a spell of anxiety.

We already knew something about what caused the night dread and insomnia, the two forms of sleep disorder for which his parents had consulted us. The image of something that bites and sucks, projected, symbolized, and personified by the little plate, brought about the anxiety crisis. Thus, we observed how the defenses against destructive tendencies functioned within him. The first defense mechanism comprised expulsion, projection, and symbolization. Then came the violent destruction of the affect-loaded object, which was feared as a persecutor. Let us now continue narrating his play. In doing so, we will witness how he once more showed that this act of sucking and biting was ultimately addressed to his real mother, as well as to his internal mother, who was symbolized by the little plate.

Roberto filled the sink with water until it overflowed and spilled on the floor. With his hands, he pushed the water that had fallen towards the mother, stepped on it until it soaked the soles of his shoes, and then walked on the dry part of the linoleum. He made sure to leave tracks that led directly to his mother. As the puddle grew, and he observed that he no longer left footprints when walking, he spilled more water, repeating the activity described, until the last footprint reached his mother. He then climbed on top of her and embraced her with an enveloping gesture, as if he wanted to pick her up in his arms. When the play with the water began, and while it was filling the sink and causing the flooding, he wanted me to hold his hand. This excluded the mother, who continued to sit in the playroom next to the bathroom, away from his action.

We already knew that at night, whether he was alone or with the babysitter, the boy felt anxiety. He would feel his mother's absence and needed to know the path that would take him to her. The footprints were a symbol of the traces of memory he had of the positive image of his mother, which were erased when the terror of the negative image washed over him. He had communicated the reason for the fear, and was now expressing his need of me. He wanted my help in order to find the correct path; the one that would lead him to his mother when he was terrified at night. He also showcased the need for an unconditional supply of aid, by demanding I never let go of his hand, even for a minute, while he manipulated the water that would allow him to reach his mother.

Let us take a closer look at this second part of his game with the water. Upon flooding the lavatory, he also communicated to us that he was urinating during the night, whenever he felt anxious. When his mother was absent, he would feel an overwhelming urgency to seek her out, which would lead to urination. The enveloping form of the embrace and the gesture of snuggling close to her reproduced the initial form of bodily contact with the mother after birth, thereby showing that he needed to return to unconditional supply, this time from his therapist, in order to heal. In this, as in other cases, crossing the boundary between the bathroom and the playroom symbolizes birth. The way in which the child crosses it teaches us a lot about the characteristics of childbirth and the child's first contacts with the outside world.

The presence of the mother in the office facilitated the dramatization of the divisions between good and bad, external and internal. However, without her, the boy would have still expressed this, but would have used the analyst, a toy, an object, or any detail of the analysis room instead.

Case 2, Hernán, age two

I will now summarize the first hour of play of another two year old, this one suffering from insomnia and rocking. This last symptom was so acute that, due to the intensity, violence, and consistence of the movements, the parents had to upholster the child's crib with cushions, thus minimizing the damaging blows to the child's head when he crashed against the bars. It was also necessary to upholster the room with rugs, so that the friction would deter the movement of the crib somewhat. These courses of action were taken because neither the parents, who slept in the adjoining room, nor the nursemaid, who slept with him, could fall asleep with the noise of the rocking crib filling the air as it moved and collided with the bedroom walls. Insomnia was a daily occurrence and sedatives were ineffective at preventing the incidents.

Hernán was the youngest of four siblings, and the only one with symptoms. The parents seemed deeply attached to each other and to their children. They lived in the same building as various uncles and aunts, who also lived with children. These children had banded together to form a large community. Within it, Hernán was referred to as "the sick man."

One piece of information stood out from the initial interview with the parents. It was the only one that could have been significant enough to explain the symptoms. Hernán was born twenty days before the calculated date, because labor had been scheduled for a day that was comfortable for the family community. The mother initially resisted the doctor's suggestion to induce birth at a set time, but the pressure of her environment and the confidence that her doctor inspired in her eventually convinced her to submit. In a subsequent meeting, we realized that her lack of defense for her child going to term was due to pregnancy being more difficult and complicated with Hernán than it had been with her other children. In the later development of the child, there were apparently no other disorders. He wound up looking so healthy and pleasant that it was difficult to imagine him with such distressing symptoms.

Hernán entered with his mother and began to play while she sat near him. His game consisted of distributing and grouping the toys on the table based on similar characteristics. When he would form a group, he would say, "They sleep." He placed chickens with chickens, buckets with buckets, balls with balls, and Play-Doh with Play-Doh. The last group he formed was made up of puppy toys. He separated the smallest one, put it in my hand, and closed my fist around it, leaving the little dog inside. He observed my hand carefully and suspiciously, forcing it to close tighter and tighter, as if he feared I would open it. Then he said, "You make him sleep."

What did he express with this game? Each group was a family, and all members were asleep. But in one of the groups—his own—the youngest did not sleep. This inability to sleep represented his symptom, and he trusted me to teach him to sleep by keeping him inside me. To put himself in my hands so he could sleep was to accept the therapeutic help, to show that he needed it. The way he placed the puppy toy in my hands and hermetically sealed it in showed his unconscious fantasy of the symptom and his potential for healing it. He needed to return to the mother's womb, and for me to not repeat what she did, thus keeping him safe in my hand. After this new birth—once he had received what was necessary from me—he could sleep.

The distrust and fear that I would repeat the mother's behavior, letting the situation get out hand, was expressed in that careful and distrustful observation with which he checked to see whether or not my hand had kept the puppy toy he'd entrusted to me. We see that for him life was divided into two parts: life before the disorder and life after it. His daily life was also divided into two sections; namely *before nighttime* and *after nighttime*. So, he divided the session into one part focused on a quiet game, and another part in which everything was invaded by anxiety. Turning on the light was the limit of his pleasant life. After that came night and the eruption of sucking, biting, anguish, urination, loneliness, and fear of the lack of a safe path back to the object. This ignorance was a consequence of not having elaborated depressive anxiety, a process which was prevented by the excessive amount of destructive, abnormally channeled tendencies. The *first child* expressed that the fear of losing the mother caused dread at night, and insomnia was a defense against that dread. The *second child*, on the other hand, expressed his unique situation of feeling different from everyone around him by being unable to sleep, and he placed himself in my hands in order to learn how to deal with it.

In the two cases that I have related, the session was merely diagnostic, and the children were then referred to another therapist.

Case 3, Adolfo, twenty-one months

We will assess the playtime of a slightly younger child, Adolfo, who also suffered from sleep disorders. His observation was followed by treatment with the same therapist, which allowed us to confirm the accuracy of the first conclusions. He was a twenty-one-month-old boy who woke up in anxiety at night. In response, he would usually make his way to someone's bed, preferably his mother's. He also suffered from compulsive thumb sucking and had not yet accepted toilet training. The training had begun at five months. During the first attempt, which coincided with the initiation of weaning, he was kept on the toilet for two or more hours at a time. When he failed to learn, the parents temporarily abandoned the training. The training resumed at eleven months, this time coinciding with the definitive loss of the breast. Since Adolfo would not sit still and could easily escape the confines of his chamber pot, the parents kept him tied up, again sometimes for over two hours.

The first session that we will relate was strictly observational, as the mother merely sought guidance in the education of her son. The relief the session brought on convinced the mother and the therapist (Elizabeth Garma) to initiate an analysis, despite a lack of experience with the effects of this type of treatment on children under two years of age. We will first summarize a basic description of the events that transpired, and then we will analyze their meaning.

Despite his young age, Adolfo did not show difficulty in separating from his mother. He entered with the therapist, and the mother remained in the anteroom. The first things he picked up were a playpen and a crib with a baby doll in it. He then went to the anteroom to look for the mother and brought her to the office.

Adolfo sat on the floor and surrounded himself with the crib, the doll, the bathroom, and a sideboard with dishes. The therapist was sitting next to him. He happily indicated that a baby was sitting on the toilet, then repeatedly placed the doll on and off the toilet. He then tried to undress a small doll by cutting a ribbon that tied her clothes together, possibly alluding to having been tied to the urinal when he was younger. When he did it, he sighed with relief and joy. He asked the therapist for help in doing this, and also asked that the mosquito net be removed from the crib. He fed the doll, covered it, and then physically attacked it. He undressed another doll and put it next to the first one, claiming they represented him and the baby. He paid attention to the water dripping from the sink and spoke the word "water," after which the therapist further twisted the faucet knob. He used the intensified water pressure to wash everything around him, then wiped the objects dry. He bathed a doll, wrapped it, rocked it next to his chest, laid it down, and covered it. He spilled the water, seemed stricken, and wiped it off at once with the rag. He looked at the clay, then took a pencil and paper and tried to draw. He rose and slid the chair and table to the center of the room. He sat down and asked the therapist to sit in the other chair. He washed the objects again, then went to the couch covered with toys and took a baby doll sitting on a desk. He bathed her, too. When it was time to conclude the session, and he was told that he should leave, he fell to the ground and refused to do so. He only agreed to leave when he was told that he would return the next day.

The fact that Adolfo had entered without his mother, despite being so small, was an indication that he resorted, with infrequent intensity, to the denial of reality as a defense against growing anguish. This is how he was able to, at first, deny the reality that this was a new, and therefore fearful, situation, as well as ignore the suffering imposed on him by the separation from his mother. The playpen he initially chose, the one from which he removed the baby, symbolized the prison, the fence, the limitation that he felt in his development—made obvious by the discomfort that he would later show us—and also the need to get out of a state of confinement. So, in the game he played, Adolfo detailed his difficulties according to their urgency.

If this session had been verbalized by an adult, they might have said something along the lines of:

"I have annoying symptoms that restrict and hinder me in life. I have come to get rid of them." The adult would then list these annoyances, either prompted by our query or spontaneously. This is very much the same thing Adolfo did with his games. When he returned to the office, he surrounded himself with the crib and the baby, which signified his sleep disorder, the bathroom, which was a clear analogue of his conflict with toilet training, and the sideboard with the dishes, which inevitably represented the oral conflicts that led him to sucking on his thumb. He expressed joy when he saw a doll on the toilet and tried to pick it up and sit it down over and over. This repetition expressed the successive attempts his parents had made to gain control over the toilet training process, as well as his need to actively complete the task for which he had suffered. That is why he expressed such joy when he overcame the fear and the doll accepted the toilet training.

It seemed that, of all his symptoms, the most manageable was control, since he could handle a few activities by himself. He could not, however, go about undressing the dolls and removing the mosquito net. When it came to these activities, he would ask the therapist for help. Asking for help carried a desire for the therapist to aid him in freeing himself from something he could not hope to escape alone. He longed for the therapist to remove his internal mother that bothered and restrained him. The mosquito net was a symbol of the anxiety that enveloped him at night. Another factor related to this nighttime anguish was a fear of the great beating, which he gave the little doll once it was lying down.

The rest of the game dealt with toilet training. The dripping was clearly urine leakage, and the act of cleaning was an attempt to regain control. In the same vein, we can interpret the concept of control in what his analyst pointed out: he tended to place each object back in its proper place after using it, which was uncommon for his age.

The inclusion of the baby doll and the desk at the end of the hour showed his desire to be older. His sister was six years old and could already acquire knowledge. She understood the circumstances of her life, due in large part to what adults had taught her. The adults in *his* life, however, did not explain things clearly to him because they considered him too young. So, he longed to be like her.

Ultimately, it seems that Adolfo's healing fantasy consisted simply of being loved, fed, and nurtured, so that he could grow up and understand himself. When the session came to an end, his desire to stay with the therapist showed us how much this boy needed treatment, as well as how relieved he must have felt to be able to express his conflicts with preverbal language.

Cases 4 and 5, Ana and Luisa, age two

I consider the following two cases to be of special interest, and so will present them simultaneously. The patients were girls of around two years of age, who were under the pressure of recent mourning. The first had lost her brother and the second, her mother. The two sessions were held at different times, in the same office, with the same therapist (Susana L. de Ferrer), and using the same play material. Each of the patients used the provided materials in a different way, but both used them as a way of expressing their basic conflicts.

Ana was brought to the consultation as a result of several weeks of insomnia. The triggering situation for this symptom was the death of her three-month-old brother, which had occurred at night. The mother had given birth to two premature twins three and a half months prior. Both boys, the twins had been born before the seventh month of pregnancy. One of them had died at birth, while great effort had been undertaken to keep the second alive until the third month. At this age, the surviving infant had already started sharing a room with Ana. The girl witnessed the moment when the father, upon entering the room, discovered that his son, who he had left safe and sound in his crib just hours before, was dead. Following that extremely dramatic episode, the symptom that motivated the consultation began. Ana started suffering from insomnia, which was preceded by an episode of nocturnal fear.

Before her delivery, the mother had to take care of her nephews and father-in-law, in addition to caring for her daughter and her pregnancy. This circumstance triggered feelings of helplessness and abandonment in Ana. These feelings were later reinforced by the circumstances of the birth, as well as the months that followed, during which the parents were almost exclusively concerned with the premature child.

The events I will describe were observed a few days after the death of the child, and the therapist was the same one called for consultation when the premature babies were born.

The toy drawer prepared for playtime contained cubes, balls, rings, saucers, cups, and a small doll. The girl's game consisted of tossing out all the contents and keeping only the small doll, which she tried to place in the therapist's palm repeatedly. She would open and close the therapist's hand in order to place the object and remove it. At a certain point, she dropped the doll, after which she expressed great panic. She proceeded to urinate on the office floor, and, frightened by what had happened, burst into intense tears. In that state, she ran out of the office in search of her mother, who was waiting for her in the waiting room.

In this hour of play, the girl repeated the traumatic situation that her siblings, with whom she identified, had gone through. The symptom was a consequence of this identification. She was afraid that, in her dreams, the same thing that happened to them would happen to her. She asked the therapist to keep the doll in hand, expressing her wish that her siblings had remained housed in her mother's womb for a longer time, and had thus avoided death. The dropping of the doll, the lack of protection in that moment, expressed the loss she felt at the premature birth of her siblings. The act of urinating on the office floor had the same meaning and, as we were able to discern later, also reflected her anxiety at seeing her brother repeatedly placed on cots and tables when his diapers were being changed; a situation she construed as dangerous due to the risk of the child falling. In addition, her father, while he was in her presence, repeatedly verbalized the fear of this happening, as well as the need to take precautions. The girl feared that the same dangers that her siblings went through would be repeated with her, resulting in the same final consequences. By not sleeping, she could watch over and control the dangers that had caused her dread and that she felt enveloped by.

Her healing fantasy consisted of feeling protected enough to ward off danger, so she had the therapist protect the doll by keeping it in the closed hand. This girl knew the truth regarding the fate of her two brothers, but had not yet become aware of the relationship between her symptom and her fear of sharing their fate. Her psychoanalytic treatment had to show her the reality of their death and lead her to elaborate it, as well as alleviate the underlying anxieties that caused her to react with insomnia. This symptom was explained by the need to stay alert so that what her siblings went through would never happen to her.

The second girl, whose play session we will describe below and who we will call Luisa, was also two years old. For the first hour of her play session, which she attended on the same day as Ana, Luisa was offered the same toy drawer. The contents were exactly the same, yet her play was completely different. She emptied the drawer immediately, showing no interest at all in the toys. She was focused, at all times, in inserting herself into the drawer. When she finally succeeded, she asked that the pried-off lid be placed on top. She remained like this for a long time, in silence. She then asked for help to get out of the drawer. As soon as she received the approval, she ran out of the office in search of her father. She led him from the waiting room by the hand and stood with him in front of the door. There, she focused her attention on an ornately carved chest of dark wood. She asked what was inside and requested that the lid be lifted so that she could explore its contents.

Knowing Luisa's story makes it easier to understand the meaning of this game. Her mother had died a year before, after six months of serious illness. Due to this, Luisa was transferred to her grandmother's house, where she spent the last months of her mother's illness. She was not told about any of this because she was considered too young to understand her mother's health problems and potential death. She was not even informed of the truth when her mother's health began to rapidly decline. When the mother died, the father joined Luisa at her new home. Both he and the grandmother were silent about everything that had occurred. A year after the wife's death, the father began to consider the possibility of remarrying. This decision increased the girl's preexisting difficulties. The reasons for her consultation, namely her inhibition of play, complications in her daily routine, and issues with her environment, worsened in the face of this new reality. The characteristics of her game showed that the child's most primary interest was to be told the truth regarding something she already knew deep down: the death of her mother. Her efforts to unravel this mystery were expressed in the game where she entered the drawer. We saw her identification with her mother when she placed herself in the drawer and asked for the lid to be placed on top. Through this action, she was trying to experience what she'd felt inside herself. In the same vein, the fact that she asked that the lid of the drawer be lifted and that she be aided in exiting was her way of expressing her desire to escape that conflict, which she felt she could not do alone. Her difficulties were intimately linked with that forbidden truth that she had been denied access to. Though she felt the sting of the consequences—not seeing her mother ever again—in order to heal, she needed to be clear about her fate. This was symbolized by her desire to know the contents of the chest. This was what she expected from treatment: acquiring knowledge regarding her and her father's truth. It was also why she brought him back to the consulting room and placed him in front of the person she was questioning regarding the chest-drawer.

Case 6, Virginia, age two and a half

Virginia was a two-and-a-half-year-old girl who presented feverish spasmodic bronchitis between the ages of three and four months. This condition recurred frequently, and was often accompanied by anorexia, weight loss, marked general decline, and intense paleness. She repeated the same process over and over, with almost no healthy intervals. She was always treated with antibiotics, but remained symptomatic and unable to heal. She came to treatment for the first time when she was three months old. This time frame coincided with weaning and with an economic disaster for the parents that threatened to split them up. During that initial consultation, the analyst warned the parents that she was unsure about treating Virginia *per se*, but that she would see her in order to perform a diagnosis and refer her to another therapist. Therefore, she did not conduct any interpretations. She made age-appropriate toys available to the child and added some others that she found useful after the initial interview.

During the first session with her parents, Virginia arrived accompanied by her mother, who had previously explained the reason for the consultation: the girl was small for her age, pale and thin, and had large, expressionless eyes. Her face, according to the mother, was reminiscent of a doll's face. The girl repeated this same cliché, which undoubtedly originated from the mother. She separated from her without expressing any emotion, a behavior that, in such a young girl, indicated a serious affection disorder. The girl needed to deny the depressive anxieties caused by separation from her mother, as well as the paranoid anxieties that every new situation usually arouses. The weakness of the ego made intense denial the only available recourse for facing them.

Virginia grabbed a fork, a toy car, and a toy plane, then babbled something. Taking a spoon, she said the words, "Little spoon." Next, she took a knife and whispered, "Knife." She placed all of her silverware next to her. She took the toy plane and said: "My mother is coming to get me." At the end of this sentence, she seized a pink plane, looked at the wheels, showed them to the therapist, turned them, and moved the plane backwards without letting go of the therapist's hand.

We will stop at this point in the session in order to analyze it in detail. Stammering something incomprehensible, then clearly pronouncing "spoon" and, less clearly, "knife," was Virginia's way of delineating the things that she knows well, the ones she is unclear about, and the ones that are incomprehensible to her. Since the therapeutic situation was an unknown factor to her, it seemed she lacked an understanding of the process taking place between her and the therapist. By acting this way, she was trying to make the therapist understand her utter confusion. Her anguish in the face of this new situation led her to test a reality where she could potentially have everything. This is why she took the silverware and placed it near herself. Ensuring that she could dispose of her toys, she grabbed the toy plane which, according to the following verbal associations, she clearly used to represent her mother. The first association surfaced when she said, "My mother is coming to look for me." This represented an expression of the fear that this might not happen. Here, we note a resurfacing of the anxiety that she'd denied when separating from the mother without affection. This was confirmed when she focused on the plane's means of movement: the wheels. She felt abandoned by her mother and feared that she would not come looking for her. The intensity of that initial, denied anxiety was expressed again during the following game, where she tried to magically erase the separation by turning the plane backwards and having it retrace its steps.

Now, let us continue analyzing her game. She paired two small toy planes, one pink and the other light blue. She placed a white car in front of them. The choice of color, the way she placed the objects, and the spatial relationships between them are all factors that allow us to suppose that she personified the white object as herself. This makes sense, since its whiteness symbolized one of her symptoms: paleness. The other two objects were clearly her parents. In her game, the white car is in front with the parents, as a couple, next to her. We know that the most intense traumatic situation in the oedipal conflict is that of being the excluded third party. We understand the airplanes as a representation of the united parents, and this is not merely due to their placement and pairing. It is also due, in part, to the girl's choice of pink and light blue, colors that, in our environment, commonly symbolize the feminine and the masculine. If we accept that the game has the value of a verbal association, we can say that Virginia associated the abandonment she experienced when her mother would leave with the abandonment she felt when her parents were together.

Then, she took the little white car, brought it closer to another, took both in hand, and rolled them together, while saying: "The cars." She picked them up, turned them to face each other, overlapped them, and separated them. She then took a target, held it in her hand, and moved it back and forth successively and rhythmically. She moved the two cars together, distancing them from the target. She paired the cars again, spoke unintelligible words, then pushed one car's wheels against the other's. She said: "The planes." She paired the two planes together and attached them to the two cars.

During this game, the therapist remained seated on the floor against the wall. Virginia played in front of her. Once more, the spatial configurations, as well as the fact that the white car previously signified Virginia herself, both suggest that these cars symbolized, at that moment, her and the therapist. Specifically, they signified a relationship Virginia did not fully understand, whose characteristic was that of moving rhythmically. The wheels were a symbol of the lower parts of the body: the genitals. The last part of this game, when she formed the two pairs, was the synthesis of the same situation, one which she insisted on partly due to lack of interpretation, and partly because repeating the urgency points is one of the characteristics of the game. She was basically telling us that, in order to compensate for her abandonment, she would do with the therapist (and her sister before that) what the parents did when they were together and she was alone.

We will now continue the retelling of the session. She took a cup and a plate. Then, she turned the cup upside down. She modified its position, placing it face up. With a knife and a fork, she pretended to eat. She took two knives and sharpened them against each other. She then took the fork and put down the spoon. She held the little pink car in one hand and moved it rhythmically from front to back, over and over, leaving the white car behind her. She picked up the little blue plane and said, "Here she is." She took the cup and saucer, yawned, and set them down next to the silverware. She placed the blue plane between her legs and made it roll up her thighs, toward her genitals. She then placed the blue plane on one thigh and the pink on the other. She put the blue plane down on the side with the cutlery and the pink one down on the side with the pink car.

We will analyze this session fragment in detail. Putting the cup upside down on the plate, then modifying the original positioning by turning it face up, is a gesture through which Virginia could express that she often felt empty, but that now she was in a receptive position. Placing the cup face up was a way of telling us that she was willing to be filled again. So was her next association, where she took a knife and fork and pretended to eat. The cup was a symbol for the breast that lay empty. She asked the therapist to fill it again, so she gathered the cutlery and pretended to eat. Thus, in this fragment, we saw her repeat her request that the therapist accompany her, feed her, and fill her with her genitals, modifying the image of emptiness that seems linked to her original objects. The knives that she sharpened symbolized the teeth, to which she seems to attribute the loss of the breast. In addition to the increase in oral aggression caused by the loss of the breast, her desire to bite suggests that the appearance of the teeth was closely linked to weaning, although her mother did not give any data in this regard.

If we consider the standard development of a child, we can deduce that the early loss of the breast led Virginia to a precocious interest in the genitals. In the material, this is represented by the pink car that Virginia moved rhythmically, placed closer to the blue plane (representing the father), and then took to her genitals. The cup and plate that she left beside her cutlery mean that she unconsciously bound the breast with food and teeth. The search for genital union to replace the loss of the oral relationship is expressed when the airplane is placed between the legs. Since this happens from the moment of the appearance of the father in the Oedipus complex, it shows the fluctuation between father and mother. Virginia placed the little plane that symbolized the mother on one thigh and the one that symbolized the father on another, moving the latter until it was close to the genitals. She identified with the mother by contact, and needed the father as an object of gratification, seeking to incorporate him through the vagina. This attempt failed because this union was fraught with the same danger that accompanied the abrupt breakdown of the mouth–breast relationship.

The material that followed consisted of Virginia taking a fork and a knife and pricking at both sides of her body. She scraped her head, tapped her own ear, and said: "Knock, knock." These actions broaden our understanding of her unconscious illness fantasy. We now know that Virginia feels all this conflict inside her head: an exhausted chest, teeth that bite, a hard, cutting penis that hits. The tapping of the ear is a clear reference to what she overheard during her parents' intercourse. These real experiences intertwined with her fantasies to configure an internal world that, as we see in this hour of play, painted genital union as dangerous as chewing or biting food.

During the previous genital phase, the scene is dominated by fantasies of the parents' continuous intercourse. The unavoidable end result of this stage is frustration, and this reinforces the sadistic conception of intercourse. This form of discharge, masturbation, and sexual games is then carried out through these fantasies and the consequent guilt. In Virginia, the situations mentioned prevented the normal elaboration of these anxieties, leading her to the denial of reality and the somatization of the conflict, as we will see in the following material.

Before continuing, I want to point out another noteworthy characteristic of the spatial settings in Virginia's games. She remained seated, unmoving, and refused to investigate anything in the room. She would not even ask any questions. This is clear evidence of the disorders in the functions of her ego, the degree of inhibition of her epistemophilic instinct, the increase in her paranoid anxiety, and the fear of the denied external world at the beginning of her session.

We will now continue retelling the play. After striking her head and ear with the cutlery, she put a fork into the cup. She stirred the empty cup, making it clink. She placed the two planes next to the pink car, pushed them, then put them between her legs. She lifted her skirt and dropped her panties, exclaiming "Ah!" while looking at herself in the mirror. During these actions, her breath was heavy, which showed signs of intense anxiety and despair. She tossed the pink stroller at the therapist, then put it between her legs and looked back at herself in the mirror. She pushed the mirror toward the floor, reflecting her shoe, but pushed too hard and scratched the floor with the mirror as she rolled the car between her legs. She yawned, looked at herself twice in the mirror, and vocalized something like "sh, sh, sh." She then took the cup, yawned again, hit her genitals with the mirror, leaned on them as if trying to put herself inside the mirror, and then scraped the mirror with the cup.

During this time, she was no longer using the little car to symbolize her masturbating in front of her parents during intercourse. Instead, she turned to the mirror and her genitals, because, at this moment, the original objects had lost their symbolic function due to increased anxiety. She communicated what she felt when she masturbated, fantasizing about intercourse with her parents and feeling flooded by an arousal that scared and drove her crazy. We can assume that the noisy breathing reproduced the panting of the parents during intercourse and the sensations of it when masturbating, as well as the performance of these imagos in spasmodic bronchitis. We came to understand that, for Virginia, bronchitis, weight loss, and anorexia were produced by the performance of unconscious fantasies regarding the parents' dangerous intercourse: intercourse that was continuous and that she could not control with masturbation or play. Thus, she tried, as a last resort, to control it within her body. In these bronchial processes, fever played a fundamental role, which was understood in the light of the unconscious fantasies we have detailed.

We stated that the cup represented the breast, the loss of which Virginia had not been able to elaborate. She expressed this by scraping the floor with the cup turned over, delineating another one of her symptoms: a "scratchy feeling," like a phlegmy, bronchial infection. The idea of her parents joined with her own personality during the crisis. She felt them inside herself, panting from within her, scraping her insides, and not letting her eat. In a dramatic way, this symbolized the failure to work out the loss of the breast through masturbation. She took a cup and a plate in one hand, and, with the other, tried to push the mirror away. But she squeezed it in such a way that it broke the support. She then touched the broken part of the bracket and stared uneasily. She placed a cup between her legs, took the mirror, and tried to glue the support she had broken. Once more, this showed her healing fantasy.

The failure of incorporation due to the intensification of depressive anxiety is expressed through the symbolization of the mouth with teeth and the toothed vagina. We can see this in her actions: placing a fork inside the cup and holding it on the edge, inserting the handle of another so as to make it enter and exit rhythmically, and, in the process, creating an amalgam of the movements of smooth intercourse and rough, brusque chewing. Since the therapist was merely an observer, the girl expressed the anxiety and despair of feeling unable to resolve her conflicts alone by staying static, blinking, closing her eyes, swaying, rubbing her eyelids, scratching the back of her neck, and scratching her genitals. She also moaned, put her hand inside her panties, and fell asleep that way. She staggered, almost falling to the ground, then woke and turned her back on the therapist. She held her head in her hands, moaning. She then sighed, took a deep breath, rubbed her eyes, genitals, face, and mouth briskly, and made respiratory efforts. Her hair had fallen over her face and her eyes were red and wet. She continued to rub her right eye. For a moment it looked like she was going to cry. At the end of the hour, she urinated.

She turned her back on the therapist, as she turned her back on a life with illness; an illness which forced her to remain in bed, restrict contact with the outside world, reject food, and deny herself anything enjoyable. Her diagnosis, however, was not pessimistic. She demonstrated, especially during the first part of the session, a sufficient capacity for play and connection that led to the expectation of therapeutic success. In addition, the anxiety so denied at the beginning of the session was manifesting itself, until reaching a crisis of anguish, which is a very good prognosis in a girl of that age.

From a technical point of view, the cases mentioned so far should fall squarely into what Melanie Klein refers to as "early analysis." However, the specific technique that I detail in these pages erases those limits, as well as those that separate the analysis of children from that of adults. This method is applicable, without modification, to all age groups. I will endeavor to prove, through examples, that the only difference is the way the child communicates with the therapist and, in part, the way the interpretation is verbalized. I say "in part," because the differences are minimal.

In order to illustrate this, I will present the first hours of the analyses a five-and-a-half-year-old girl who suffered from constipation, an eight-year-old boy whose symptoms were encopresis and enuresis, a six-year-old girl with a phobia of lameness, and an eight-year-old epileptic boy.

Case 7, Ema, five and a half years

Ema was a five-and-a-half-year-old girl who was brought to analysis for six months. She suffered from chronic constipation. Her environmental situation was unique: She was brought to treatment by the person who cared for her, whom she believed to be her mother. In fact, her mother had died during childbirth because of eclampsia, which had caused Ema's premature birth by cesarean section. At birth, she was severely underweight and she remained in an incubator for a month, cared for by the establishment's staff. The particular traumatic condition of her birth added to the oral frustration, due to lack of a maternal breast, which was replaced by poor hospital care. Ema represented this part of her story in a drawing (Figure 7.1). The month she remained inside the incubator increased her paranoid and depressive anxieties.

Figure 7.1. Ema's hospital with incubators.

We will relate the first hour of her treatment, in which all of this became very evident. Ema took a toy machine gun from the objects the therapist had made available, mimicked the sound, and carefully checked the front of the barrel. She placed it on a raft together with two toys depicting natives, and let them sink, saying, "Danger, they are both drowning." She symbolically expressed the repetition of her birth. Due to the characteristics of the game, it was clear that her idea of birth was always linked to a specific fantasy: to be born, one must fight against death and suffer abandonment.

Her mother, before she died, entrusted Ema's care and safety to a friend of hers. This was, at the beginning of the treatment, the *real* mother for the patient. Her father was away when Ema was born, never really took care of her, and a long time transpired before he met her. However, as time passed, and the father became closer with the daughter, a situation of continuous conflict arose between the adoptive mother and the paternal grandparents. Both sides fought covertly for possession of the child. This situation was aggravated by the difference in economic resources between the two families, which Ema noticed. Her adoptive mother was poor and her grandparents very rich. The problem was also worsened by the way in which she was treated, with a lot of attention and time spent on seducing her, and not enough spent on genuine affection. The girl sensed this, as well as her father's indecision, which fluctuated between the two environments.

She expressed the conflict that this situation created when she took a top from the drawer and spun it, pairing its rocking motion with movements of her own. When the top was about to stop spinning, and started wobbling, she said: "Which way will it fall?" Before it had a chance to topple, she lifted it, leaving it suspended in the air. This symbolized the lack of security and stability she felt, which was amplified by the treatment she was subjected to in the family environment. On certain occasions, she was told she would continue to live with her adoptive mother. On others, she would stay with her grandparents. In essence, she was always "in the air" and never got to settle down.

She was brought to treatment for intense constipation. She would spend five or six days without a successful bowel movement, despite having been subjected to all kinds of diets and drug treatments. We will relate how she expressed her symptom, as well as how she showed clear knowledge that this was the reason why she had attended therapy. She took a sheet of paper on which she traced the route of the trolley (Figure 7.2).

Ema said, "It's the trolley that goes from your house to mine." She marked the stops with thick knots. While she was drawing, she said, "The trolley stops in Plaza San Martín, which is where I live. But I don't know why they make people get off a little earlier … They push each other out at the same time … and then the trolley is completely empty …"

The journey of the trolley through the thick knotted stops represented, for Ema, the journey of the fecal material through the intestine.

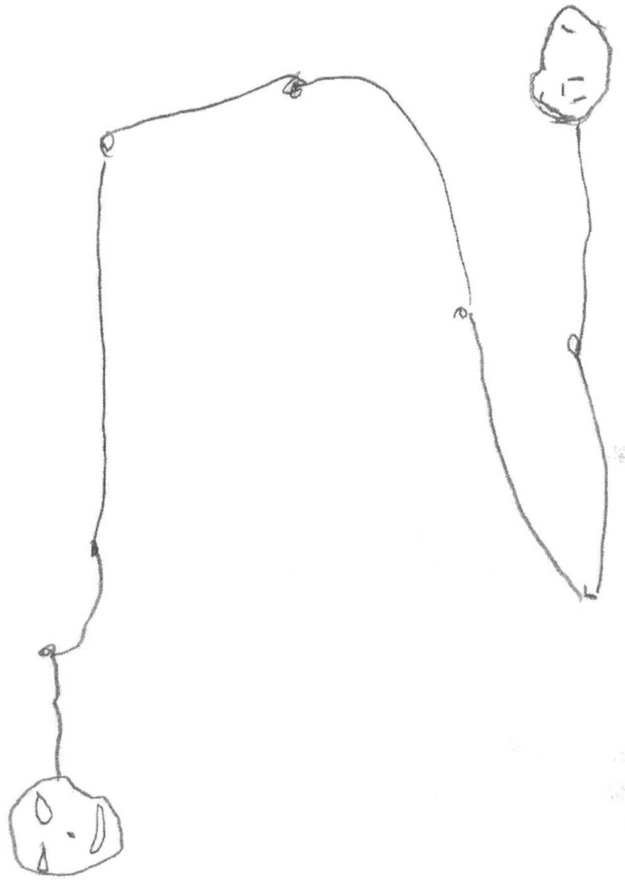

Figure 7.2. Ema's trolley connection to her analyst.

Through this, she showed us her unconscious fantasy: the act of defecation and fecal matter. These elements represented the fetus inside the mother's womb (Ema herself) as a bad daughter; that is, as destructive, unwanted fecal matter. By stating, as she drew, that people exited the trolley a little before the final stop, she was showing her knowledge of the way she had been born—abruptly expelled from her mother's body before she died. In the end, the trolley was left completely empty, just as her mother had been left completely empty of life. To stay with her until the end would have meant dying with her, but the idea of having abandoned her left Ema loaded with an intense guilt, which contributed, in part, to her symptoms. This was further showcased when she finished off the drawing with the deathly image of a skull to mark the final stop in Plaza San Martín.

This unconscious guilt is what she expressed in her body through constipation. Through this symptom, Ema identified with her mother. If she retained the fecal matter—a symbol representing Ema herself as a fetus—she could assure herself that she had not abandoned or killed the mother. Not letting out the fecal matter was, for her, a way of perpetuating the fantasy of having a living fetus inside a living mother.

During her first hour of play, after expressing these conflicts, we saw her anxiety intensify. After drawing the skull, she tore the paper in two and crumpled it. A dirty paper, which belonged to her, torn in two like used toilet tissue, clearly personified her own self. She felt dirty, mistreated by the divisions that her internal conflicts created in her, and aggravated by the adults who disputed her conflicts, which only worsened the divisions. At this moment, she felt herself to be part-objects of the two-family nuclei that seduced her and disputed her, but found that neither side managed to constitute a single good object, a total good object. This made her take refuge in an idealized object: her dead mother. During that first hour, she expressed the unconscious fantasy of her illness, as well as her need to get rid of the dead mother. Like she'd done with the paper, she longed to tear up the dead mother's role, ball it up, and throw it across the floor of the office. Thus, she placed her illness in the hands of the therapist.

During sessions, she would constantly reproach herself. It was evident that she felt that each clarification of the truth, whether it dealt with her mother, her father, her adoptive mother, or her grandparents, was tearing her apart. To Ema, this was a rebirth that entailed as much suffering as the first. Her reproaches were nothing more than a continuous request for love. She rightly demanded that the therapist give her all the love that her mother could not give her. This hour makes it very clear to us that, despite the lengths the adults around her went to in order to hide the truth from her, Ema was always aware of her mother's fate. In Figure 7.1, she showed how she conceptualized her time in the incubator while the other babies were in the nursery, as well as how she processed the fact that her mother was accompanied only by the doctor at the time of delivery.

Case 8, Fernando, age eight

In the previous case, we saw how Ema, a five-year-old girl who suffered from persistent constipation, successfully symbolized her difficulties in evacuating the intestine. We will now show how Fernando, eight years old, represented the opposite symptom: a lack of urinary and fecal control. The therapist Manuel Kizzer included buckets, colored pencils, scissors, Play-Doh, pencil sharpeners, marbles, glue, and tape in the diagnostic drawer. The first hour of play was diagnostic, and, therefore, the material was not interpreted to him, but we can see his conflicts represented in the flow of his play.

Fernando took the buckets and built a boat with them (Figure 7.3), claiming he would later build the dock. He created a large tank with a water outlet (A), then said that there was a "leak" at that outlet and a garbage dump on top (B). He pointed out that everything accumulated there and that the problem must be solved with a valve. If we consider the tank with its water outlet (A) and the garbage can (B) as the projective symbolization of the belly and its contents, and we take into account

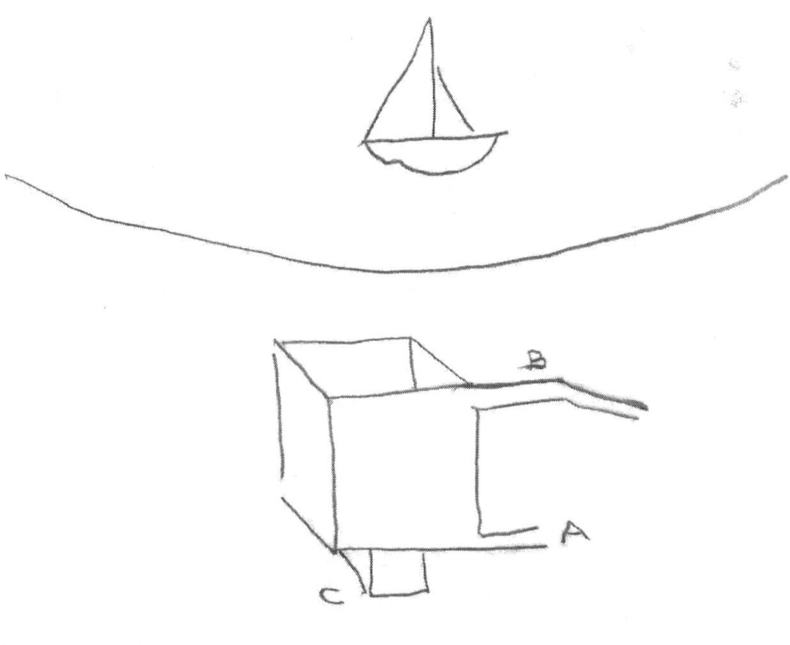

Figure 7.3. Fernando's bucket-boat on a leaky tank.

that the undersized, weak support (C) cannot hold up the contraption, we realize that this support (C) is what Fernando feels he must maintain. Indeed, we could interpret the whole diagram as a symbolization of his entire body scheme, as well as a representation of the insecurity that his annoying symptom produced in him. The ship coming to the dock represented him coming to treatment, to have both enuresis and encopresis fixed.

Case 9, Beatriz, age six

Beatriz, a six-year-old girl, was tested twice: once, when she was four, for suffering from a phobia of lameness, and a second time, when she was six, for a phobia of school. We will relate the first hour of the former analysis (by Héctor Garbarino).

One day, when Beatriz was two years old, she was sitting with her mother at the door of her house. She saw a lame man pass by and began to cry in terror, pleading with her mother to return her to the house. From that moment forward, she would not leave her house unless she was verbally assured that she would not encounter anyone like that. The phobia gradually progressed to include situations that were somewhat related to the original. For example, Beatriz could not bear to see children with a bandaged leg, or anyone who had difficulty walking. The therapist learned from her mother that Beatriz was born after a prolonged labor, during which she'd suffered from suffocation. She had not breathed immediately and had been kept in an oxygenated incubator for twenty days following her birth. When her mother put her to the breast, she had difficulty latching on. She cried and refused to suck properly. Due to these circumstances, a nurse from the sanatorium helped her mother. The mother claimed that without that nurse's intelligent and unconditional support, she would not have been able to breastfeed the child. Though it began with the aforementioned difficulties, breastfeeding then continued with no problems until nine months. Beatriz's restlessness and tears, however, did not stop.

When Beatriz was one-and-a-half years old, a sister was born. The pregnancy began when the patient was nine months old. This is a period of special complexity in *every* child's development. But it is especially important in this case. I frame it thus because the event coincided with weaning, and was based on a bad start to the relationship with the mother. When the mother returned home with the new baby, Beatriz cried for hours, clinging dramatically to the bars of her little sister's crib.

Shortly before the onset of her symptom, the child's maternal grandmother died. Since she slept in the same bed as her grandmother, the circumstances of the death were particularly traumatic for Beatriz. The death occurred overnight and suddenly, but, according to her mother, the girl had remained asleep and unaware through the ordeal. When it was explained to her, at a later date, that her grandmother had gone to heaven, Beatriz asked to die so she could go play with her. Her phobia of lameness coincided with her sister learning to walk. It became really evident the day her sister took her first steps on her own. From all the information the mother provided, it seems important to point out that the dead grandmother's sister was lame and that Beatriz did not see her frequently, neither before nor after the grandmother's death.

Beatriz was a pretty girl, with an expressive and friendly look. Once inside the office, however, she began to stare at everything around her with fear. After a few moments of hesitation, she took two little dolls and looked back and forth between them, as if comparing them. She put them down, took a telephone, and held it close to her body, then tried to stop the dolls from standing.

Let's analyze this fragment. In her anxious inspection of the room, Beatriz showed her distrust of the analyst and her fear that the analyst was the same as her parents. The desire to communicate intensely with him was expressed in the alternate observation of the dolls, followed by bringing the telephone close to her body. When she stopped the doll from standing, she showed her concern and announced that her symptom was somehow related to it. Let us remember that the appearance of the symptom coincided with the first steps of the sister, and that the pregnancy of the mother, in turn, coincided with Beatriz's own first steps.

Beatriz continued the game, trying to place one of the dolls in a bathtub and failing. She restrained the dolls, then took a stick of clay, broke it in the middle, and asked: "What am I going to do with this game?" In this new fragment of Beatriz's game, we come closer to understanding the meaning of her phobia. She expressed the wish that her sister had not been born; this being the doll that she tried to introduce into the bathtub. The tub itself was a symbol of her mother's womb. She did this immediately after having restrained the doll. But the sister exited and stood up, like the dolls she tried to stop from standing, and her destructive impulses arose, driving her to break the plasticine bar in two. This carried the meaning of breaking her sister's legs. Her problem now was how to fix what she had destroyed. This is why she asked the therapist to teach her how to repair her doll's lame legs, which were a displacement and condensation of the damage to her sister and her grandmother. By displacing the conflicts with her sister—which clearly stemmed from the parents' intercourse—to the image of disabled people, Beatriz transformed them into persecuting objects that she must avoid. By inserting hatred and fear into these images, she was able to continue living in peace with her sister. The mother claimed that Beatriz adored her sister and, in a sense, she was right.

From what has been explained so far, we can infer why Beatriz chose disabled people as the object of her phobia. This coincided with her sister learning to walk, which, as Beatriz walked, increased her jealousy, envy, and rivalry. Her sister became someone to be feared because she could move freely. The death of the grandmother, which occurred in those days, meant, for Beatriz, the reality that death exists, which increased the fear that her destructive fantasies could be fulfilled. Being disabled and being dead became two real events, and the moment she saw a disabled person, her sister's lameness and her grandmother's death linked the two concepts in her unconscious. The parents' story, wherein Beatriz incessantly cried and clung to the bars of the crib the day her sister arrived home, evokes the image of someone holding on to something sturdy so they won't fall. All these contents were clarified in the course of the treatment. The systematic interpretation of the material, formulated in the transference plane and its relationship with the original objects (parents, sister, grandmother), determined a considerable improvement in Beatriz's phobia. This prompted the mother to discontinue the analysis two months after it started.

The school phobia, which appeared two years after this treatment, was also closely related to her sister, from whom she had become inseparable. She always remained by her side, which prevented her from any action and paralyzed her.

Case 10, Gerardo, age eight

Gerardo, eight years old, suffered epileptic seizures four or five times a day. His education was disturbed by his continuous absences. He walked into the office alone and seemed uninterested in toys. He began to draw a house, going out of his way to get all the details right, and adhering to a standard expected for his age. He carefully colored in the picture and, when finished, drew multiple large dark clouds over it. The first ones were very close to the upper edge of the sheet, and those that followed got closer and closer to the roof of the house. When he painted the last one, the boundary between that cloud-laden sky and the roof of the house had been lost. Then, he said, "The storm is coming; the roof is collapsing." The appearance of successive clouds, each one drawing closer and closer to the house, symbolized and dramatized the foreboding time preceding a convulsion, with the storm that destroyed the house representing the convulsion itself, and the collapse being the fall as a consequence of the seizure.

"The storm has arrived," he said to me, "the house is collapsing." He asked me to teach him how to make a house "that does not collapse." His unconscious fantasy regarding his illness consisted of an uncontrollable force that was alien to him—the storm—from which he felt a foreboding aura. He could not fight against this force, and it would eventually knock him over and produce the convulsion. His healing fantasy consisted of the therapist teaching him to control that force, so he could avoid the convulsions and the collapse altogether.

Commentary on Chapter 7

Alan Sugarman (USA)

Reading this chapter from Arminda Aberastury's book on psychoanalytic technique offers a wonderful view into a child analytic pioneer from both a different culture and a different era. It is fascinating to see her struggle with issues that are still quite germane today while approaching them from a very different theoretical vantage point than one sees in typical North American child analytic literature. She begins this chapter on play with a bold assertion about the capacity of young children for insight. At the time that she wrote this, she reports the common belief was that because children expressed their problems via play, a preverbal modality, they lacked awareness "of the disease or the will to cure it" (this volume, p. 123). But she challenges this notion, claiming that "as early as the first session of an analysis or a diagnostic observation, the unconscious fantasy of illness and cure emerged" (this volume, p. 123). She uses the rest of the chapter to present case examples that she believes demonstrate children communicating their unconscious fantasies of the etiology of their problem, their desire for help with it, and a specific fantasy of how they need to be healed.

In these statements, she is challenging the belief of many English-speaking ego-psychologically oriented child analysts that young children are incapable of insight. Perhaps the clearest exposition of that perspective is Kennedy's (1979) conclusion that five year olds do not have the developmental maturity for insight. Secondary-process thinking is not well established; implicit memories are still in the process of consolidation; past and present become easily confused, as does fantasy and reality (Sugarman, 2003). Kennedy, in contrast to Aberastury, saw children's capacity even for self-observation as quite limited and usually used to maintain a current sense of well-being rather than self-understanding. She also stressed the limiting factor of children's immature sense of time leading to merger of past and present so that "real insight of how the past affects current experience will be extremely rare in the under-five" (Kennedy, 1979, p. 17). Yet, many of the case examples in this chapter are of children much younger than five with Aberastury claiming they have awareness of the cause of their symptoms.

This contradiction between her and Kennedy is partially based on what Aberastury sees as "evidence" for the child communicating their unconscious fantasies. Throughout her clinical examples, she makes immediate interpretations (to the child and in her own mind) of the symbolic meaning of the play. A contemporary and non-Kleinian reader is left with mixed feelings about them. On the one hand, one feels awe and admiration at her ability to read the unconscious communication in the play. On the other hand, many will question how much her Kleinian orientation leads her to see a particular meaning that may not be there. Such doubts seem credible given her rather dated view of the function of play. She agrees with Freud whom she reports to have "discovered that, if a child plays, it is *always* indicative of a need to work out traumatic situations" (this volume, p. 123, my italics).

This understanding of play ignores the importance of inborn constitutional capacities that always emerge in facilitating or average expectable environments. There is a vast modern-day literature documenting the adaptive and development-promoting functions of play. It is a crucial developmental attainment that promotes the capacity for mentalization and all the self-regulatory functions that emerge from being able to mentalize (Mayes & Cohen, 1992; Sugarman, 2003, 2008). Certainly, child's play may be used to work out traumatic situations. But that is only one of many possibilities. Likewise, many of her understandings of the symbolism in the case examples may be correct. But, again, a few of her examples raise questions of other meanings. Most non-Kleinian child analysts would be reluctant to be so definitive about material in the first session.

Nonetheless, most contemporary North American child analysts would agree with her that even young children can attain insight. They just differ in how they define insight. Aberastury advocates direct interpretation of what she understands to be the unconscious fantasies in the symbolism she ascribes to the play. The implication is that doing so makes the unconscious fantasies conscious to the child. This is a topographic model of mutative action used by classical Freudians and Kleinians to explain that psychoanalysis cures by making repressed mental contents conscious. The analyst acts as a decoder of this repressed content. In contrast, contemporary ego-psychologists emphasize the importance of fostering a process of insightfulness whereby the child analyst helps the child to realize that he has an internal world that arises out of important interactions with the external world and fantasies about it. Play is used as a vehicle to promote this awareness. "Via insightfulness, the young child does not gain access so much to repudiated mental content as to a key psychological process that has been derailed by internal conflict" (Sugarman, 2003, p. 331).

Despite this key difference, both Aberastury and contemporary thinkers (Ferro & Basile, 2006; Sugarman, 2009) agree that child analysis and adult psychoanalysis are far more similar than different. "However, the specific technique that I detail in these pages erases ... those [differences] that separate the analysis of children from that of adults" (this volume, p. 142). She was forty years ahead of her field in reaching this conclusion. But the difference between her theory and more modern theories of mutative action leads to vastly different explanations for the similarity. Aberastury sees the two treatments as being the same because the emphasis is on analyzing unconscious mental content. The child expresses the content in play while the adult expresses it in free associations. In both modalities, the analyst decodes the latent meaning and interprets it.

Contemporary child analysts understand the similarity in different ways. Ferro and Basile (2006), for example, stress that the two modalities are essentially the same so long as the interpretive emphasis is on the here-and-now. And Sugarman (2009) argues that child and adult psychoanalysis both have essentially the same process despite some differences in technique (use of the couch, role of the parents, emphasis on free association). He also thinks that they share the same mutative principle—promoting the process of insightfulness.

Finally, Aberastury was prescient in her finding that analyzing children does not require the preparatory phase that Anna Freud originally believed necessary before she developed defense analysis. Aberastury was clear that one can interpret unconscious meanings, even to very young children, from the get-go. "It is essential that, *from the first moment*, we assume the role of therapists. This helps the child position themselves as a patient as well as become conscious of the unconscious fantasy revealed in interpretation" (this volume, p. 124, my italics).

In summary, Arminda Aberastury was both a brilliant pioneer in child analysis and a prisoner of her era and theoretical model. She both anticipated many technical advances in child psychoanalysis but was constrained by the Kleinian model so prominent in her country during her era. Nonetheless, her sharp clinical acumen and case examples continue to offer pearls of wisdom from which we can all learn.

CHAPTER 8

Subsequent work with parents

Once we have the crucial elements assembled from the history given by the parents and our experience of the child, and have made our diagnosis of the case based on them, we must arrange another interview with the parents to give our recommendation. Whether or not they attend the meeting and fulfill their obligation to complete the assessment process is a factor that should have been ascertained before ever seeing the child or thinking about treatment. I want to make it clear that, in regards to any case, psychoanalytic treatment is the most effective form of treatment; but only so long as the effort required of the parents does not exceed what they can be humanly expected to provide for their child. It is neither advisable nor convenient to create new anxiety by offering the parents a solution that is inaccessible to them.

Our analysis must stem from the understanding that a parent likely does not know what psychoanalytic treatment *is* and may think that, given a few hours or weeks, everything can be solved. We must also remember that a person is generally unaware of the cost of an analytical session and will often make calculations based on comparisons with other societal roles such as tutors or medical doctors. We know that the scarcity of psychoanalytic treatment is the most common argument that parents use to resist placing their child in the care of an analyst, but there are parents who really *cannot* cope. Families that have a large list of obligations and low income must make very real sacrifices to pay for long and expensive treatment. For this reason, when it comes to these cases, I will only suggest psychoanalytic treatment if I consider it absolutely essential for the child.

Suppose we are consulted for a mild, transient sleep disorder. If there is a suitable family environment and economic conditions are broad enough, treatment can and should be suggested. This helps resolve the fixation points that, in the future, could trigger a more serious neurosis; especially if external circumstances become adverse. But, if the economic difficulty is real, and the growth of the child is monitored with frequent interviews or in a mothers' counseling group, the possibility of leaving the symptom untreated without great future risk can be considered. Many times, the symptom of a child is manufactured by the mother or, at the very least, maintained or aggravated by her.

Clinical example: Miguel, three and a half years old, and his parents

On one occasion I was consulted about a three-and-a-half-year-old boy, Miguel, who urinated in his bed at night. Until then, everything about his life and current family structure had been encouraging. However, the mother had suffered from enuresis, which drove me to inquire about her behavior regarding her son suffering the same symptom. I learned that she still put him to bed in diapers, although the son had been asking her to take them off for quite some time. The next day, she would wake up feeling an intense obsession with the state of the child's bed, and would check whether it was wet or dry first thing in the morning. I assumed that the mother's externalized anxiety about the memory of her own symptom played a fundamental role in maintaining her son's. As she was fairly informed on these issues, and the overall family picture did not seem askew, I proposed a test. I suggested to the mother that, before seriously considering treatment, she remove the diapers and warn the child to not wet the bed. Then, I told her to wake him up in the middle of the night and walk him to the bathroom to urinate, but no more than once a night. I also clarified that, according to our current understanding of neuroses, enuresis is not considered a symptom until age four. This information was intended to alleviate her anxiety.

The child reacted with relief and satisfaction, accepting the conditions. A few days after starting this routine, he stopped wetting the bed. We might wonder why a symptom that is often so rebellious was, in this case, so easily solved. I believe that the mother's relief at knowing that the problem was not as serious as she'd originally thought favored the child's improvement. Because she had a good relationship with the son, she was effective in complying with the instructions. In addition, the child had developed normally, his symptom had been exacerbated by the mother's anxiety, he had a united parental unit, and related well with both parents.

As we have pointed out many times, we must consider the complementary relationship between internal and external factors in all cases. When it comes to an internal conflict such as conflict over growing up, we must consider the environment. If the environmental factors are positive, the symptom can be treated and overcome. If negative external situations have been added to this same internal conflict—for example, a lack of contact with the mother, the absence of the father, unfair punishments, or inappropriate demands—the symptom becomes so structured and ingrained that we might not be able to solve it as effectively. In any case, the suggestion should always be made to the parents—and hopefully accepted by them—to closely monitor the child's evolution and initiate psychoanalytic treatment if another symptom appears or relapses.

Referral to mothers' counseling groups

The mother can't always react like she reacted in this case, because, generally speaking, her conflicts prevent it. When this occurs, we must refer her to a mothers' counseling group, where conflicts are interpreted and resolved and the baby's life is reoriented. Mothers' counseling groups offer optimistic possibilities for the prevention of infantile neuroses. This is especially true if the mother joins when she is pregnant, or when the child is young. The earlier she solves her problems, or else is informed about the appropriate conditions for the good development of her child, the greater her chances of forming a positive relationship with her child.

The key to the further development of the child lies in the first year of life. When Freud highlighted the importance of childhood trauma for later development, he was particularly referring to the first five years of life. This concept was partially based on the belief that the Oedipus complex emerged around age three or four, and that the superego was subsequently formed as the heir to the Oedipus complex.

What we know today about development leads us to suppose that the child's relationship with both parents is already set in the first year of life. In the second half of the first year, with the flowering of genital tendencies and the establishment of the oedipal situation, a circle closes, and object relations within that circle form the oedipal triangle. This is the beginning of heterosexual tendencies in women and homosexual tendencies in males, as both begin to relate to the father's penis and partially abandon the mother's breast. In our experience, the difficulties that arise in the first year of life have the most serious ramifications in the future. The child who loses a parent before the first year of life is over is much more likely to develop psychological conflicts than the child who suffers this same loss at age seven.

Our knowledge concerning the first stages of development allows us to assess accurately whether an achievement, a behavior, or a difficulty is normal or pathological. It allows us to adapt the stimulus to the moment of development in which it can perform with the least interruption. By using a framework within which we can include normal or pathological development in the object relationship, we can assess the normality of the child's relationship with the objects according to their level. The latest theoretical contributions on the child's relationship with the mother, the inclusion of the father and siblings in the emotional life of the child, the awakening of interests, and the initiation of the symbolization process, all allow for a healthy orientation to the infant's needs. This orientation will undoubtedly afford the best prevention of future disorders. Thus, we come to the inevitable conclusion that early guidance from the mother is the best antidote to the formation of symptoms that might otherwise develop from minor difficulties. For example, mothers whose older children had varied sleep and eating disorders were able to verify that, after attending a group of mothers, the disorders ceased. They also reported a lower frequency of more serious negative character traits.

In children from one to five years of age, modifications in the mother's attitude, while not equally effective in all cases, are still very important. If the child is undergoing treatment, the maternal counseling group can support the child's treatment. If the child is not in treatment, the group makes it a priority to interpret the mother's feelings of guilt, the intensity of which invariably depends on the severity of the child's illness; and this interpretive activity relieves the guilt and that enables the child's behavior to improve.

In the cases of children older than five years, we also recommend the mother's admission to a counseling group. This is because the indubitable relief of guilt she experiences favors a better attitude towards her child. This is especially true in preadolescents, and is crucial in understanding their conflicts, coming to terms with their new instinctual needs, and accepting their growth.

When the child suffers from asthma, acetonemia, a tendency to fall and hurt themselves, recurrent angina, disorders in development due to the arrest of basic functions like walking or speaking, and inhibitions in school learning, the solution is to look for the unconscious roots that have determined these symptoms. And to make the unconscious conscious, we have only one truly effective method to accomplish this: psychoanalysis. In these cases, when changes in the mother's external and internal attitude are not enough, psychoanalytic treatment of the child will be necessary. Psychoanalysis is both therapeutic and prophylactic, since experience shows that the improvement of the child results in a decrease in family tension, which, in and of itself, prevents new disorders.

In cases where the child's indication for psychoanalysis is urgent and cannot be achieved due to the parents' real economic difficulty, the mother should instead be guided to the mothers' counseling group where she will receive counsel from the leader and the other mothers in the group. We must clarify that this solution is partial, transitory, and should only last until the parental unit is financially stable enough to afford treatment. It may seem cruel to tell this truth, but postponing the knowledge causes nothing but harm to the child and the parents. If we are dealing, for example, with an epileptic child, and we believe that only psychoanalytic treatment will lead the child to be free of the symptoms, we must defend this conviction even when it is not easy to do so. In Nora's case (see Chapter 12), the parents had to make great sacrifices to simultaneously afford the girl's individual treatment *and* the mother's guidance group. However, if they had not done so, the girl's illness would have reached such a degree so as to be incurable with any type of therapy. Not to mention that, according to what we saw, the next few years would have most likely seen the second daughter succumb to an illness as intense as her sister's.

In most technique books about child analysis published to date, there are references to the difficulties that parents add to the already complicated task of analyzing a child. However, we must be able to count on their participation from the beginning of treatment, because a child is not a socially or emotionally independent being.

For many years it was argued that, unlike the adult, the child lacked an awareness of the disease and the neurotic disorder that prompted treatment. When I understood that a child not only *knew* they were sick, but openly displayed the unconscious fantasy of illness and healing from the very first hour, and made their *own* decision to accept the therapist, it became abundantly clear to me that it was most often the parents that decided to stop or interrupt treatment. They would pretend the child did not want to come and take advantage of holidays, trips, or the disappearance of symptoms to temporarily interrupt the sessions. During each case, I always wondered whether the parents would keep the child in analysis for the necessary time or—as was the experience of all child analysts—remove them at the most crucial time.

Original approach to parent meetings

In the early days of my work, I met with parents quite frequently. I listened to their descriptions of their child and I dispensed advice. The evolution of psychoanalysis has increasingly led me to not overvalue the data parents provide on the child's daily life or to provide advice. Back then, if they asked me for advice, I gave it to them, always influencing them in favor of the urgent needs of the child. Although, at the time, the suggestions provided effective results, they later brought me negative repercussions as they invariably presented as hostile and persecutory clients. This happened even in cases where the analysis had been objectively successful. The reflection on the latent meaning of the interviews led me, little by little, to the technique that I will delineate in these pages.

It was during the analysis of a four-year-old boy—a child who had killed his month-old cousin—that I better understood the role I should assign parents in order to overcome the difficulties I have pointed out. As far as I could tell, these difficulties stemmed from a confusion of their role with that of the therapist during a preliminary section of the analysis, in which they had to collaborate by changing situations or attitudes. I concluded that it is not advisable to give advice to parents—so long as the child is in analysis—even in the case of extremely misguided situations, such as co-sleeping, corporal punishment, seduction, etc. I maintain that it is only the child's improvement that effects a real change in the family environment. Therefore, I work only with the child, in a two-person relationship, as I would in adult analysis.

A fundamental topic in child analysis is the management of parents and their inclusion in the treatment of the child. Although, with the discovery of the play technique, it became possible to understand how the young child's mind worked, interpret the conflicts, and solve them, the success of therapy, however, was often not accompanied by an increase in the confidence of the parents. On the contrary, they often interrupted the analysis of the child for futile reasons and in an abrupt manner, without giving us enough time to let the child work through the separation.

Even though child analysts have repeatedly pointed out this technical difficulty, no papers as yet attempt to understand or solve it. They have limited themselves to studying it as an unavoidable stumbling block, maintaining that the child does not go to treatment of their own volition, and that its continuity does not depend on the child. Years of experience in child analysis led me to confirm this fact, but I resisted the idea that it might be unsolvable. I always thought that the difficulty must arise from a technical deficiency that, born of the adult technique, had not yet given us the key to solve this problem.

One of the fundamental obstacles is the need to handle a double, and sometimes triple, transference from parents and child. As I have already pointed out, for many years, I followed the classic rule: I interviewed the parents prior to treatment. To a certain extent, these interviews helped me acquire an idea of the evolution of the treatment, as well as supplying me with the tools to advise them. The experience made me see that this was not a good solution to the family neurosis, since the reasons for the misguided behavior were unconscious and could not be modified by conscious norms.

I understood, for example, that when the father or mother relapsed into co-sleeping or corporal punishment, I suddenly became a purveyor of persecution in their eyes. The guilt they felt was channeled into aggression, which made treatment difficult. In addition, the increased guilt led them to seek my punishment or my censure by treating the child even worse. The conflict was aggravated by its lack of interpretability, since the parents were not in treatment. The issue eventually led to the interruption of the analysis.

Gradually, I began distancing myself from the parental interview and abandoning parent counseling entirely. At the beginning of my career, if I were asked to analyze a child who slept with their parents, I would advise them to give the child a separate room. This turned out to be a mistake because the advice acted as a negative external factor. It abruptly interfered with family life, shattering an internal situation in the process. Without being privy to the child's participation, and without understanding to what extent the process was essential to the child's neurosis, I had no way of knowing the effects of the separation. Experience taught me that when children, even very young ones, elaborated the conflict for themselves, they would also demand the change, and this had the added advantage of conviction from previous analysis. Thus, I did not interfere, preventing the parental transference situation from the beginning. This also allowed the parents to adapt to the new relationship with the child. Since interpretation is the basic instrument of psychoanalytic treatment—specifically the interpretation of transference—it is evident that a relationship with the parents that lacks interpretation leaves them free to pursue any type of elaboration.

Practice taught me that the effectiveness of counseling depended on the presence of the therapist and that, separated from the therapist, the parents continued to deal with the child's conflicts as they had done before. However, they also had to deal with the added aggravation that, if the child's symptoms relapsed, they now knew that the child was sick and understood the cause of their illness. The therapist was thus transformed into a superego, and guilt generally turned into aggression.

When I tried to modify external situations, my mistake was acting as if the parents did not have conflicts. Under this false assumption, I encouraged their support in the positive transference that they established with me. But, by making this choice, I failed to consider a fundamental unconscious factor: the growing rivalry they experienced with the child. They stopped being parents, instead becoming rival children in search of help. One child was the privileged one, the one in treatment, and the other was injured, had no treatment, but had to pay for the other's improvement.

Added to this rivalry was the one they felt with me. They saw me as a parent who steals the affection of the child and makes amends for the original parents' mistakes. All these contradictory feelings led them to act in a compulsive way. Many times, even though they consciously wanted to, they could not bring themselves to follow my advice. They were prevented from doing so when the suggestions interfered too much with their own conflicts, or when their confidence in me was contaminated by the contradictory feelings that I have indicated. As this whole pattern of transference could not be interpreted, it was not understood. It remained repressed and led them to fluctuate between absolute obedience and systematic rebellion.

This complicated and subtle network made it increasingly difficult to handle the interviews, which are generally spaces where idealization or love holds sway. Rather than positive elaborations, however, our interviews were full of resentment and frustration, which often led the parents to destroy the treatment of the child in an attempt to defend and sustain a part of the child's personality. Another important fact was that, when the child's therapist asked the parents for changes to help or hasten the improvement and they could not keep to them, they felt like failures as parents.

Evolved technique in meeting with parents

The understanding of these problems and the desire to alleviate or solve them led me to change the technique. I changed it because I understood the following:

1) My previous performance was not useful for the child
2) It disturbed family life
3) It ended up damaging the treatment.

I decided that, as long as the parents put the child in treatment, I would let them adhere to their usual behavior, avoid influencing them, and not point out defects or mistakes in their child-rearing.

A father who hits his son might stop doing so temporarily, based on our advice. However, at any time, he is liable to repeat the previous behavior, or similar behavior, if this change is not based on an understanding of the reasons that led him to act like this in the first place. If a mother tends to tuck her child into the marriage bed, our advice to not do so will be limited by the conflict anxiety that leads to it. But if the mother–child couple is changed by modifying one of the parties, the child—even a young one—will reject co-sleeping and will seek another form of contact with the mother. A psychoanalytic treatment enables a child, even a very young one, to modify their environment. Though a child might not always know how to verbally express themselves, and might lack the ability to make themselves understood in their wishes, changes in their behavior are usually a warning that ends up being directly understood.

This prompted me to almost completely suppress interviews with parents, except when they express such an overwhelming need for the interview that denying it would be more disruptive. In these cases, I do it under conditions established in advance: the child, no matter how young, must be directly informed of the day and time when we will see the parents, and the child must know that everything that is spoken during that meeting will be communicated to them. The parents must also be informed that the content of the child's sessions will not be disclosed, as we agreed when starting treatment. Parents, in turn, must know the conditions of this agreement. They must be aware that everything they say will be transmitted to the child, and that they will receive no information about the child's sessions in return.

Adopting this behavior leads to a real strengthening of the bond with the child, as well as a better relationship with the parents. They feel relieved by placing the entire illness in the hands of the analyst, with a consequent reduction in guilt due to sharing the burden. Furthermore, if the parents are left out of the therapeutic action—if they sit outside the consulting room, for instance—their transferential bond with the analyst becomes more manageable. This way, they are less exposed to the inherent frustrations of a contact that, while apparently deep, is only superficial and supportive, because the transference is not interpreted.

By assuming total therapeutic responsibility, the analyst does more than simply alleviate the parents' anxiety. They also adopt a more real and adequate attitude. On the contrary, if we advise them to make changes to help their child improve and they cannot comply with them, they feel responsible for any setback and their anxiety becomes intolerable enough to interrupt treatment. When the healing of the child depends not only on the action of the therapist but also on the attitude of the parents and the modifications that they make in family life, conflicts are created. The parents may feel unable to follow the rules—due to their own conflicts—and will tend to think that the treatment is wrong. The guilt will become untenable and they will resort to the psychological mechanism so well described by Klein: If something cannot be repaired, it must be destroyed. This mechanism is largely responsible for the frequent interruptions of the analysis of children. With the current technique, on the other hand, the therapist fully assumes the lead role. The parents' role is limited to sending the child for testing and paying for treatment.

Experience showed me that even very young children were capable of demanding to sleep alone, avoiding situations in which they would be punished, and shifting their need for affection to more suitable figures. I remember an eighteen-month-old boy who was analyzed for difficulty walking and a slow overall development. When the boy improved, he imposed new living conditions, such as sleeping alone and spending more time with the mother than with the babysitter. This is to say that, by breaking the neurotic bond due to the improvement of one of its members, the other was able to change and ameliorate the situation of separation. In addition, it is common that, as the child exhibits change, the parents will seek therapeutic help.

The psychoanalytic treatment of children has undergone a host of modifications. This is mainly due to the fact that we analyze children who are younger and younger, or even children without language rudiments, so it has become necessary to look for techniques increasingly adapted to preverbal expression.

The anxiety manifested by the child at the beginning of the treatment—experienced unconsciously by them as a new rupture in the relationship with the mother—is the repetition of the anxiety caused by birth. Understanding it, I decided that it was important to reproduce the original situation as much as possible. For this reason, I clarify to all parties involved that it is convenient for the child to enter alone. If, during the first session, I do not succeed, I interpret the child's reaction to me in all the details and I announce that, in the next session, the child will enter alone. I advise the mother that, if she cannot bear the separation, she should have someone else accompany the child, as her own anxiety can disturb the initiation of treatment. I point out that I will take care of the child's reactions, and this clarification is necessary because the child may cry, whine, kick, and scream. The duration of the reaction, the intensity, and whether or not it is accessible to modification through interpretation, all these factors teach us a lot about the history of the child and the way they act in the world. After this first and abrupt separation, it is almost normal for the child to enter the office spontaneously and remain in it. Later, the child may present new crises, but each more fleeting and controllable.

Parents should bring the child four or five times a week; preferably five. The child should come on days and hours chosen in advance. They should stay with the therapist for fifty minutes, just like an adult in psychoanalytic treatment. In the case that the sessions are suspended due to difficulties the analyst might have, they will be replaced whenever possible. The same is true if the difficulties stem from the parents, because continuity in the sessions is very important.

The fees and vacation date of the analyst will be stipulated in advance. This allows parents to know the conditions beforehand, so they can organize family life to adapt to them. The analytical contract establishes that sessions suspended due to any difficulties on the patient's side are generally paid, whether due to illness, vacation, or any other cause. The continuity of treatment should be preserved as much as possible, since sometimes the anxiety aroused by the analysis of a child leads to unexpected travel plans, changes, or unnecessary prolongation of illnesses.

Having already indicated the limits of our role, and having ensured the total reserve of the material that the child entrusts to us, we must still clarify other points. Parents need to know that, at some point during treatment, the need for sexual clarification will arise. Therefore, we must ensure that they accept that condition and its consequences. They are not advised to follow a certain behavior if the children question *them*, but they are warned that it can happen and that they must be prepared.

It is also necessary to clarify the position of the therapist in terms of the religious problem. Non-practicing, but, to some extent, spiritually inclined parents often enroll their children in religious schools or give them a religious education. This confuses the child, who feels the conflict between the opposing tendencies of spirituality and nonobservance and takes responsibility for the final fate of their parents. For instance, the child may worry and think that the parents will go to hell if they do not comply with the demands of their spiritual teachers. In our experience, this has serious consequences for the child. There are some deeply religious parents who educate their children according to their beliefs, and who come to prefer that the child remain sick rather than risk a loss of faith. In this case, confusion is avoided, but not conflict.

In all cases, it is essential to clarify to the parents that loss of faith is possible within the treatment, but that this does not mean that the therapist has an active ideological attitude in terms of religion. We will clarify it as the subject appears, by analyzing the conflicts that have arisen in the child. It should also be noted that neither the moment nor the way in which the problem will arise is foreseeable. In other cases, atheist parents send their children to religious schools or make them comply with certain demands—generally the same ones their own parents imposed on them as children. Nothing would be gained by explaining to them the child's confusion when confronting the simultaneous atheism and religiosity being imposed on them. This contradiction must be solved by the patient himself.

The initiation of treatment must be done by previously establishing the basic conditions, so that the therapist can act with the same freedom as they feel with adult patients, without requiring further interviews with the parents every time a choice needs to be made.

Another issue that needs to be clarified with the parents is the position of the therapist regarding the child's origin: adoption, illegitimacy, etc. It is the experience of analysts that, when children are adopted, they unconsciously know the truth of their condition. Even in those cases in which it has been jealously hidden from them, the analysis will still lead them to make this situation conscious. When raising the problem with parents, they often refuse to tell the child the truth, or abruptly stop treatment. Parents should remain informed of this necessity, and treatment must begin only on the condition that they are willing to clarify the child's origin when the child inevitably asks. If they do not accept this condition, under no circumstances can the treatment be carried out successfully. When the confrontation of the child with the adoptive parents approaches, they usually ask for an interview.

At the beginning of the next session, we communicate the content of the session to the patient, which will facilitate clarification and alleviate the anxiety of the parents. In many other situations, where an important portion of the truth has been occluded, this interview technique facilitates clarification at the moment when the child is ready to face and elaborate the truth. The patient *and* the parents both need time to clarify something that is very painful to hold in for so long.

Gloria, age nine, adopted

A relevant case is that of an adopted girl who suffered from severe learning disabilities, one of the more common symptoms in adopted children. Gloria, nine, used to express her problems by drawing apartment houses. These houses had nine floors—her age—and the doors on the ground floor—the first year of her life—were firmly shut. On the following floors, the windows were also closed. In her associations, the concern of knowing where to enter the house was evident. The latent meaning was an attempt to find out if she had entered through her mother's genitalia—the front door, or through an ancillary and indirect route—the windows. If the door remained closed, it was because her family members had denied her that clarification. When the analyst began to interpret this material, she spoke with the parents to request that the child be told the truth. But they had not been warned and they strictly opposed it. This led to the abrupt discontinuation of treatment.

Pedrito

In Pedrito's case, when the subject of the analysis was the difference between the sexes and his fantasies about the vagina, the mother called to inform me that she was aware of having done wrong, but that she had been driven by something stronger than her will. She related that when he returned from a session, her son asked her if she had a penis and she replied, "Of course I do." Being able to include that conversation with his mother in the next session not only made it possible to clarify the erroneous knowledge that would have left him even more confused about the difference between the sexes, but also made it possible to rectify the mother without too much anguish.

Fanny, age ten

During the analysis of Fanny, a ten-year-old girl, I was presented with a similar problem. I was able to solve it by handling the interview with parents as I have pointed out. Her immediate family members were devotedly Catholic and were, therefore, subjected to very intense repression and prejudice. The father was a doctor and knew something of psychoanalysis. The mother, who was also a professional, had a theoretical understanding of what her daughter's treatment entailed, and had read a lot about it before deciding on it.

This knowledge had familiarized them with the idea that the clarification of everything concerning sexuality was fundamental. But, being themselves very inhibited, they had not dared give their daughter any answers to the insistent questions she'd asked them since childhood. A few months after starting the treatment, the patient's genital anxiety increased due to the first spurts of pubertal growth. On the other hand, the most annoying symptoms had disappeared, which is why the parents were relieved and expressed as much. One day they asked for an interview. After consulting with the patient and receiving her approval, I acquiesced. The mother was very distressed and had fairly justified fears that her daughter would create difficulties at school due to her continual use of vulgar sexual terms and her almost persecutory use of her sexual knowledge. I granted the interview, giving them the indicated warnings. In the next session, while Fanny opened the drawer and resumed a drawing she had been working on for several sessions, I related the interview in full and interpreted her behavior. The act of scaring her parents and her classmates was an attempt to show me the degree to which she feared the new sensations in her body and the knowledge about herself that came with them. For this interpretation, I relied on the minute details of the drawing. She was scared by the knowledge she was acquiring, which she still considered bad and forbidden, even as she flaunted it. That is why she formulated the knowledge in a vulgar and shocking way. She sought to be reprimanded or censored. I also discerned that her behavior was an attempt to terminate the treatment. Since she was not able to control what was happening to her body—the growth of her breasts and the new sensations that invaded her—she attempted to stopper the stream of new knowledge in her mind, in the hopes the physical changes would cease in turn. She had sent the mother to me so that I could fix the mess and was also testing whether her behavior had scared me and whether I, like her parents, no longer responded to her needs for clarification. I went on to tell her that the disappearance of her most annoying symptoms had modified her relationship with her parents and that, in a certain sense, she was seeking to return to the past by occupying them with new problems. The result of this interpretation—which she developed little by little and I repeated piecemeal every time I thought she might find it useful—was a modification in her behavior. The clarification of the deeper causes that had motivated the behavior revealed new material in the transference and within the repetition of the original situations. As a child she had longed for the possession of a penis and the current changes in her body reactivated those early fantasies. The possibility she most feared in her relationship with me was that I would fulfill that old wish.

Concluding remarks

We have stated that, during the initial interview, the roles have been clearly delineated: there is a therapist for a child who needs treatment, and there are the parents of that child and other members of their environment, who will receive not only the benefits, but also the effects of a psychoanalytic treatment. They should know, for example, that difficulties may increase at any given moment, and rapid improvement may be followed by relapse. They should be aware that, when analyzing a child, a whole history is recounted, and difficult moments sometimes arise in the process.

It is not necessary or appropriate to anticipate the results of the treatment, since only during treatment can we really assess the severity of the disorder. It is implicit that a therapist taking charge of the analysis does so because they have faith in the method. Parents generally want to be told how to help their child improve, and it is convenient to highlight the effort they will have to undertake by bringing their child four or five times a week, on time, and for at least a year. It should be pointed out to them that by doing this, they can best help the therapist.

The effort that parents make when carrying out such a long and expensive treatment must be appreciated, especially in a field where punctuality is so important and where scheduling often limits the mobility of the whole family. A therapist with this understanding position is more adapted to reality, is more efficient, and favors the success of the treatment.

In a sense, this technical change mirrors the same turn that psychoanalysis itself underwent. Concerned at first with external events, with real traumas, psychologists then focused their interest on the internal world, almost devaluing the external in the process. Eventually, they reached a final, balanced interplay between internal and external reality. Now, without disregarding the real exterior, we work with the internal—the version of reality the child provides—and we include the data of daily life that the parents give us in the analysis. We do the same with adults, when they tell us something about another person, and we associate it to the patient's relationship with us. In the analysis of adults, we do not try to change the objects that surround our patient, nor do we interview or advise the relatives, even when the patient has relationships as extremely dependent as that of a child with their parents. Instead, we lead them to independence internally and, if this is achieved, only *they* are able to detach themselves from the real external object; insofar as it is necessary.

Our findings also lead us to the conclusion that the validity of the data provided by the parents is very relative and we can learn more from the child themselves. A child, no matter how small, informs us by themselves of the evolution accomplished through treatment. When necessary, the child consciously or unconsciously provokes an interview with the parents, who complete the picture of the family group. Therefore, interviews are not necessary in discerning the effects of the treatment.

This new technique has the advantage of maintaining our role as therapists. We assume the role in a complete way, by not trusting anything but our work with the child to solve their problems or symptoms. We leave the parents in their role as parents, without disturbing the family structure with our tips.

To recap: I only give an interview to the parents during treatment when the patient agrees. What is spoken is recounted in all details to the child at the beginning of the next session. This way, we give the child the certainty that what happened in the doctor's office will remain as hermetically sealed as the contents of their individual drawer. Sometimes children *seem* to not understand what we are saying, or not care at all, but we soon see that every detail has entered their mind and is elaborated over the course of weeks or months. Although we must keep the child–parent unit in consideration, the interpretation should be directed exclusively to the patient.

Commentary on Chapter 8

Minnie Dastur (India)

In Chapter 8, Arminda Aberastury returns to the topic of working with parents to establish and sustain child analytic treatment. She gives guidelines that are not only important to beginner therapists but also serve as effective and necessary reminders for longtime practitioners. She also describes in detail the evolving development in child analysis, particularly the necessary work with the preverbal and unrepresented.

When beginning a treatment the framework needs to be set in place. After going through the child's history a meeting must be arranged with the parents. The role of the parents, their capacity to understand, and the pathology that they come with need to be given due consideration. The external environment of the child exerts a strong influence on the child. Arminda advises us: "Whether or not the parents attend the meeting and fulfill their obligation to complete the assessment process is a factor that should have been ascertained before ever seeing the child." The factors of the time space, the financial space, and the psychic space of the parents need consideration. The child then can be seen. Thereafter, there should be another meeting with the parents in which to give them some picture of what the analysis will involve and to address the pathology. Attention to this detail of the setting will protect the analysis and give the parents the confidence to support the treatment.

Arminda's suggestion of mothers' counseling groups, when analysis is not possible or there is parental resistance to it, is extremely helpful. She suggests that in such circumstances, if the future risk to the child is not too great, it might be more helpful to both child and parent not to start an analysis, particularly if the child's symptom "is manufactured by the mother, or at the very least, maintained or aggravated by her." In the clinical example of Miguel, she suggests that in such cases in analysis sometimes something more than interpretation may be needed, an issue of technique to which Stern and colleagues drew attention (Stern et al., 1998).

Arminda stresses the need of more understanding of the technical difficulty of managing the parents of the child who is in analysis and rues the fact that papers have not been published sufficiently on this crucial issue. The difficulty of working with parents has been referred to (and dismissed) as "an unavoidable stumbling block" but Arminda does not avoid the topic: She describes the risks and benefits. Giving advice or guidelines of behavior often results in the parents feeling persecuted, guilty. This can lead to aggression against the child and the analysis, and the analyst is then introjected as a harsh superego. Arminda agrees that the work should remain in a two-person relationship, as in adult analysis. Yet in her mind space, there is the parents' presence and their relationship with the analyst and the child in the here-and-now of the session—a three-dimensional space.

Arminda's open and free sharing of how her work experience has shaped the manner in which she conducts child analysis/psychotherapy makes this book a much-needed reference point in psychoanalytic work with children. She follows her own experience, taking what she needs from Klein, Winnicott, Bion, and others, but using what she finds most useful, interspersed with, amended by, and extrapolated from her own clinical experience, to form the way she works. Today's practitioners of child psychoanalytic psychotherapy will intuitively find here what they may not have quite formulated themselves, an intuition of the "unthought known" (Bollas, 1987).

Arminda's way of working is paying attention to the realistic aspect of the child's world as well as to the phantastic. A therapeutic alliance securely established with the child also enables the parents to stay within this alliance. The family is a unit and psychic change in the way of relating in one of the members effects a psychic change in the others as well. As the saying goes, "the strength of the clan is the wolf and the strength of the wolf is the clan."

Arminda brings forth for all child therapy practitioners the importance of being forewarned and prepared to work on issues of bias that are bound to arise and have an impact on the therapist's position in the treatment. These may arise out of religious beliefs, cultural experience, and attitudes towards sexuality. Particularly in countries with diverse religious and cultural practices, conflicts with the traditional beliefs and contemporary culture are highlighted by increased exposure to television movies and social media. Parents and children now live in a world truly *sans frontières*.

Arminda acknowledges that, "for many years it was argued that, unlike the adult, the child lacked an awareness of the disease and the neurotic disorder that prompted treatment." Her beautiful illustration of her work with the adopted child Gloria, age nine, shows that this is not the case.

Gloria openly displayed the unconscious fantasy of illness and healing, bringing in her need to know the truth of her adoption, which the parents were unwilling to reveal, and so they terminated the therapy. For Gloria, this is *unthought known*. The sad part is that the child is left with a part of her life unlived and probably will be left always in search of it, yet living with the projections that she must not know. Arminda leaves us thinking that, had it been clarified right from the start that these questions were bound to come up in the therapy, the parents might have been able to work through their own unwillingness. Gloria's learning difficulty is related to what she is not allowed to learn!

On the other hand, when having an interview with the parents at the behest of Fanny, age ten, Arminda was able to help them understand that Fanny's pathology is due to her shock and anxiety about adolescent changes. The child's confidence in the therapy was ensured by Arminda's later sharing all the details of the parent interview with Fanny. She reached a "balanced interplay between internal and external reality." It is a line that the therapist has to straddle with care, protecting her patient and the therapy. Arminda also stresses that as in adult analysis, we learn most from the child patient and should not rely too heavily on data from the parents.

Each therapist can reach into the experience Arminda shares with us and make some part of it work in their own way, from case to case. We need to have faith in ourselves and in our work itself.

Part III

Clinical narratives of child analysis

CHAPTER 9

Developmental delay: Clinical narratives of two analyses

I will show how the analyses of a six-year-old girl and a four-year-old girl with similar developmental disorders developed and how the data that the parents gave us was used in the interpretation to the children. I will attempt to illustrate some of the technical statements made in Chapters 6 and 7 and summarized below:

1. During the initial interview, the anguished parents often forget fundamental details of the child's life that are intimately connected to the appearance of the neurosis.
2. During the analysis of the child, traumatic situations arise, and if the anxiety and guilt of the parents have been reduced by the child's improvement, they will usually confirm these facts. Sometimes, they even expand on them with new data, which allows us to more accurately reconstruct the circumstances within which the symptom or problem originally arose.
3. If, during treatment, the analyst has interviews with the parents, has warned the child about meeting the parents beforehand, and

has delineated the proper conditions with the parents and the child before they take place, the following must also be ensured.

a) The analyst must not inform the parents of anything that happens during the sessions.
b) Everything that the parents say must be transmitted to the child during the next session, and used for interpretation.

In the two cases that I will detail, both girls suffered from a marked delay in language, a symptom that was a consequence of a profound disconnect with the outside world. The first involved Patricia, age six, elder sister to a four year old and a two year old. The second concerned Verónica, age four and three quarters, youngest of four siblings. In both cases, the siblings were healthy and had no developmental disorders.

Patricia, age six

The stated reason for the consultation was Patricia's marked delay in language. Since the time Patricia was three years old, the parents had sought consultation for this symptom, but the pediatrician who attended her had not given any importance to her disorder, constantly hoping that it would resolve spontaneously with age. It was the inevitability of her enrollment in elementary school that spurred the pediatrician to resort to psychoanalytic treatment. Later I discovered another symptom: anorexia.

The parent interview

Patricia's mother came alone for the initial interview. Her father was a businessman, and though he always ensured his daughters were financially satisfied, he played a nonexistent role in their emotional care. In regards to treatment, he acted the same way. He managed everything related to payment, fees, and attendance, but never accompanied Patricia and showed no interest in her progress until late in the analytic process. Their maternal grandmother lived with them. She was an elderly woman with stunted mental faculties, who became an extremely negative figure in Patricia's emotional development.

Patricia was six years old and could only verbalize the words *mama, papa,* and *ata* (the name for her grandmother). She used the three words appropriately but also used *ata* as a contraction of *aqui* (here) and *esta* (is), which she used to express the appearance and reappearance of objects or people. In addition, she emitted a series of inarticulate sounds through which she expressed the desire to mention objects or situations that were completely incomprehensible to her. She also suffered from serious anorexia and her level of play was well below her age. Her mother noted that Patricia suffered from being unable to express herself and was jealous of her sisters, who spoke and played normally.

Patricia was a desired daughter, and the pregnancy and delivery seemed to have occurred normally. Her mother did not remember how many hours had elapsed between the time Patricia was born and the time she was put to the breast for the first time. Similarly, she had no recollection of her daughter's feeding rhythms, but she made sure to point out that the child securely latched on to the breast from the first moment. Breastfeeding continued smoothly until seven months, at which time, Patricia's mother abruptly weaned her because she had become pregnant again. Apparently, Patricia did not initially react negatively to this sudden loss. She accepted the bottle and all seemed well. However, as time passed, she began to have difficulties with meals. These issues persisted and intensified, eventually resulting in serious anorexia.

The mother also had a hard time recalling the dates Patricia stopped language development and began toilet training. She was under the impression that these milestones were achieved at later stages and she added that she had not been especially picky about cleanliness. All the data we received regarding the moment in which the control began, its characteristics, and how it affected Patricia, stemmed from the girl's analysis, and were later confirmed by the mother, who added important data she remembered by then.

At around one year of age, Patricia began to walk. Around that same time, she uttered her first words. When she was born, her sister was seventeen months old, and was already fully developing her language skills. Her mother had no recollection of Patricia showing curiosity during pregnancies and childbirth, nor had she witnessed any masturbation. Her level of play was low for her age, her language difficulties were apparent, and both of these hampered her relationship with her sisters and other siblings. Her suffering, jealousy, and envy were as evident as the stark difference between her and her healthier, prettier sisters. After the initial interview with the mother, it was decided to have Patricia attend sessions four times a week.

Setting and communication

I will focus, in particular, on the way in which Patricia expressed her unconscious fantasy of illness and healing, as well as on the methods through which she communicated to me her suffering—mainly from toilet training and its contextualized circumstances.

For the first session, an assortment of miniature cars was placed on a low table, some with pull strings and some without. Next to them sat a small toy garage, buckets, paper, lead pencils, colored pencils, erasers, scissors, glue, a whistle, dolls, plates, cups, and cutlery. In the center was an automatic pencil sharpener with a transparent, plastic waste tray.

The first interviews with Patricia

Patricia was a thin girl with a sad countenance, and was obviously inhibited. From the moment she entered the office, she showed great distrust, but agreed to separate from the mother on the condition that we leave the door open so she would remain visible. After a few minutes, during which Patricia observed everything around her, she grabbed the cars and lined them up one after the other. She "drove them" in and out of the small garage repeatedly. Then, she took a pencil and placed it in the sharpener. She inspected the hole very carefully every time she went to sharpen a pencil. After inserting the pencil, turning the handle, and curiously inspecting the lead, she watched the sawdust fall into the transparent container, Patricia took a piece of clay and covered the hole. She then tried to place the pencils in the plasticine-covered opening and pointed out that the congestion meant nothing could enter anymore. She repeated the game several times. At that moment, I provided her with my first interpretation:

"You close the openings in mom to prevent things from going in and out of her, and that's why you also need to keep an eye on her."

She shook her head, but as she denied the interpretation, she upended the container and emptied its contents, namely sawdust and pulverized lead, onto a small piece of paper. She wrapped the paper around them, forming it into a tight bundle and reinforcing it with several papers. She went on to place it in her individual drawer, which she closed securely.

Patricia then began to examine the room and pick up toys. First, she looked at the objects attentively. Then, she showed them to me and, by means of her three-word vocabulary and a litany of hand signals, asked me to name each of them. I observed that she chose well-known objects, like beds, chairs, and the like. She also gravitated toward the cars she had used at the beginning of the session. Her inquiring gestures were like the verbal questions most children ask: They already know the answer, but they hide the desire to know something that seems censored or distressing to them. I interpreted that Patricia wanted to know why she could not speak and the other children could. This was mirrored in the act of presenting me with the cars that did and did not have strings attached, and with the inherent question as to why her mother had made her like that.

Without responding to my interpretation, she asked to go to the bathroom, making hand signals indicating that she needed to urinate. When her mother saw her exit, she accompanied her to the restroom. On their way back, I could hear the mother chastise Patricia for soiling her hands with pencils and plasticine. When she again entered the room, the child was very anxious and made hand signals indicating that she wanted to leave immediately. I interpreted the following to her:

"You want to leave because you are afraid that I will transform into a bad person who puts hurtful things inside you, like the dirt on your hands and your mother's reproach. You imagine them to be things that your mother has put in you, which have made you unable to speak."

In an attempt to communicate, she put the dirty bits of her hands in her mouth and sucked on them, looking at me questioningly. Then, she sucked the clean part of her hands, smiling, but, at the same time, sporting an anguished expression. I said:

"While we're here, you and I are going to find out, little by little, why you cannot speak, why you smile even when you are sad and scared, and why you are afraid of me and your mother." Near the end of the hour, right before she left, she ran to the couch and kissed it. Then, she quickly exited without making eye contact with me.

Discussion

In this first hour, she expressed her sufferings and her symptoms through her play actions, which symbolized the mother's body and her own. Closing the hole meant, in addition to the interpretation previously given, that she had closed her own hole—her mouth—because of the sufferings experienced by her mother's pregnancy, and that she must close another hole—the anus—in order to submit to her mother's control. Second, she showed that her difficulties with urinary containment were linked to the idea that she felt destroyed or incomplete. This was expressed in her intense and sudden need to urinate after my interpretation of the cars with and without strings. Third, she expressed her belief that these difficulties were due to her mother placing bad things inside her—the product of intercourse represented by the crushed pencil lead and sawdust, or that these elements had become negative because of her own destructive fantasies—clearly expressed when she sucked the part of her hands covered in dirty pencil lead. Then, she showed me that she needed to place good things inside herself—the clean part of her hands—in order to heal her difficulties. Finally, she expressed her capacity to love and her desire to incorporate something from the therapist-mother, as evidenced by her kissing of the couch in an attempt to take part of the office home with her, and thus something of me. This was made possible by the projection of her love onto me. She felt I could help her clean away her impurities and thus kissed the couch.

This is easy to understand if we remember that her breastfeeding was initially good. As in the first object relationship, the child projects love and hate onto the mother, and receives, in return, satisfactions and frustrations. Her mistrust in her mother's ability to help her, as well as her acceptance and her rejection of me, became evident during our interactions.

Later sessions

In later sessions, Patricia placed materials she had initially associated with internal anatomy in hermetically sealed packages. She locked them in her individual drawer and, during each session, she would conduct thorough inspections on the contents, anxious and paranoid that they could have been destroyed, stolen, or damaged during her absence. This behavior was interpreted every time it appeared. For her, the materials represented the product of the sexual relations of her parents, namely what the mother had inside her. Essentially, they represented penises and the substances within them that are involved in making children; the same materials the parents had placed inside her and her sisters. They served to symbolize her conception, as well as why she felt incomplete, inadequate, and intensely jealous of her sisters, who were favored by her mother. In the transfer, by enclosing these contents in little packages and inspecting them each time, she expressed her jealousy of other patients and her fear that I would not defend her from the assaults and thefts they might inflict upon her. When something went missing from the packages, and she lost the omnipotence offered by the hermetic closure of the contents, she reconceptualized the materials as persecutors. She would shake them off, or ask me to "get them off her." She represented, through these substances, her fantasy of her inner world, including how it was constructed, the imperfections it held, and how she wanted to "string" them together, fully integrating all the elements.

As her analysis progressed, those substances were enriched, because she added others that she considered positive: milk and coffee. With them, she represented the fantasy of being born again, under different conditions, not unlike the result of the two substances being mixed to create a drinkable solution. She played with a large pot, sneakily removing all the materials in her individual drawer that she considered positive and placing them inside the container. She left what she considered negative inside the drawer. To the substances in the pot, she added more and more of what she considered "good"; including, for example, sugar, which meant love and beauty to her, or coffee, which meant positivity and success.

When, in the course of many sessions, the group of positive materials reached a "point" of goodness that she considered sufficient, she dumped them back into her individual drawer, overwhelming any bad elements in a wave of positivity and symbolizing that the time to be reborn was at hand. This single pot game was later expanded with a newer version, one in which she filled three smaller equal pots and fluctuated over which materials corresponded to each of them. In this way, her actions symbolized the mother's three pregnancies and her wish that all three children had been born equal.

In a later phase of the analysis, she abandoned the game with substances and symbolized the same situations with toys, and those toys were representing groups, instead of individual content. The toys selected consisted primarily of collections of cups, jugs, pots, and other assorted objects, which were selected and grouped according to their durability and how well they could be fixed. Through these games, she manifested her reparation fantasies and her ability to enact repairs on herself.

In the last phase, Patricia used groups *and* individual content. For example, she played with large bags full of toys, which varied according to her acting fantasies at the time, and which represented feelings that could have been verbalized as, "I need to have a penis inside me to be able to speak," "I don't know if a woman is entitled to a penis," and "I want you to give me a penis that fixes my insides and heals me."

These contents had an evident secrecy to them, similar to that of the hermetically sealed packages at the beginning. The importance of the secretive aura became so entrenched that it led us to some extreme situations. For example, during this period of her analysis, when playing with toys and substances, Patricia tried to force me to stay in the next room so that I could not watch her. The isolation to which she sentenced me during that section of the analysis turned out to be simply the transferential repetition of what the child had felt in regards to her mother, when her mother had gone to the sanatorium to have the second sister and external events had increased her anxiety and destructive tendencies.

The game she played made me understand that toilet training began in the absence of her mother. When she revived it in-session, she expressed it through a game wherein she fed and cared for a doll, showing me clearly all the anguish she had experienced. For this game, she chose a doll who, in addition to having her mouth open, had another opening through which she urinated. Patricia's loving and caring attitude changed abruptly after a few sessions. At first, she would dress and feed her with affection. Before she left, she would make sure the "baby" stayed in the crib, safe and warm. Without warning, she began to cover it in dirt, grime, and paint. She took to undressing it, subjected it to starvation and cold, and turned it into a dirty, naked, battered plaything, leaving it on the tiled bathroom floor. I could do nothing to prevent the mistreatment, as I had to stay in the next room while she was performing the cruel acts.

Patricia made me play the role of the absent mother, who did not come to her aid when she was abused for being a dirty child. This isolation she condemned me to, and her displeasure at the thought of seeing me, corresponded to the need to blind herself to the traumatic event; in addition to representing the anger toward the mother who had abandoned her. In this game, Patricia's doll was *her*: bad, dirty, abandoned, full of filth. This was how she felt when the analysis began; when she'd gone to the bathroom to urinate and sucked the dirty parts of her hands. At the same time, she was playing the role of the nanny, continually fluctuating between the evil she suffered and the evil she caused. During this period, she showed curiosity and jealousy toward the other children under my care, even wanting to force their drawers open to see what they contained. I observed that Patricia expressed her loneliness and her mistreatment through her own physical dirtiness and, within the transference, through her curiosity and jealousy toward the other drawers; in this case, clearly symbols for her sisters. Owing to this, I theorized that toilet training must have been severe and must have started when her sister was born.

Another parental interview

Consequently, I asked Patricia's mother for an interview and asked if the toilet training could have coincided with the birth of her sister. She remembered then that, when she'd gone to the sanatorium for her second birth, the nanny had severely restrained Patricia, forcing her to learn. When the mother returned from the sanatorium after eight days, Patricia could control her urine and fecal matter.

In this same interview, she sadly recalled an episode that she connected with the arrest of language development. In the days following her return from the sanatorium, Patricia made great efforts to pronounce her sister's name. One day, when she was sleeping in her crib having suckled, Patricia, clinging to her mother's skirts, had uttered her sister's name for the first time. With a shrill voice, and removing the M, she yelled: "Onica!". The mother broke down in tears as she recalled that her reaction was to hit Patricia on the palms and scold her for nearly waking her sister, instead of appreciating the milestone she had so laboriously achieved. She also recalled that, since the delivery took place at night, Patricia did not know of her departure. When she woke, she did not find the mother and the situation was never explained to her.

This interview with her mother was transmitted to Patricia in the following session, and the traumatic events recalled by her mother were added to the interpretation of the aforementioned games. Once again, we were able to see the interaction between external reality—poor treatment at the hands of the nanny and the mother, and internal reality—the devaluation that Patricia showed in regards to her contents and materials.

Discussion

We saw from the first session that Patricia thought she was different from her sisters, and had been born incomplete. She symbolized this idea through games where she was represented by a car without a string, and during which she was forced to compete with cars that *did* have a string; in this example, a clear representation of her sisters, who were verbal and well-spoken. She thought that her mother had placed bad and insufficient things within her, expressing it during two other instances of play. During one, she filled three pots, which represented her and her sisters, with materials. But, while one pot only contained scraps, discarded objects, and decomposing trash, the other two had succulently designed toy meals inside them. This game was accompanied by anxiety attacks. She vacillated between entertaining fantasies of stealing the contents from the other pots, and spiraling into paranoid ideas about whether or not her own material had been stolen when she was away.

During the second game, she poured the contents of all the pots into a huge saucepan. She carefully strained and separated the things that she considered harmful, until she was left with a perfect set of contents. Only then did she begin to play at rebirth, which consisted of emptying the drawer and putting the contents inside.

Another of her fantasies was that of emptying her mother, then filling herself—a large bag—with the things that her father gave her—airplanes and cars. However, the anxiety of mixing the good with the bad, as well as the fear of taking something from her mother, conspired to destroy her in a way she was not able to repair. From the moment she regained her faith in her own ability to restore the games through groups, unbreakable or fixable, the bags full of objects began to emerge within her, and she began to speak. If she could restore, she could do things, fill herself up, and allow herself to be aggressive, since she could remake what she'd destroyed.

She imagined that, if she were filled with her father's contents, she would gain the ability to speak and become intelligent. At first, she expressed these fantasies through her games, using substances. Later, she manifested them by making bags that she filled with cars and airplanes, and which she kept hermetically sealed in her drawer. They represented, for her, the female genitals filled by penises. She and her mother would be full of her father's penises, but the bag had to be hermetically sealed, otherwise someone might steal them.

External stressors

I will now relate how Patricia experienced the successive frustrations that followed the mother's pregnancy and the abrupt weaning. From Patricia's perspective: 1) her mother had deprived her of the breast in order to manufacture her second daughter; 2) in order for the second daughter to be born, the mother had abandoned her to go to the sanatorium; 3) during that absence, she was forced to give up her fecal matter and was treated harshly; 4) when her mother returned from the sanatorium, she tried to overcome her destructive tendencies and recreate her sister by pronouncing her name, but her mother hit her and prevented her from speaking, which meant a confirmation that her mother had been turned into a negative force by all her aggressive fantasies; and 5) if she could not restore, she could not destroy, which forced her into an excessive and premature defense against sadism that simultaneously consisted of an interruption of her contact with reality and an inhibition of the development of her fantasy life.

Patricia submitted and gave up her feces, but kept for herself the words that carried the same magical meaning of destroying and restoring: feces, urine, and children. At the same time, she punished her mother and expressed the aggression against her environment with a symptom that distressed and worried her parents and herself. Progress in language development was initially evident only during the sessions; while in the house, she maintained her verbal isolation. She was hiding her words because she wanted to conceal all the negative thoughts and aggressions that, in fantasy, she had wanted to dispense upon her mother and sisters. With the words, she kept those secrets, those hermetically sealed packages. This is why it was easier for her to talk to me than it was for her to speak inside her own house, where the real situations of anxiety caused by her envy and jealousy continued.

Her first game, in which she stuffed the hole in the pencil sharpener, also symbolized the closing of her mouth, the sealing off of her anus, and the desire to close the mother shut. I was able to understand later that it was also a closing her own genitals, so the father's penis could not enter.

She did not speak because, if she did, she would get to know her own internal world. This is also why, when she began to speak, she was incorrectly pronouncing the words. To speak was to reveal not only the negative elements, but also her fantasies of incorporating the father as an object of love. She used to pronounce the words backwards, which was a way of both masking her thought process and representing the introjection of the word that she then projected onto the outside world.

The prohibition of speech meant the prohibition to expel her sister, and also the inability to hide from her. When she said "Onica," removing the "M" that the name has in common with the word "Mother," Patricia was denying that her sister was the product of her mother's union. She had to keep within her body the words that, for her unconscious, were equated with defecating, urinating, and giving birth to children. The equality of bodily substances, which has been pointed out so many times by Melanie Klein, was very evident during the analysis of this girl. The substances that she handled represented fecal matter, urine, menstrual blood, mother's milk, or father's milk. They belonged to the mother as well as to herself. In her games, when she exchanged the substances from one package or pan to another, she was representing combining her interior with that of the mother, or eating the mother's products—the products of adults—in order to identify with them. This is why she added substances like coffee, which was forbidden in her house.

These games were often interrupted when anxiety reared its head, due to both the risk of irreparably destroying the food and the danger that retaliation might be forthcoming. At this juncture, it is important to note that, though I have placed emphasis on the behavior of the mother and the nanny during toilet training—as well as during the days before and after the mother's delivery—I am, under no circumstances, claiming that this behavior alone is capable of producing the language arrest and additional symptoms. If I have highlighted their behavior, it is only because, in the course of the transference relationship, it showcased its own importance. I think that, at that point in her development, Patricia's fragile internal situation made these events traumatic enough to cause such serious symptoms. Patricia was seven months old when her mother abruptly weaned her, and that weaning was prompted by her new pregnancy. What we know today about the development of the child, those facts that clinical experience confirms on a daily basis, allows us to understand that the oral and urethral sadism that prevails at that time was increased in this case by the abrupt weaning and pregnancy of the mother.

The oral phase, aggressive and sexual forces

When a child is born, the oral phase is structured, which is essential for the survival of the human being. This is not only determined by the food supply, but also because the process provides the stimuli that will allow them to reestablish a bond with the mother, thus overcoming the birth trauma.

Teeth represent instruments that make possible the fulfillment of the destruction fantasies that dominate in this sadistic, cannibalistic oral phase, and their appearance determines the abandonment of the oral bond and the need to remake it through another area of the body. In this period of life, the discovery of the vagina in the female, and of the need for penetration in the male, initiates the genital stage in which the penis–vagina union will replace that of the mouth with the breast.

Aggressive sexual strivings at this stage can be satisfied only with fantasies and masturbatory acts, including all the infant's play activity. The impossibility of the total fulfillment of the needs in this period of life forces a regression to the moment of birth, in which oral, anal, and genital tendencies were available to unite with the mother. From there, a new phase is structured: the primary anal expulsion phase, which generally coincides with standing up and becoming interested in fecal matter.

In Patricia's case, the bad relationship with the breast shifted to the penis and to the total figure of her mother, as the possessor of her father's penises, making her more feared and hated. In normal development, the displacement of the mouth to the vagina causes it to be burdened with the anguish associated with the previous bond with the breast. The fact that her father was psychologically absent increased Patricia's difficulties and inhibitions to receive from the penis what she had lost from the breast. This interaction of internal and external factors was also evident in forced toilet training, which coincided with the mother's absence when giving birth to her sister, and in the harsh way the training was carried out, which made Patricia feel that she had been prevented from female identification through the theft of her own offspring: feces and urine. In Patricia's mind, the mother's pregnancy had increased all the fantasies of assault, evacuation, and destruction of her contents, and had triggered a fear of revenge for the object being attacked this way.

The demand for control of elimination and cleanliness—especially at that moment in which these fantasies were occurring—was experienced by Patricia as a ratification by reality that the fulfillment of her fears was possible. This reinforced her need to enclose and keep something for herself—her words—as was evident during both her first analytic session, and the subsequent sessions wherein she enclosed her contents in hermetic packages, or covered the pencil sharpener hole with plasticine.

Regarding the mother's reaction to Patricia pronouncing her sister's name, it's possible that the situation would have been less traumatic if this experience had not been coupled with previous ones, and filtered through Patricia's experiential consensus of meaning. Instead, it became another fulfillment of deeply unconscious fantasies by reality. The increase in depressive anxiety due to the reinforcement of her attack fantasies (the teething) combined with the evidence provided by reality of the feared disappearance of the mother (her depressive anxiety) plus the feared evacuation of her body, ratified by abrupt and severe control (her paranoid anxiety) all conspired to create an intolerable situation for Patricia. The external events, in turn, became more traumatic because they added up and accumulated and, more than that, because they acted as confirmation of her most active fears at that particular moment of her development.

In Patricia's case, abrupt switching and criss-crossing of developmental stages rather than smooth transitions seemed to be hallmarks of fundamental traumas. Weaning took place abruptly as a consequence of her mother's new pregnancy. Additionally, the toilet training was carried out by the nanny very suddenly, coincided with the absence of the mother, and was a consequence of the sister's birth. The absence of the father made the normal elaboration of the loss of the breast even more difficult, replacing it with the penis. Two experiences of loss, of the breast and the inside of her own body, were linked in Patricia's mind to the birth of the sister. This occurred in a much more intense way than is normally expected.

Anorexia and language inhibition

The two symptoms, anorexia and language inhibition, were the expression of her difficulties with the outside world. They showed her fear and rejection of social connection. At a deeper level they referred to the genital connection that would have allowed her to overcome the loss of the oral bond. When her sister was born, Patricia felt she lost her mother. The nanny violently removed the products from inside her body and, when Patricia tried to repair the fault of her sister's birth by remaking her through the spoken word, her mother punished her and forbade her to speak. In her fantasy world, her mother was forbidding her to repair her sister, condemning her to live in a destroyed world and keep her words inside her.

The anorexia that she suffered from is explained by the increase in paranoid anxieties. It also manifests itself through the fear of incorporating good things and transforming them into bad and destructive things—fecal matter and urine—due to a displacement of the vagina to the mouth. Within this situation of anguish and disappointment, which occurred in front of her mother, the figure of the father would have the ability to help her overcome depression. In this case, however, the figure consisted of a psychologically absent father who did not help her work out the loss of her mother. In addition, there was no other male figure in her immediate environment that could replace him. This led to Patricia identifying with the person most closely linked to her mother—her grandmother. This reinforced the identification of her intellectual limitations and her feelings of disability. The inhibition in the development of language was caused by a displacement from the corporal to the mental. Preserving the mental contents was Patricia's way of compensating for having been forced to give up the material contents; namely the fecal matter, urine, and potential children.

The role of transference, incorporation, and language acquisition

When she went through the transference situation, she was able to incorporate something positive—the breast—and then she could also incorporate the penis, which enabled her to pronounce words and continue the development of language. In seeming confirmation of this, we noted that the first words she added to her vocabulary during the treatment were "no" and "yes," and arose from the interpretation of her transference bond. In his article on negation, Freud (1925h) interprets the "yes" as accepting, swallowing, assimilating, incorporating, and sees the "no" as expulsive, spitting, rejecting life, and expressing the instincts of life and death. When Patricia said her first "Yes," she made the decision to live in the world. Her "No" signified a rejection of the words that came out of me, as well as a rejection of the mother's content, repeating her original situation. She expressed her general rejection situation in front of the world, and her submission to the traumatic situations mentioned. Saying "Yes" meant changing her position before the external world. It was the act of receiving my words, and incorporating the breast and the penis—a primal scene—which allowed her to structure a new internal world. It is rather obvious that this incorporation, which was expressed in the verbalized "Yes," heralded the healing process.

Patricia announced her intentions *before* pronouncing her first words, through the act of leaving her individual drawer ajar and opening the little packages that she had hermetically sealed during the first hour. An obvious example of the importance of the individual drawer! The drawer represented the mouth that she speaks with, the vagina that receives the penis, and the mother that conceives a child.

Of course, the attitude of opening up to me, of giving and receiving, was not always consistent. We suffered setbacks during analysis and many times returned to the attitude of total isolation and confinement. The refuge she found in her internal world, as well as her difficulty with the formation of symbols, were evidenced by the games she played, which consisted of toying with substances that were not age-appropriate. The whole external world was, for Patricia, the image and likeness of her internal world, made up entirely of urine and fecal matter.

We have already stated that Patricia thought she was different and incomplete, and that she symbolized as much through her various games. She imagined that her imperfection and emptying were due to the bad things that her mother had put in her, as well as the lack of incorporation of the father's penis. Eventually, her healing fantasy emerged: a desire to fill herself with the substances of her mother and mine. However, only the decrease of anxiety and guilt, and the fusion of the extremely good and persecuting imagos, allowed her to realize this fantasy. This resulted in effective bond transference and a better relationship with the world.

Summary of the course of analysis

During her first analytical sessions, Patricia rarely played with toys. She preferred to handle substances like pencil lead, sawdust, flour, and water. Through these choices, she symbolized her mother's contents, her own, the mixture of both, her hunger for her mother's contents, and her identification with her mother. In another game, she separated the substances she imagined adults often handled from those that she attributed to children. She expressed her guilt and fear of persecution when she stole from and angered adults.

During the second phase of her analysis, she played with my wallet, seizing all the contents and selling them to me later, at exorbitant prices. Having paid for them, she would refuse to give them back, essentially "tricking me" in the process. After these games, she would suffer a crisis of anxiety and rage, and would run out of the analysis room as if she were afraid of me. She then made bags that she filled with toy cars and airplanes, keeping them tightly closed and in reserve. She piled them up inside her drawer, always expressing fear that someone would steal or damage them.

The progress in Patricia's symbolization increased her possibility of connecting with the external world, which changed for her as her internal world was analyzed and modified. She was able to relate better with her sisters and with some of her friends.

I should point out that, in this case, the circumstances in family life were made very difficult by real external situations, and Patricia did not suggest any changes to improve them. The progress of her adaptation to reality was the result of the analysis of her internal world, and she learned to manage *herself* better within family life and her school environment. However, she could still not be considered a totally "normal" child.

Verónica, age four and a half

Verónica was the youngest daughter of seemingly healthy, well-matched parents. Their children seemed to be normal. But their pediatrician, Prof. F. Bamatter was alarmed by Verónica's language delay, which triggered the suggestion of psychoanalytic treatment. Her analysis took place in three stages.

The first parent session

During the initial interview, the father and mother both looked very concerned about the disorders of their daughter. They readily answered my questions and informed me in detail about the reason for the consultation. They remembered very little of the girl's story. Any details regarding her daily life, how she spent weekends, or even what she did for birthdays, were very brief. At times, they seemed to grasp the seriousness of their daughter's disorder. This was especially obvious when they mentioned some of the symptoms that led them to infantilize and be overprotective of Verónica. At other times, they would deny the severity of the situation and refer to the symptoms as choices, behavior disorders, or whims.

When they consulted me about Verónica, her male siblings were thirteen and twelve years old, and her sister was ten. All three of them were apparently healthy and, according to the parents, had presented neither developmental disorders, nor interruptions in schooling. They wanted me to analyze Verónica because they found her impossible to educate. When they explained the reasons why she was being brought to treatment, they said that she had a language delay, and that any words she had acquired by the age of two, she had lost gradually. They understood her, but no one in the environment could recognize the sounds she made as words. In addition, even when the sounds were understood, they did not coincide with the objects or situations with which they should be related. They stated that Verónica was very nervous, that she suffered from fits of rage and crying, and that this occurred specifically when people failed to understand her, a very common situation. When strangers appeared, all these symptoms worsened and she became especially upset and out of control. They highlighted her most intense phobias concerning flowers and dogs, which made it impossible for her to adapt to the rural environment in which she lived. They added that she always seemed scared, would never look straight ahead, and would stare at people's hands incessantly. The darkness terrified her and, when night approached, she would have a crisis of terror. Strangely, and despite the terrifying episodes, she would go calmly to bed afterward, without even requesting that someone accompany her. They had, at times, the feeling that Verónica did not recognize them and could not differentiate them from strangers.

Verónica was a desired child and the pregnancy went smoothly. The delivery only lasted one hour, and, according to the mother, was totally normal. After three hours, they attached Verónica to the breast and she latched on effectively. Breastfeeding lasted three months, at which point the parents started combining mixed feeding with gradual weaning. They did not remember when she had stopped suckling. She ate well, although they did not remember the details of her feeding schedules or her rhythms. They noted a consistent lack of physical activity and motor skills and remembered Verónica as a quiet baby who never protested or asked for anything. She had difficulty while learning to walk and expressed a fear of falling. Her first steps had been shaky, and the parents did not remember when she'd taken them, but they guessed that it was around the end of the first year. The learning was slow, and it took until two years of age for her to successfully walk. After that, she had no incidences of consistent falling.

She spoke her first words at the age of two according to the parents' report (and at the age of three according to the pediatrician's report) but progressively lost them. She remembered fragments of songs in French, which she hummed with remarkable intonation and accuracy, but whose lyrics she could not articulate well.

It was after the loss of verbal communication that they started to find her lost in thought, talking to herself. It was also then that she began an evening tradition at sunset of waiting for the arrival of the moon. The few words she spoke at that time did not seem connected to her feelings or expectations.

Her parents compared her to a "double," imitating people without ever being herself. She had never uttered a suitable word or phrase. Her parents and her brothers spoke French and Spanish, and her service personnel were well-versed in Spanish, as well. The parents did not remember anything concerning teething, but they figured it had developed smoothly. Regarding toilet training, they said it was achieved easily and without corporal punishment. They remembered it occurred particularly early, though they did not recall the exact date they had started teaching it. The pediatrician's report mentioned some isolated losses of urinary control. The parents vaguely recollected a time when Verónica's sleep was disturbed, but claimed she currently slept well; though never for more than five or six hours.

She had never shown any type of sexual curiosity, they had not seen her masturbate, and, to their knowledge, she had not participated in any such games with her brothers.

In the latter part of the interview, we learned much more about Verónica's disorder and many of the added details were of great interest to us. At one point in her development, which the parents did not remember with much exactitude, she used to wake up at night terrified, but this had not happened lately. Her day-to-day life seemed very standard. She woke up early and had breakfast alone. She would eat the food out of a cup to avoid spillage, as she had since she was young. The parents could not remember when she had removed bottle and pacifier from this eating routine. After breakfast, she played alone, not being able to leave the garden due to the phobias.

When I asked them what Verónica was playing, they related the following two games: the first consisted of taking a doll in her arms, then leaving it, only to pick it up again; the second consisted of repeatedly bringing individual objects to her mouth, prioritizing those made of metal. As we can see, the two games had the same characteristics, and could very well have been games played by a one-year-old baby. Verónica would occasionally try to play with cubes and more advanced puzzles, but would quickly become impatient and give up the game, destroying what little she had done. She tended to reject, ignore, or break toys.

Following her morning routine, she had lunch at midday with the whole family, and seemed to adapt well to their rhythm. She seldom took naps. Though she drank tea with her brothers and spent time with them afterward, she wouldn't really play or hang out. When night came, the darkness would terrify her. In spite of this, she meekly went to bed alone and without protesting. In the morning, she did not ask to be woken, even if this meant waking herself up very early. She waited patiently for someone to dress her and get her ready. As she had no motor skills, Verónica's mother dressed and undressed her. She also washed and bathed her as if she were a baby. The idea that Verónica might bathe herself was never considered, as her mother did not believe she could do it alone and, thus, had never given her the option.

Her life on weekends changed very little. The parents would visit friends or plan events at their own house, but this started upsetting Verónica. Due to her anxiety, they avoided social outings more and more. Her birthdays were not particularly celebrated, since she did not show interest in anything, and few things could get her excited. New stimuli were the only exciting things for her. She had no positive affective response to any traditional stimulus and, at times, her mother had the impression that Verónica did not recognize her. She suffered from unexpected fits of rage that no one around her could alleviate.

At the end of the first interview with the parents, the treatment was decided. As they did not live in Buenos Aires, it was necessary to find an adequate location that would not disturb the family organization too much. Given the seriousness of the case and the type of disorder, it was completely counterproductive to separate Verónica from the family. But, on the other hand, the seriousness of the case dictated several years of treatment. If her mother stayed in Buenos Aires where her ill child could see me, Verónica would be separated from her siblings and her father who had to stay in the country, thus dismembering her family. So this was not possible, either. I proposed that we conduct treatment only during the months the family considered least damaging to the dynamic.

They chose periods in which the older children were studying in school, and left the vacation months free from treatment. All this was resolved with them before starting the sessions. The daily routine was not modified at all. I proposed sessions six times a week, anticipating that the treatment would last for years and that the results would not be predictable.

I warned them that, during treatment, they might feel hopeless or doubtful on multiple occasions and that, even then, I could not dispense any information regarding the case, or offer any advice, no matter how sorely needed. I suggested that, in those moments, they continue with their educational modality as they had so far, and that they adapt their behavior to Verónica's changes, to the extent that they believed it necessary. The entire first period of analysis passed without any parental interviews. The one exception was on the day of the farewell, in which the mother told me about some changes that she had noticed in her daughter, and during which we decided the date on which Verónica would restart the treatment. Shortly after, I received a long letter from the father, which I will transcribe later, during my description of how I used this information.

The first analysis

The first analysis period lasted four months and the six-times-a-week sessions were consistently fulfilled. They were interrupted for a month, and restarted some time later, again six times a week for five months. They stopped again, this time due to the summer holidays, then were taken up for the whole of the following year. There were no interruptions until November, at which point we ended the treatment.

The first break

After the first four months of analysis we decided that we should forgo analysis for a time, as a test. The decision was taken in consideration of the toll the treatment was taking on the parents, and because improvements had been achieved more quickly than expected. We resolved that we would restart treatment only if Verónica encountered additional difficulties, or the parents noticed any serious setbacks.

As the mother had external and internal difficulties preventing her from allotting the necessary time and contact crucial to raising her daughter, the parents hired a young governess to exclusively care for Verónica. She turned out to be a well-endowed person, who understood that she should support Verónica in her achievements, but knew to refrain from pushing or forcing her. The activities Verónica carried out included exercises and games tailored to strengthening motor skills, a modicum of school learning that consisted of letters and numbers, free drawings, small crafts, and housework, which included setting the table, making desserts, sewing, and embroidering. The most enjoyable activities for Verónica and the ones which best showcased her abilities, were those feminine activities in which she approached an appropriate age level. As a result of this period, she was able to enter a small school, as a listener, at the first grade level. Her rudimentary education resulted in some improvement in her affective contact with other children. She even played some games with them. With her brothers, the relationship remained excellent.

During that period, I saw her twice, and heard about her progress from her parents. The improvements were permanent and she continued to progress. Sadly, I am not able to offer a series of photographs her father provided me, where you can see the progressive improvement of her expression, and her transformation from the sordid, dramatic girl I met on that first day, to a happy, seemingly normal child. As the situation stands now, she is a girl who is fluent in Spanish and French, and suitably adapted to the demands of her environment, but who still plays too little and has trouble learning at school. However, the same difficulty that she showed for the use of words now appears in the handling of numbers and letters. She is capable of repeating and copying them, but does not grasp their meaning. I will go on to relate the experience of her treatment from the beginning.

Sessions with Verónica

Verónica was four years and eight months old. She was slim, tall for her age, and her gaze was blank. Although she had been described to me as a very strange child, and I had read her pediatrician's report at length, her appearance still shocked me, as did her screams of anger and fear. There was a dramatic and sullen look to her face; something between a blank stare and a frown, which shaped her mouth into a strange smile.

When her mother introduced her to me, she shook my hand, bowed robotically, and entered the playroom without showing anxiety, as if ignoring the separation from her mother, who remained in the waiting room.

On a low table, I placed cups, plates, cutlery, buckets, several dolls, some pieces of clothing, string, knitting wool, and glue. I doubt it is possible to reproduce the sheer monotony and difficulty of those first few months of treatment through the written word, but I will try.

During her first session, and without looking at anything around her, Verónica went to the tap and let the water run. She put her hands in contact with it. She freaked out when she touched the water, laughing and screaming in equal measure. Her shifts in expression were swift and unpredictable. She muttered commands *at* the water, as if the substance itself were an invisible character, all the while laughing and screaming. Here, the changes were also sudden and extreme. At the moment when she seemed most terrified, she spilled water from the sink, and remained paralyzed when it touched her feet or legs.

I interpreted the changes in her reactions to the water as extremely positive or negative characteristics of her contact with me, and as a repetition of what she felt with her mother. Verónica communicated that she was interacting with me in order to treat me well or poorly, depending on her whims. When her orders were not fulfilled, or she did not feel understood, she threw the water aside and became paralyzed in fear. She seemed to not understand my interpretation, but she opened the door and looked at her mother. While she was away from her mother, she had felt left alone, and felt bad and scared. Sitting there with her, trying to understand her, I was like the water at which she smiled. I interpreted that those orders she gave to the water were also addressed to her mother and to me; two people who were wanting to get rid of her by separating and distancing ourselves from her. If we did not respond to her wishes or we failed to understand her, she would get angry and throw us out of herself. But once we were out of her, she was afraid that we would chase her and hurt her. This is why she would remain still, in an attempt to paralyze us inside her.

Her limited relationship with the world was expressed in the consulting room, through her unique relationship with water. The ignorance and rejection of everything that surrounded her, and of the contents of the drawer she was staring at, clearly delineated for us her position before the outside world.

I interpreted the water as aspects of her mother and me, which she imbued with positivity or negativity by speaking to them. If they did not respond to her command, they terrified her and she threw them out of her. But, while on the outside, they scared her even more. She thought they could do her a lot of harm and paralyze her while she tried to paralyze them. She felt that she could not get rid of them, whether they were inside or outside.

This game of opening the door and playing with water was repeated, with very slight changes during several sessions. Though it appeared that she was not listening to me, the look of terror on her face when she opened the door and spied her mother, all the while smiling at me, made me understand that, at that moment, the fear was referring to her mother. I completed her interpretation by telling her that her mother, who was far from her and leaving her by herself, was like water that scares. I told her that I, accompanying her and trying to understand what she felt, was like good water, which she was smiling at. Each time her hands touched or spilled water, I would reformulate the interpretations according to the expressions on her face. The increase in fear and muscle tension when the water was outside the sink was striking. I interpreted this action as an attempt to remove from within her, from her mother, and from me, all that which terrified and paralyzed her. These were the things she couldn't talk about. I also interpreted that when she whispered sounds, she was pitting both competing "waters" against each other, making her mother and me friends or enemies at will, taking us out or putting us inside her. However, if we did not respond to her wishes, she would despair.

I was very impressed by a reaction she had during one of those sessions. I had been lost in my mind and had stopped interpreting for a few minutes. A stream of water directed at my eyes brought me out of my reverie. I interpreted that she needed me to always observe and understand what was going on in her mind: By waking me up like that, she was asking me to always stay alert, so I could understand and heal her. I understood that the bond that she had formed with me was sufficiently established that she could attack me with the water, wake me up, and dispose of me at will. This modification in the transference relationship was of the utmost importance, since her mother had described her as a quiet baby who never asked for anything.

After splashing water at me, she left the tap running for the whole hour. The sink overflowed and the water spilled to the floor, without causing her any anxiety. I interpreted that she felt a need to unconditionally flush away my breast and my milk in order to heal. I also inferred that the water that flowed continuously were my words, which could not be interrupted or broken, like the umbilical cord that joined her to her mother while in gestation. She could now modify what happened. There, inside her, she could redo it with me, and would become angry if the flow of my words—the nourishing milk that entered her mind and fed her—was interrupted.

During the next session, she ate garbage from the floor and sucked on water that was spilling from the sink. I interpreted that being in that room was like being in her mother's uterus, and she ate from me to feed herself. However, she was forced to take rubbish and bad water that she expelled, as she thought she should have done inside the mother.

After eating the garbage and drinking the water from the floor, she had a crisis of despair and fear. I interpreted to her that she felt that I—as her mother—attacked her from within with dirty water and garbage, forcing her to have that filth inside her and preventing her from being cured of it. I also interpreted to her that she did not speak because she feared that garbage and dirty water would come out of her mouth, and that she felt a need to keep everything inside her even when it was negative, because bad was better than nothing. When she wanted to get all that out and couldn't, she shoved and screamed, just as she kicked and screamed when she wanted to speak but couldn't. To ascertain this, I used the information her parents had given me when they told me of her kicking and screaming response. I also interpreted that putting those pieces of garbage inside herself was an attempt to transmit that she could, through emitting the little pieces of words—or screams—attempt to communicate, but that they were not enough to put together complete sentences.

After the performance, she would to turn her back on me, which I interpreted as an effort to not see what was being shown to her, because it was too embarrassing. Remembering that one of her symptoms was not looking straight ahead and staring at people's hands, I interpreted the positive part of her turning her back on me. I told her that not looking at me in the face also meant that she was less afraid of me attacking her, and that she did not need to observe my hands to prevent what I might do with them.

Other times, she did not react like that, and escaped from the room. I interpreted to her that she was doing it because she was afraid of me and of hurting me, and longed to escape from the insight that meant staying with me and uncovering what was inside her.

I also interpreted the flight as a way to preserve *me*. It was clear that she disappeared to avoid attacking me, due to the escapes being accompanied by a desperate incorporation of water from the tap; an act which I interpreted as a rediscovery.

These reactions (and my previous research on teething) made me think that the delay in walking and language development was linked to teething. Later events also led me to find a link between teething and walking, but I did not obtain new data from the parents to confirm this hypothesis.

Verónica used to go to the bathroom to urinate and defecate, leaving the door open so I could watch her while she evacuated. She wanted to make me understand what she felt when urine and fecal matter came out of her, and to ensure I was there to observe what her parents did. This was the way she expressed her anguish and loneliness before the primal scene. I also interpreted that she was afraid of being emptied and that my presence reassured her that she would have an unending supply of substances, should she ever run out. At this time, I was again the therapist and she was the abandoned child.

The separation from her father, imposed primarily by me in order to heal her, seems to have registered as a repetition of the prohibition she felt from her mother when attempting to approach him. This reinforced her bond with her breast mother by denying her mother's genital aspects. There was a relationship between what her parents said regarding the ease with which control was achieved early, and the fact that she held back her words, which had taken on the meaning of the body products she was forced to release by submission and fear. The words would have the meaning of the products of the genital union, and would be closely related to the primal scene; especially since the learning started during the second half of the first year.

The second period of analysis

My hypotheses were confirmed when Verónica returned to treatment because of a regression during which she lost the ability to walk and speak that she had acquired when in treatment. During this regression, a symptom appeared that the parents said was the repetition of one she had at nine months. It consisted of a kind of throat noise accompanied by a sobbing spasm. Teething, loss of walking, and inarticulate sound were intimately linked. During the first period, after the aforementioned times she went to the bathroom to urinate and defecate, she used to react by prolonging the act a lot. She would smile at times, taking on an expression of triumph. I interpreted this as a manic denial of her omnipotence in the face of her fear of being empty and alone; a loneliness embodied by the act of her parents' copulation.

Verónica went back to playing with the lavatory, repeating her first games. She seemed just as freaked out as she was at first. This time, I mainly interpreted the dissociated aspects of her relationship with me, being careful not to point out the division between the mother and me. I introduced the dissociation between the breast mother and the genital mother and added that she was feeling all this with me—the union of mother and father, the woman with a penis—because she was scared that all this would happen inside *and* outside her. She splashed water from the sink, peed herself, and wanted to exit the room.

I told her that I was there as a person, in addition to being in her mind, just as the water was both outside and in her mind at the same time. She then looked at the drawer of toys, which she had never touched.

I interpreted that the contents of that drawer that she did not touch were like everyone else that she ignored, myself included. Leaving everything inside her mind, she couldn't see the toys in her drawer, and could not take things from it outside. She could do it with the water, which was like the breast milk that she knew; a substance she could put inside and take out of herself at will. She feared that all those things would come out of her mind, slip into the outside world, and that, as they escaped her control as did the water, she would not be able to transform them at will. Those things also represented me, everything that she was ignorant of, and everything she did not dare explore; in essence, the genital mother. She needed to accept that these concepts existed outside of her mind and her will; that, while she stood in the room, she was also inside the mother's womb, curious but afraid of seeing something other than the breast with milk-water that she already knew. Blinding herself to the other things that were within her mother and within me—the father's whistle, feces, children—was the same as refusing to look at the contents of the drawer.

The water that appeared and disappeared according to her will represented the breast, which she could have inside and outside herself according to her hunger. The things that she did not explore were dangerous, she did not know them, and she feared them because she did not know how to handle them. This is why she resorted to denial; it had the power of killing perceptions.

The game with the disc

The next session, Verónica brought me a record. She seemed very excited and the mother told me that it was impossible to pry it from her hands. When she came in, she placed a pencil in the center hole of the record and spun it in quick, nervous movements. She put the nail of her index finger on the part of the disk with grooves and, bringing her ear close, she made as if she were listening. She then took my hand, and repeated the same scraping motion with my index finger, obtaining a similar sound. She made me listen to it, she listened to it, and then she made a similar movement with my fingernail on the smooth part of the record. As it had no grooves, it made no noise. I interpreted that she was showing me that her body contained sounds, words that I had to look for, areas that spoke and that I had to search for as delicately as we had searched the disc. I interpreted that, like that record, she had enclosed sounds inside and wanted me to find a way to bring them out.

Verónica spun the disc hard, and it fell to the ground and shattered. She picked the pieces up and anxiously showed me the sharp bits. She placed the edges or spikes against my hand, forcing me to feel how much they hurt. I interpreted that those broken pieces were the sealed words, which pricked her from the inside, made her suffer, and would not exit her body. Those particles were like ideas that could not be converted into words, with all the pain that this difficulty of expression meant. She showed me how she felt; that her words were broken pieces that prick or hurt and that she alone could not put them together. They also represented the cutting teeth that bisected her words; words that, when screamed, would be thrown out along with her pain. Just as the broken record no longer makes music, she had stopped creating words because she, too, was in pieces. She felt that everything was irreparably destroyed inside her, and that the debris was cutting and prodding her. She simultaneously felt that everything outside was *also* broken, like the disc. In response to my interpretation, she approached me and she took in my breast area with a very anxious expression. I interpreted that she was afraid that my breast was also broken and she could not heal it or make it speak. She reached into her drawer for a rubber jar and handed it to me, along with the pieces of the record. I interpreted that some confidence had been regained, when she identified my breast as a part of the outside world, ascertained that it had not disappeared, and trusted that I could paste the pieces of words back together with my milk. Adhering herself to me, she was supporting her whole body against mine.

I interpreted that she wanted to insert all of herself inside my body; not just her words. She longed to be inside me, imbuing herself with the words that I spoke. I added that she now dared to look inside herself, and place herself inside me, because she had regained faith in that healthy milk, linking it to the water with which she played in the first few sessions as well as to my breast. I also interpreted that to be confused with me was to have my breast and my milk, to have my words, and not to suffer the jealousy and anger that she felt in front of me and all those who spoke.

Verónica returned to the game with water, and seemed to hallucinate. I interpreted that now all of me was like the water; that if she felt understood and loved by the water, it would feel good to have it inside and outside herself, but that if she didn't it would become bad and terrible, morphing into the thing that takes her words away from her. She played with the water, filling her hands with it and looking at them with a rapt expression. I interpreted that she placed water, milk, and words inside her, bathing in them and possessing them.

It seems important to point out that Verónica placed the broken pieces of the disc inside the drawer, representing something similar to Patricia's packaged, pulverized sawdust.

In many instances, Verónica interrupted her games in order to carefully inspect the pieces, as if she expected something in them to have changed due to what was happening within her. I interpreted that she was ascertaining whether the water, the rubber, and the contact with my body had repaired the pieces and that, if so, she could be sure that the words had been repaired inside her, allowing her to speak. I also interpreted that those broken pieces inside the drawer were the broken pieces inside the mother, before Verónica was born, and that she was looking for a way to glue and fix the mother's belly with the pieces that made her, so she could come out healthy again. She took the jar of glue and rubbed paste on her hands, on the pieces of the broken record, and on the walls. I interpreted that now her whole room was my belly, with her inside, and that she was trying to fix me as she wanted to fix mommy's belly while inside *her.*

At the next session, Verónica entered the room and spoke with a clear voice and an interrogative accent. "Madame?" she said. I interpreted that she was wondering how I had remained in the office while she was not with me (the external mother) and was showing me how inside her (the internal mother) she had hidden me so I could complete her. She was expressing that, in her loneliness, I had managed to remake myself within her. Her interrogative voice was a way of questioning whether the words I had successfully placed inside her also meant that all of her was fixed. She found the pieces of the record inside the drawer and tried to play each piece, then pressed them together with glue, but was unable to rejoin them. I interpreted that she was afraid that something was still broken inside her and me, like the record. Inside her, only the word "madame" was fixed, and that there were still many broken pieces, like "mom," "dad," and "together."

I made that interpretation, trying to include the couple at the time of her conception, but her lack of response showed me that her mind was not on the pair. It was, instead, hyper-focused on her and her mother, as well as on our relationship. I performed the interpretation because it was the penultimate session, and I thought that the idea of seeing the father and mother united at home would be special for her. After all, she had separated from them to come to Buenos Aires and follow her treatment. Later, I understood that time and space were confusing for her, and that the concepts of travel and of her parents' union did not make sense as linked to each other; nor did the past link with the present and the future.

On the day of the last session, Verónica brought a bouquet of flowers for me saying, "*C'est pour vous, Madame.*" She seemed very excited, but she spoke clearly and it struck me that there was so much affection in her eyes. This was surprising, seeing how expressionless she had been at first. I interpreted then that, before leaving, she was showing me that she kept me inside her; that my person could enter and leave her like those words she took from inside her mind and spoke with her mouth. She was transmitting to me that taking my person inside her had allowed her to overcome the fear of flowers, and that she brought them to me so that I could understand that she now felt empowered to face the countryside full of flowers which she originally feared. Those flowers—which had been the object of her phobia—symbolized a faraway field of people, removed from me, where she would meet her parents, her brothers, and her problems. During this session, she repeated the act of gifting me the flowers several times. I interpreted that she repeated this game in order to gradually overcome the fears of moving away from me, by symbolizing the act of taking me inside her through her words. Before leaving, she asked me to bring out a plastic bottle, unbreakable and hermetically sealed, with which she had played a lot in the previous sessions. This reassured her that she had not broken our bond. She wanted a real object that personified me and would help her face her difficulties when she needed me. It was the expression of her need to take me in and out of herself.

When we said our farewells, the mother told me how much Verónica had practiced that little phrase, rehearsing the gesture of taking the flowers until she had it just right.

What we have revealed about Verónica's history gives us an idea of how her internal world was evolving. Now, we will see how these changes were reflected in the external world. No element showcases this more aptly than the following fragments of the letter the father wrote me a month after Verónica returned home.

Fragments of the father's letter

1) *Handles things with care and skill, including wristwatches, lighters, glasses, chalk, etc. She seeks to disassemble the music box in order to know what it contains, then immediately brings it to be fixed.*
2) *She talks a lot and understands almost everything. Sometimes she says words that surprise us. She knows what she wants and she manages to get it. She excels at small assignments, such as picking things up off the floor and putting them in their place, taking scrap paper to the wastebasket, looking for cloth and drying the area off when she spills water, and looking for specific toys, like boxes, dolls, records, or books.*
3) *She dresses and undresses herself, and gets into bed alone when she is tired. If she prepares a bath for herself, she undresses on her own and bathes without help. She does not like having her laces undone, and insists that they be tied at all times.*
4) *She entertains herself by drawing on and cutting paper. As I write to you, I can hear her say,* "On va manger." *And, indeed, it is time to eat. She recognizes people, even if she has not seen them for a long time. If she is playing with my lighter or watch, and I ask for it back, she willingly and easily returns it. She likes certain foods, and, if she knows how to name them, she comes into the kitchen and asks for them. She tunes the radio to the programs she likes the most, but has little patience and perseverance to listen or overcome any difficulties; she is easily discouraged. When she first arrived, after the treatment, these advances were not appreciated, but a few days later, we began to see the changes.*

Before, she seemed to ignore her mother. Now, she is very affectionate with her and demands to see her. She continues to sleep little and does not seem to need more.

Discussion of the process

If we analyze the changes the father points out, the most important are clearly the ones regarding her attitude toward her mother and toward objects. Let us remember that, during the first hour of treatment, Verónica separated from her mother without showing any affection, and that her parents claimed she did not seem to be interested in anything. In her games, she expressed the reason for this affective anesthesia: It arose from those terrifying internal imagos which she was unable to confront in reality, and so she denied the existence of reality. The dissociated image of her mother was a consequence of the lack of fusion of the instincts of life and death, which took her to extreme positions and away from her reality, and which left her feeling unseen and unrecognized. Within this form of object connection, concepts like paralysis, violent expulsion, denial, idealization, and omnipotence exist as defense mechanisms for the ego, and deny the real object based on the fear that reproduces the characteristics of the internal object. They cause a true breakdown of perception.

The care for objects that the father pointed out to us indicated a great progress in the relationship with the world, and a first step in the elaboration of the depressive phase; the reduction of sadism to preserve the object. The repair tendencies seen in her achievements in toileting and hygiene and her eagerness to fix things also meant progress in working out the depression. The music box that she disarmed was a representation of herself. The father took the role of therapist there, similarly to how I had taken the role of the father and played with the music box just as he had done.

Verónica's curiosity about the interior of objects like the mother's body had previously been heavily repressed. When there cannot be a normal degree of aggressive possession and exploration of both the mother's body and the external world, any symbolic relationship with the objects associated with the mother (and therefore with contact with the external objects and with reality) is lost. But now her curiosity about her mother's body was freely expressed through the examination of the music box. This was proof of the relief of her destructive tendencies, thus corroborating the first achievement noted.

Like Patricia, Verónica submitted, giving up her feces and urine—the early and easy learning—but keeping the words, which have the same magical value. Also, the progress in her language development suggested that the depression had been elaborated, at least partly, and that it had improved her communication with the world. As the father said, she now "knows what she wants and manages to get it." This period of analysis lasted four months, and progressed at a rate of six sessions a week.

In the second phase of the analysis, she played for many sessions at riding the elevator, having realized that the playroom was in my home.

I interpreted this game as an attempt to work out the separations imposed by the treatment. She tried to elaborate, through the relationship between one floor and another, the relationship between space and time. The passage from the ground floor to the first floor represented, for her unconscious, the trip from the country to Buenos Aires to find me, as well as the reverse trip to reconnect with her family. This game had multiple variants.

Sometimes she tried to place me inside her while she was isolated on one side of a fence, and other times she was the one who wanted to place herself inside *me*. As I have pointed out, in addition to interpreting the meaning of being alone in the elevator and confinement as an expression of her connection difficulties, I actively prevented her from being left alone inside the elevator, as this could have been a situation of danger. She also did not agree with placing me alone in the elevator.

In this game, the second floor also represented the second period of her analysis and the progress made. The setbacks, on the other hand, were symbolized by the descent to the ground floor, with the approach to the exit door taking on the meaning of the interruptions in her treatment. Through the union of time and space, she expressed those periods of treatment, as well as the journey to rediscover her father.

I interpreted that she wanted to make me disappear and appear at will. Moreover, instead of me participating as my own person, she would control and place any object that represented me. In this second period, she progressively drew up the distinction between the external and the internal world, both in terms of objects and herself, and made efforts to establish a relationship between time and space. She showed me how she mistook "today" for "yesterday" when she pushed the "up" button to go "down." She had progressed in language by acquiring new words and using them appropriately. She would say, for example, "Madame," while taking me by the hand to her mother, to whom she now referred as "Mother." It's important to note that this did not happen as it had in the first stage of her treatment, in which she had mistaken us for each other. Now, she accepted the existence of a real mother and of a therapist who was *like* a mother to her.

During one of the sessions in the office, Verónica pretended that she was listening to something that, due to the rhythm that she imposed on her body, seemed like music; but this method of pretending was very different from the first period of hallucinations. The difference was that, now, she was able to evoke an internal image and make it appear or disappear at will. On the other hand, during the first period, she was completely at the mercy of her hallucinations. This meant that she began to handle her internal objects in a way more suited to reality.

Since the mother and father had told me that, when Verónica listened to the music box with her father, she would utter the word "lady," I interpreted that listening to music and approaching me to listen was like when she was with her father and listened to the music box which he called *la boïte á musique*. It was a way to express that she missed me, and that she suffered from not having me with her at her parents' house. Making and listening to music with me was a way for the father, Verónica, and myself to be united, so as not to feel the pain of having to be separated from either. She was transmitting that, in order to see me and heal, she had to separate herself from him.

With her music, she brought us together inside her, because seeing us separated outside her made her sad and scared. I also interpreted this in relation to her father and her mother, from whom she also separated when she came for treatment. At this moment of her analysis, the music itself represented what, during her first period, was the glue with which she had symbolically joined the fragments of her words within herself. She used to take the pieces of the disc and, when the fingernail went through the grooves, pretended to listen to music, saying, *la boïte á musique*. If we recapitulate the substances she used for symbolization, we can safely say that the water was replaced by the disc, the glue, the contact of her body joining mine, and the music was replaced by the rubber that binds and joins. She essentially synthesized physical and psychic contact with music and thought.

I gave her a long review of these meanings. She then brought me some scissors and stated that I should feel free to cut out and separate the pieces, because I could trust her to glue them back together. She wound up a music box that she brought from her house, and, as it played, she desperately bit into objects. If the music stopped, she would stop biting. I interpreted that now she felt free to tear with her teeth, as she was sure that she possessed something that unconditionally symbolized unity: music.

At the end of that period, which lasted five months and consisted of six-times-a-week sessions, her mother told me that Verónica was now able to foresee the consequences of her actions. As an example of this, she pointed out that, at the beginning of treatment, waiting in line during car rides would set Verónica off, and it would be impossible to make her understand that she simply needed to wait for the people on front of her. Now, she claimed, Verónica was able to integrate into a queue without the need for prompting and without showing impatience.

Her mother also pointed out to me that Verónica spoke more often and used words adequately. She could recognize shapes and could follow the contours with her fingers, a fact that I interpreted as an important step towards abstraction. She also told me that the child was beginning to recognize colors, and that this had occurred following the recognition of shapes. She insisted on recreating our games in her own house, routinely naming objects and colors correctly. The mother also pointed out that Verónica knew all the people in her environment and used their names when referring to them. As for sleep, she told me that, although Verónica rested for slightly longer than before, she did not sleep as many hours as her brothers. She noted that the tantrums were less frequent and that, in general, she was easily adapting to the daily demands of reality. She seemed affectionate, consistent in her reactions, and willing to obey, but her level of play was still very low and she suffered from frequent depression.

The third analysis

Verónica started her third period of analysis after a six-month hiatus. The original interval of two months had been extended by four due to various difficulties on her end and mine.

During her first session after this interruption, I related what her parents had told me. In stark contrast to her previous sessions when

I had encountered a girl who was virtually mute, and who looked at me as if I were a stranger, by this time her physical appearance was excellent, she had grown a lot, and she had a healthy air to her. There were no traces of the expressionless girl who had started the treatment. Her current look was one of anger and resentment.

Verónica hesitated before entering the office, observing everything with great distrust and carefully inspecting her individual drawer, which I interpreted as an act fueled by a fear that, after all that time, things had changed in me, in her, and in the relationship between us. I think that this setback in her relationship with me was a consequence of her long separation, as well as of the anger that it caused her to have to leave her father yet again. Upon entering the office, she denied my existence as an attempt to deny her own illness, which had forced her to separate from him. Upon leaving the office, she was shocked, and hesitated to enter my room again. I observed that she had the same expression when she left my room as she did when she went to an adjoining one that she had designated as her father's. During this period, her gait became shaky, and the anxiety attacks became so acute that we sometimes had to interrupt the sessions before the fifty minutes were up.

Her mother called me in distress, expressing that she did not understand what was happening to her daughter. According to the mother, throughout the day, Verónica would eagerly count down the minutes until the session, but when she arrived back home, she would seem terrified. She also claimed that the child talked at length about her father and yearned to return to the country.

I communicated the mother's words to Verónica and added to my interpretation that she was partly angry with me, due to the need to separate herself from her father in order to come to treatment; a process she clearly likened to her mother's supposed prohibition of contact with her father during her younger years. The fact that my presence, as well as the presence of broken things in the office such as the shattered record, forced her to think about everything that she had not yet fixed (symbols of things the teeth cut). Registered as a punishment of sorts, she wanted to run away from me and from what she saw while she was with me, as she did when I started treating her.

Verónica became practically silent and I noticed in her such difficulty walking that, at times, I wondered if there was some neurological disorder that had escaped previous investigations. I pointed out her waddle and told her that she should speak with her mother so she could be examined by a doctor, who had not seen her since she'd been in Buenos Aires. Her expression was one of great suffering, and she agreed with a thankful gesture. From a biological perspective, the medical examination found no irregularities.

Along with the staggering gait, Verónica began to make a strange noise with her throat. The sound seemed, at times, to resemble choking or a tic. The mother pointed out that this difficulty in walking occurred only with me. Outside, the girl ran and played as usual. She also stated that, in terms of language, it was as if we were interacting with two different girls. Outside the office, Verónica spoke in fluent French and Spanish, acquiring new words every day; but while inside the office, she refused to utter a single syllable.

I conveyed this to Verónica and I interpreted that she was trying to show me something that had happened when she was little and could barely walk, during a time when she could not speak and suffered a lot. During the sessions, she would have crying spells. I endeavored to keep her in the office, as she had already arranged that her mother would not wait for her, but would instead come pick her up at whatever time she decided.

After that period and the continued interpretation of her anxiety situations, she began to stand up and experiment with walking. She spoke the word "Dad" and called me "Mom."

In one of those sessions, Verónica staggered in to my treatment room and threw herself on the floor. She remained motionless, staring at the ceiling, resting her arms against the sides of her body. She went on to emit, at regular intervals, a small, sobbing, snore-like sound, which was accompanied by respiratory spasms. I was sitting next to her, and when she extended her arms to me, I received her in mine. I felt it necessary to continue the experience. I interpreted that she felt like a baby in the arms of her mother, an adult who remembered what had happened in those moments of her life when such desperate spasms had taken her breath, voice, and movement away. Her attitude in my arms was that of a baby of no more than three months of age.

I brought a hammock chair into the office and took her in my arms, responding to the way she behaved. She cried and despaired, hallucinating and fighting multiple invisible assailants. Sometimes her body would tense up so much that it would become rigid, only to go completely flaccid a moment later. The sudden transition made me feel that if I had put her on the ground at that very moment, she would have collapsed. I interpreted again, this time telling her that she felt like she did when she was drinking in her mother's arms, but that now she was showing how afraid she was. I related to her that she suffered from not being able to stand, walk, or speak; that she felt her needs were unsatisfied because she could not make herself understood and, thus, could not fend for herself. I gave her these interpretations repeatedly and in detail, matching them to her attitude and position in my arms, and relating them to her bond with her mother in the past. I pointed out that she no longer behaved like she did then: like the quiet baby her mother had described to me. I noted that, instead, she now expressed all her hostility and fear of being attacked. Now, I could ask for help from her, because she trusted me and I felt myself inside her, protecting her.

Verónica left the office and went to the next room and said the word "Dad." I interpreted that we were with the father in *la campagne* (the countryside) and, at that moment, I was the mother who allowed her to be with the father. On the other hand, when I kept her in the office, I was the doctor who separated her from the father. Now, the trips designed to bring her to treatment, which she had previously elaborated with the elevator material, took on a new meaning: my evil separation of her and her father and, more deeply, her own separation of the parents. To interpret it, she returned to the office, separated the broken disc, and tried to exit again. I interpreted that, during those months away from me, I had taken on the role of the good doctor—the unbreakable plastic bottle she took with her—and upon returning to the office, I had become the bad doctor, who forced her to stand next to broken discs that represented her fear of teeth that break and puncture.

This situation persisted during many sessions, in which she traveled from one room to another, and only occasionally did she succeed. I kept her in the office for the fifty-minute session. I interpreted that, while in my office, she escaped the dangers of teeth breaking and destroying, and, while in the other room, she represented the danger of receiving her father inside her. As this material was interpreted, it became clear that the consulting room and the adjoining room represented her relationship with her mother's shattered breast, as seen in the broken discs. My room, in turn, represented the transferred relationship with the father, seen in the symbols of the penis and the vagina. The modification of that original situation (wherein the mother forbade her from approaching the father) through this new transference was evident in her growing confidence, as well as in the fact that she entered the office with me and willingly evoked the memory of her father. When entering and leaving each of those two rooms, she wore an entranced expression, as if she could not recognize either place.

I understood that she could not join the memories of her father with the memories of the moments she had spent with me. It was as if there were two Verónicas that she could not bring together: the one who lived in the field with her father, and the one who visited me to continue treatment due to her mother forcing her to separate from him. I interpreted this game as an attempt to elaborate the distance she felt she'd created between her father and herself, as a consequence of the treatment: a separation that was experienced by her as a repetition of the one imposed by the internal image of the mother. When Verónica tried to replace her, she felt it was forbidden. This anguish was displaced to the flowers and the dogs.

The longing for the father that I allowed during treatment modified the original prohibition. Verónica was now able to ask her father for the repairing penis, since during the regression period she was able to allow herself to express oral needs and longing for contact in the transference. I also understood that in her mind, time and space were jumbled. The real, physical distance between her and her father was transformed into a distance between past and present moments, and she could not grasp all the memories that lay between them. This interpretation impressed her deeply and, with a face full of wonderment, she stared into space. "Image," she said. I interpreted that she was telling me that she now possessed images: She could remember and visualize moments of union between her father and her mother, her father and me, herself and me. This way, she could keep us together in her head and her heart, as memories.

I felt that the same Verónica loved and remembered the father and me, the mother and the father, the country and the city. She was, at the same time, the Verónica who lived with her parents *and* the one who dealt with me in this office. This possibility of recovering lost moments in images and in memory meant enormous progress in her mental life.

Concluding remarks on the two narratives

In the case of Patricia, memories of traumatic situations that occurred in real life emerged throughout her treatment, and were confirmed by her mother; a fact that allowed us to understand the origin of her symptoms.

In Verónica's case, no memories appeared, but through the intense transference regression and the repetition of symptoms, which the parents placed as having begun during a specific period of her development, we can assume that her neurosis erupted at nine months with the appearance of teeth, the beginning of walking, the emergence of multiple phobias, and the strange snoring and shortness of breath. It is possible that a future analysis can provide us, as was the case with Patricia, knowledge of the real external events concerning the period of life linked to these symptoms.

Commentary on Chapter 9

Jill Savege Scharff (USA)

Arminda takes us deep into the consulting room as she develops a relationship with Patricia and Verónica and their parents. Both children had normal deliveries and breastfeeding for some months, and both had delayed language and both felt incomplete and imperfect. Patricia experienced a loss of the breast at seven months when her mother became pregnant with her sister and then she was abruptly left with a harsh nanny at the time of the delivery, whereas Verónica was the youngest sibling of brothers, there was no abrupt loss but more of an emotional absence since her mother remembered little about her first year except that she was a quiet, easy baby, and eventually became preoccupied with other things and left Verónica with a nanny, but one who was good. Both children, for different reasons and in different family contexts, suffered during the toilet training time of development and both of them gave up their body products on demand, but kept their words for themselves. Both girls played with putting a pencil in a hole: Patricia sharpened the pencil and wrapped up the precious sharpenings to keep in her drawer, like a parental union to be protected and hidden; Verónica put her pencil in the hole at the center of a music disc which created a scraping sound, and when she dropped the disc it shattered as if the realization of genital union destroyed her mouth–breast union. But the primal scene was not on Verónica's radar, and those types of interpretation fell flat, because her interest was in recovering the breast mother, which denied the mother's genitality. The Kleinian influence is evident in the language of interpretation in both cases.

First we meet Patricia, saying nothing but driving cars in and out, and putting the pencil in the hole, and stopping up the hole, then looking at the difference between cars with and without strings attached, after which she went to the toilet. Arminda concentrated on the idea of Patricia stopping up the mouth and the anus to be free of her mother's control. I was thinking about this girl's feelings about why she did not have a penis and how that connects with her imperfection. Later the sealed-up sharpenings are given the meaning of being bits of penises, babies, and the analyst's other patients as products of sexual relations. When Patricia wraps up bits of cars and planes instead, she represents the attempt to incorporate the father's penis. She also played with putting good and bad things in a pot, as if to recreate her own mental contents and make them good. I was also thinking of the pot as her female body and of her identifying with her mother and making her own babies in the pot. I felt so sad to learn of her mother's punishing her for mispronouncing her sister's name, especially because it led to her to completely stop speaking. Arminda uses Patricia's play with opening and closing her individual drawer to illustrate the importance of the drawer as a representative of the mouth, the vagina, and the fertile mother.

We see Verónica as a terrified child, yelling and screaming in rage, not at all the quiet baby her parents described at birth. She must have taken in fragments of badness but could not integrate them in words, and screamed as if that was the only way to get them out. She didn't play with toys in a drawer but played with water, letting it run, spilling it, drinking it, and walking in it on the floor, with pleasure and terror. Water play seemed to express a return to the amniotic fluid before all her abnormalities were apparent, a reveling in the breast milk, a representation of an aspect of her mother and of her analyst, an expression of the transference, and a longing to be inside the analyst's body. I was fascinated by the use of water to communicate instead of words: Water seemed good if she liked Arminda's interpretation and bad if she did not; water could wake up the analyst and get her to pay attention! As she trusted Arminda, Verónica reenacted her first months of life, actually lying in her arms and taking in a new experience of an attentive mother who put words to all that was happening. Adult analysts do not offer this degree of physical contact, but can draw from this example to do it metaphorically through provision of a comfortable private space and a reflective mind capable of understanding the terrors and longings of the infant on the couch.

Readers trained in therapy that is based in attachment or defense interpretation might recoil from the interpretive focus here. We have to remember that Arminda is treating very disturbed children with developmental delay and she gets to know them over four or five sessions per week. Like Melanie Klein before her, she tunes in to their level of primitive, preverbal thinking where fantasies appear to be realized in reality. Others of us may really appreciate that and integrate it into our own practice, as Arminda did with her reading of Klein, which is better than falling under the spell of the creative play interpretive technique, as I did during my training in child psychiatry when I had just read Klein on the early genital stage. I had a first session with a conduct disordered four-year-old girl aggressively chopping up clay to make hamburger meat which kept falling apart. There are so many ways to address this—feeling anxious about seeing me, trying to tell me about her wanting a solid meal, showing me how her attempts to integrate fell short of her intentions, and so on. I hate to admit that I interpreted this play as her attack on her parents' union. No wonder the child fled the session crying. I can't now remember the associations that led me to this interpretation and which might support it, but the point is my interpretation was the result of an aggressive incorporation of a brilliant theory, and technically hopelessly premature and incomplete.

The content of this chapter gives us insight into the mind of children like these and helps to show how an experienced child analyst can enter into that inner world, and how she interprets the inner conflict effectively with the cooperation of the child. It also gives us a full and deep experience of the connection between parental expectations and behaviors, bodily experience and infantile fantasies, which is of use whether we treat children or adults.

CHAPTER 10

Focus on three clinical reenactments of birth trauma

I will present the material from three treatments and one mothers' group to illustrate the working through of birth trauma. I will not recount the treatments in full but select the fragments that best depict the birth trauma that was described by parents and symbolized by the children in play, fantasies, behavior, and associations.

Marta, age four

Marta's parents consulted an analyst, Mercedes F. de Garbarino, when she was four years of age, for help with a combination of enuresis and a series of emergent character disorders. They pointed out that she was very disobedient, had a distaste for strangers, could not bear to be in their presence, and would either hide from them, or manifest her aggression in some other fashion. She tended to behave like a baby, demanding her mother carry her from place to place. She had also showcased an extreme reservation to exposing her feet or genitals. For all these reasons, it was decided that she should undergo treatment.

During the first few months, Marta refused to be separated from her mother. Due to this, she had to undergo analysis and interpretation while seated on the mother's lap, her back to the therapist. As she did not speak or play, the interpretations were based solely on movements and shifts in positioning. Marta reacted to the analysis by curling up into a ball and progressively immobilizing herself, until she reached a completely fetal position. Her main symptom—her rejection—was clearly evident in her unwillingness to face the therapist, and, indeed, her interpretations. She defended herself against these by snuggling into her mother's lap and adopting a protective position.

After a month of treatment, the mother entered the office, and announced to the therapist that she had made a pact with her daughter, and that the girl had promised to enter the next sessions alone. Immediately after this comment from her mother, Marta approached her. She grabbed onto the mother's arms and hung from them, her head swinging dangerously close to the ground beneath. This was interpreted as a movement based on a fantasy of birth, detachment, and separation from the mother.

Entering the office alone was the equivalent of losing her mother at birth. As she listened to the voice of the therapist, she snuggled back into her mother. This was then interpreted further; the girl understood the voice as an external entity connected to the forces that had conspired to place her in the reality that she so feared. She could not bear to be separated from her mother and was therefore returning and reentering her. To accept the human voice would have been to accept the existence of an outside world.

This same situation was repeated with some variations. As an example, Marta took some steps around the office, feeling her way around and touching things with her feet as she went. At times, she would try to contact the therapist by directing the objects towards her. When the therapist interpreted the girl's desire to connect to her, she climbed back up and into her mother's skirts, and snuggled up like before.

For another month, regardless of the conscious and consensual pact she had entered into with her mother, and even in light of the interpretations that had been elaborated before her, Marta could not bring herself to enter the room alone. Faced with this unchangeable fact, the therapist decided to adopt an alternate technique: that of simply *forcing* Marta to enter the office alone. The therapist decided this in the hope that the large amount of anxiety triggered by the forced entry might be equivalent to that of Marta's birth, and might thus cut the cord linking her to the mother. This measure, as we have indicated, was announced to both mother and daughter, and they were informed that it would be carried out in the next session. When the therapist pointed out that, during the next session, Marta would *have* to enter the office alone, the girl reacted with great anguish. She then repeated the movements she had made back when the mother had verbally commented on her prior agreement to enter alone.

The analyst realized that, during those previous two months, she, the patient, and the mother had *passively* avoided facing the anguish of birth. Now, through this separation, they were taking *active* measures. By severing Marta from her mother and taking her alone to the doctor's office, they were forcing her to enter the world. By abruptly cutting her cord, the therapist repeated the midwife's dexterous maneuvers during Marta's birth: The infant had been born with the umbilical cord wrapped around her neck and under her arms; and the cord had to be cut before the girl was able to be fully extracted from the womb. This cut had imposed the world onto her before she was biologically prepared for it, contributing to her difficulties in adapting to postnatal life. We will now relate how the child dramatized her birth when the therapist announced the indicated technical measure.

Reenacting the birth trauma

From the previously described position, Marta retreated into the protective folds of her mother's skirt. She slowly slid one leg out, extending it, then bringing the foot to the floor. She did the same with the other. She slowly let her body droop to the floor, leaving only her head nestled between her mother's legs and her mouth viciously sucking on her mother's clothing. While Marta slowly and methodically carried out this movement, the therapist interpreted her new birth, step by step.

Marta's first points of contact were, of course, her feet. With them, she sought to get closer to the therapist. This form of bonding—through the feet rather than the mouth—allowed her to connect to the therapist, while also remaining attached to her mother. The therapist based this interpretation on the behavior Marta had exhibited towards her mother. Throughout that first period, during which she sat huddled in her mother's skirts, Marta suckled and bit her fingers, as well as two of her mother's pieces of clothing—a button near the navel, and the end of her belt, which, in this case, represented the umbilical cord. By keeping her bond with her mother intact through her mouth, she could seek and explore the outside world through other points of contact.

The moment she finished the performance and the therapist's voice dissipated, Marta rose and positioned herself on her mother's lap once more. When the interpretation resumed, the voice reemerging with it, the patient restarted the previous set of movements. It was interpreted that, stimulated by the announcement of the separation, Marta was expressing to the therapist that she needed more direct help to achieve it. She was pleading that the voice carry out the work of the midwife, while also announcing the unconditional food supply—the protective, motherly, milk-adjacent presence—that she needed to receive in order to safely discard the mother. The fact that she remained hanging from her mother's legs by the head was clarified in later analytic sessions.

The behavior was interpreted in the following ways: Marta longed to remain attached to the mother and repeat what she felt when, despite pushing, she could not exit the womb. She essentially felt held in place by the cord. In the following session, when separated from the mother, Marta hung on the back of an armchair, supporting herself with her arms and swinging without detaching herself from the chair. Once more, this lack of separation from the chair symbolized what she experienced when the cord obstructed her, preventing her from separating from the mother.

During the second session, following the symbolic severing of the cord, Marta remained glued to the door. She screamed, cried, drooled, and gnawed on her fingers. Mucus poured out of her nose and slid down her clothes and extremities, unobstructed by a despondent Marta. The session culminated with Marta drenched in a mixture of saliva, mucus, and tears that covered the entirety of her clothes, hands, and face. She seemed eager to recover all the substances that had sustained her inside her mother.

The interpretation was simple and clear: By cutting her cord, the therapist had forcibly removed Marta from her mother's womb. In a desperate attempt to deny that separation, the child had clung to the office door in very much the same way she had held on to her mother's skirts.

During the next session, her anxiety partially diminished, Marta tried to turn around and look at the therapist. She couldn't bring herself to do it. She only managed sideways glances, turning toward the door often to try to open it. It was pointed out to her that her difficulty with looking at the therapist, and, indeed, at anything around her, was due to her feeling like a newborn who fears the unknown.

Included in the layout of this particular office was a small marble threshold, placed next to the door. The rest of the floor was made of wood. Marta placed one foot on the marble, and left it there for a long time. She then placed the other foot down, and lifted up the first foot. She alternated the contact over and over, switching back and forth between feet, until one came to rest in front of the other. Squeezing them together like this was the only way that both feet could fit on the marble at the same time. While making these movements, and still glued to the door (analogous to the mother), Marta was faced with the office (the outside world).

Marta then removed one of her feet from the marble and barely brushed the wooden floor. She quickly returned it to the marble, hesitant to place it on the wood fully. After several tentative attempts, she managed to completely rest her foot on the wooden surface. Following this set of actions, she was provided with an interpretation. She was told that she was trying to feel the outside world, which included her therapist, but needed to do it little by little because she was very afraid. The cold unknown of the outside world was symbolized by the temperature of the chilled marble. In truth, and in Marta's mind, this outside world had not been very welcoming. This perspective was due to the circumstances surrounding her birth, and because her first contacts with her mother were negative. Upon interpreting the events, Marta stood up, leaned her head against the door, and looked directly up at the ceiling, her eyes slowly scanning the wallpaper.

We will now try to express Marta's unconscious fantasy of illness, as well as how it conditioned her symptoms; mainly, withdrawal from the world. Due to her birth trauma and her initially negative experiences with the world, everything associated with her birth caused her to fear both rejection and the unknown.

At this time in the process, the mother remembered that she had rarely taken Marta in her arms. She used to let the child "cry out" her woes, and, on one occasion, at eight days of age, had even allowed her to cry a full night without relief. She also recalled that breastfeeding had lasted until eighteen months and that, when the brother had been born, Marta had been immediately weaned and taken from her parents' bedroom. During this period, she had begun to walk, and fell often. She'd also suffered from blackouts, a symptom for which a biological cause was never ascertained.

During the treatment, she exhibited all these difficulties with the therapist. However, as per my own interest in the particular way in which Marta symbolized the trauma of her birth, I have limited myself to recounting the fragments of the sessions in which these birth issues are more evident. I want to emphasize, however, that within the subsequent material, it was noted that the initial suckling of the button (standing for the navel) and the belt (the umbilical cord) was meant to simultaneously maintain an oral bond with the mother and a genital bond with the therapist. This way, Marta could dissociate the image of the breast mother from that of the genital mother (in this context, the therapist). Her foot symbolized the fantasized male genital through which she sought to unite with the genital therapist/mother figure.

This allowed us to understand one of the symptoms indicated by Marta's parents, her extreme modesty regarding genitals and feet.

Daniel, age four and ten months

Daniel, four years and ten months old, who suffered from conduct disorder and night terrors, was brought for treatment with Jorge Rovatti. Daniel tended to somatize and, at a year and a half, during a feverish episode, he had seizures accompanied by episodes of fainting.

Both parents came to the initial interview. They assured us that he was a wanted child, but that the mother had experienced severe anxiety during the nine months of pregnancy. She'd feared that she would not be able to carry a healthy child to term. He was pulled from the womb with forceps, following a prolonged and turbulent anesthetized delivery in which the cord wrapped around his body. They put him to the breast at forty-eight hours. They pointed out that the child was eager to breastfeed, but since the mother produced very little milk, they had to complete the feeding with a bottle.

Teething occurred at seven and a half months. At eleven months, Daniel began to walk, showing an initial tendency to fall. At a year and eight months, he had achieved control of his urine and fecal matter, but only at two years and five months did he obtain nocturnal fecal control.

When he was one, the parents took a month-long trip abroad, not telling Daniel about it because they considered him too young to understand. At that time, he articulated his first word, which was his own name.

After a year and a half, they enrolled him in a kindergarten, but he could not attend because he became ill. When he was three years old, he suffered a fall that caused the breakage of two teeth. This coincided with the mother's new pregnancy. At the time, there also emerged two episodes of sleepwalking that added to his nocturnal turmoil.

After the first interview with the parents, psychoanalytic treatment was decided at the rate of four times a week. As I explained, we will also limit ourselves to exposing sections of the material from a session in which birth trauma emerged as the central theme.

Previous to this, Daniel's games had centered upon his fantasies of the primal scene and the pregnancy. After interpreting that situation, Daniel walked to a closet in the office that is usually kept closed, and verbally expressed his desire to open it. The therapist, understanding the child's need to include it in his play as an element of symbolization, agreed to open it. Then, Daniel entered the closet and asked the therapist to close the door. Soon afterwards, he requested the therapist open it.

As the door opened, the therapist found Daniel crouching, with his eyes shut tightly and his arms crossed over his chest, in a squatting fetal-like position. The therapist then verbally interpreted the following to Daniel, based on previous material (which we did not transcribe for the aforementioned reason). In the face of all the dangers and fears Daniel felt, he needed to return to the interior of the therapist/mother/wardrobe, mimicking the environment inside his mother's uterus before birth, but now with the added ability of ordering the door to open and close on a whim. He was thus trying to elaborate the circular, traumatic situation of his time stuck in the birth canal because of the cord and his emergence thanks to forceps.

Next, Daniel took a ball of yarn that was inside the closet and asked if he could use it. The therapist offered him an interpretation, consisting of an affirmation that Daniel needed to reestablish the bond that had joined him to his mother through the umbilical cord (the yarn) but with the therapist instead. He then asked the analyst to close the closet door again, but when he began to do so, Daniel had an anxiety attack.

"Maybe you can open it later," he frantically affirmed, adding, "When it's time, can I get out?"

Then, he grabbed a small tin pan (a symbol for the placenta) and twisted the handle (the cord) giving it the shriveled shape of the post-birth umbilical cord. He kept twisting the handle, saying, "When everything is twisted, it is time, and you can't see the light." At that moment, the therapist offered him the following interpretation. At the precise moment Daniel was about to leave his mother's belly, the cord twisted around him like the twisted handle and prevented him from being born and "seeing the light." After pointing this out, Daniel took the ball of yarn and said, "This was it. Do you tie me up now?" rectifying the situation through its analysis.

During the next session, Daniel returned to his symbolization of the umbilical cord, this time through a new element. He used gum, which he stretched and twisted in a manner similar to the handle of the frying pan, after which he ate it. Through this act, he expressed the need to separate from his mother by cutting the cord with his teeth (eating the gum) and, at the same time, he showed his need to introject her in order to separate from her in reality.

Diego, age nine

Diego was an adorable nine-year-old boy. The middle child of a young, apparently well-matched couple, he was born in the eighth month of pregnancy, and the delivery was quick. The parents did not remember how long after birth Diego had latched on to the breast, and said that breastfeeding had lasted up to seven months, with the aid of a bottle. At first, he resisted solid food, accepting it later without major problems.

He began to walk at seventeen months, showing difficulties in coordinating movements. It took until the age of three for his gait to be considered "normal." He too spoke very late, uttering his first words at the age of four. When he was six, his intellectual performance was low enough for concern, so his parents consulted me to confirm a prior oligophrenia diagnosis. After a careful introductory analysis of the child, I advised a psychoanalytic treatment that began immediately. He lasted a year and a half, at a rate of five-times-a-week sessions, and was forced to interrupt treatment once because the therapist, Emilio Rodrigué had traveled to another country. The progress in his first analysis was remarkable, but this was not the case for the next two, which were interrupted for different reasons. During these latter treatments, however, the achievements of the first treatment were, at the very least, maintained. Shortly before starting this last analysis the parents consulted me again. The parents had informed Diego of their impending travel plans—they would be gone for two months. From that moment onward, he began to regress both in his school learning and in adapting to the environment.

The fragments transcribed correspond to the first two sessions of the fourth treatment. These moments take place immediately after the interview with the parents, wherein it was made clear to them that Diego had linked his first therapist's travel to another country—which was a definitive abandonment—to the treatment they were about to undertake currently. I also reminded them that when the first analysis was interrupted, the child had been told that the therapist would return, but he was unable to do so after all. Thus, Diego had been accepting the treatments that followed as temporary and on that condition. Furthermore, when the first therapist's absence became definitively permanent, no one had clarified it to Diego. This explained his current fear that the recently announced, two-month voyage by the parents would *also* turn into a definite absence.

The new therapist Eduardo Salas told me that in the first session Diego showed great reluctance to establish a new transference relationship. The initial distrust commonly associated with any psychiatric treatment was reinforced by the successive losses and failures. Having laid all this out for Diego in the utmost detail, the therapist showed Diego that he was anxious about his parents' next trip. During the second session, Diego explained that he'd agreed to this separation from his parents. Then his associations revealed the birth trauma that was symbolized there. He referred to a beach that had been mentioned at the beginning of the session. He spoke of riding his bicycle across the shore, only to find that the path became a steep cliff. His vehicle hurtled downward uncontrollably. The wheels twisted and shoved him off the path, forcing him to dodge clusters of foliage. He spun around a few times, finally landing on the pavement. As he spun the tale, he moved his head and body from side to side, mimicking the lateral centrifugal pull of a race car.

At this juncture, it is crucial to recall the circumstances of Diego's birth: He was born in the eighth month of pregnancy, and labor was very fast. According to his mother, the midwife had uttered something to the effect of "The boy almost fell to the floor." The associative material of the session and the historical dimension amply justified the therapist's interpretation. Diego's words expressed his experience of his vertiginous birth as an unstoppable fall that ended with a blow. The rotation within the birth canal was symbolized by the turns that he made with the bicycle, while the difficulty to pass between the plants symbolized the journey between the maternal pubic hair. The vertigo produced in the fetus when rotating within the birth canal was expressed when he spoke of the wheels of the bicycle turning suddenly. It was also revealed to him, according to the initial material, that he attributed his mental weakness, at least in part, to the way he was born. The therapist completed this interpretation by telling Diego that he feared the repetition of these situations in his new analytic experience, and the child, with an intelligent and relieved expression, answered, "Yes."

Diego then took a toy car—he claimed not to know the brand—and commented that there were no seats. He stated that the car should have seats and that, since it didn't, it was incomplete. He thus symbolized his experience that crucial components in his development were missing, that he was not finished, because inside the mother's womb some unknown process had been left incomplete. The therapist interpreted this to mean that Diego would need to reexperience that event with the therapist. This way, he could complete the interpretation and, in doing so, fulfill both the treatments that had been left truncated *and* the pregnancy that had not come to term. This, Diego symbolized in later sessions more clearly, sitting on the therapist's lap and occasionally smacking his head against the therapist's belly.

In response to this interpretation, Diego took a pencil sharpener in his right hand and a pencil with a broken point in his left. Despite having the pencil sharpener in his hand, he asked the therapist for one.

Through this bit of communication, he was symbolizing that he placed all hope of healing in the hands of the therapist—hence, the request for the pencil sharpener even when he could easily use his own—and certifying his belief that he alone could not heal without significant help.

Diego used the pencil sharpener with so little skill that he was unable to actually sharpen the pencil. The therapist then pointed out that Diego was feeling a slowdown in his own abilities. At this moment, an imperceptible movement of the analyst's arm made Diego turn away. All of a sudden, the inquisitive child looked very frightened. His expression was one of suffering.

"I cut my finger," he wailed, a fantasy that was not based in any way on the material we had previously observed during the session.

This boy was circumcised on the fifteenth day after his birth. The therapist interpreted that Diego also thought *this* trauma had influenced his condition. In essence, he was missing the tip of his "pencil" and could not return it to its original sharpness. In later sessions, during which he repeated the action with the pencil sharpener, the therapist interpreted the need to recreate the original situation with the therapist, instead of the family members, in order to recover the lost foreskin. The therapist also surmised that the hesitant reaction that Diego showed was due to his fear that all the painful events that had caused his illness would repeat themselves. He associated the detachment of the foreskin with the detachment of his first analyst and with the fear that all the losses would be repeated in this new treatment.

Silvia and Graciela, age five

The mother of five-year-old twins Silvia and Graciela entered my counseling group because her daughters refused to give up thumb-sucking. She wanted advice on how to correct this habit, and she made clear that this was the only symptom she was concerned about. I explained that the research group was not geared towards dispensing advice or judgment; rather, it was designed in the hopes of understanding the reasons and causes of common mental disorders. In the group I said that, if she was willing to sit down with us and tell us about the symptoms, we could gradually ascertain how they had originated, and slowly come to understand them together.

It soon became clear, however, that the real reason for the mother's entry into the group was her own need to elaborate trauma, namely the "terrible impact" that bearing twins by herself wreaked upon her, especially without the prior warning of her midwife. At first, she denied all the anguish that this caused her, as well as the great effort she had made to raise the children.

It was clear that she had adapted to the situation of having two daughters, kept them both equally satisfied, breastfed them until they were nine months old, and, at the same time, performed all tasks around the household. Yet, she was incapable of acknowledging the stress this had caused or the effort it had taken, at least initially. She later recalled that, in the fourth month of her pregnancy, the doctor had asked her if there had been cases of twins in her family. Although she answered affirmatively, her midwife had never directly pointed out the possibility of having them, so the mother had not thought about it further, and never expected the ensuing result.

It was interpreted that she had denied *herself* the knowledge of twins, and the midwife was not at fault. After all, the doctor's question should have been taken, in and of itself, as an alert about the possibility of twins. She rejected the interpretation by replying that, during the following visit, she had asked her doctor to clarify whether or not there was a chance she could bear twins. According to her, he had responded in the negative, and she'd been very disappointed. Still, two days before the delivery, she had been told that she would have a very large male child. Instead, two girls were born. First came Silvia. Then, ten minutes later, her sister Graciela arrived. They remained in the incubator for five days, while the mother was in the sanatorium. She breastfed them until the beginning of the sixth month, then sought aid in the baby bottle. Weaning took place at nine months. She did not give them a pacifier and both began the habit of sucking their thumb from the first month of life.

The group saw, clear as day, her disappointment at not having been granted a boy. The initial rejection of the daughters was obvious, even if the mother had completely repressed it. The area we worked on the most together during the interpretations was her reluctance to accept that she had been a good mother; she tended to devalue everything she did, always considering herself to be guilty of the initial rejection, the first five days of lack of contact, and the restriction in suckling. She could not recognize her kindness and her affection, denying all that she *had* provided her daughters and instead focusing only on the negatives. From everything she said about them, it was clear that Silvia was the entrepreneurial and bossy one. On the other hand, Graciela, who was born second, was timid and seemed to shrink in stature and personality when around her older sibling. We were able to understand that the mother supported Silvia's character traits, repeating the initial difference in privilege created on the day of their births. When the mother changed her behavior, notable shifts began to occur, since the roles that had previously been so clearly marked for each girl were being redistributed.

Over the course of one session, following this improvement, the mother related that something strange had happened in kindergarten. She said she'd connected this event to the way her daughters had been born. During a New Year's Eve party—in essence, a social, communal "birthday"—the girls were chosen to play the role of dolls. They were dressed in costumes and placed inside a box. At one point during the performance, Pinocchio wound up the doll-girls, and to the sound of music a fairy touched their heads with its wand. With its magical touch, the fairy gave them life; that is to say, it gave birth to them. While Pinocchio wound them up, Silvia waited patiently and quietly in her box and Graciela kept looking out to see "what was going on outside." When the fairy touched them with the wand, Silvia immediately left her box, but Graciela remained undecided and did not dare to leave it until after a few moments.

With this performance, they repeated the way the birth had occurred. These events were more notable when, the following week, the mother reported that the twins had woken up with fever and a rash after the performance. She claimed that the infection was intense in Graciela, the second born, but very mild in Silvia. This symptom was similar to the one they had suffered when weaning had begun at the end of the fifth month and they'd received their first bottle. At the time, the symptoms had *also* been more intense in Graciela than in Silvia.

The feeling the mother had repressed, which provoked such intense stress, was simply her guilt at her own initial rejection of her daughters, motivated, above all, by her disappointment at not bearing a male child. This conflict made her see and foster in Silvia the traits that she considered masculine and, in addition to supporting her, she began to subconsciously prefer her. By becoming conscious of her guilt, she was liberated from her preferential behavior and she was able to allow her daughters the independence they craved and needed. In the wake of this paradigm shift, the mother noted the disappearance of the thumb-sucking during the day, and the girls would only resort to it occasionally before bed.

The roles that had previously been so rigidly delineated between them became more and more elastic. They stopped being two halves of the same girl, and each of them became a girl onto herself; a girl who, while saddled by genetics with many of the other's characteristics, was an overall separate entity. It was at this time in their evolution, after a year of treatment, that the event at the kindergarten performance occurred.

With the guidance of the therapist, the girls reproduced the two separations from the mother: the birth and the beginning of weaning. Thanks to the changes that occurred in the mother, they were able to repeat the birth and weaning experiences, because the most favorable conditions to continue progressing in the independence process were to be born again, and to start weaning again. They *needed* to relive these traumatic situations to modify them and, thus, establish a new relationship with the mother.

Commentary on Chapter 10

Jill Savege Scharff (USA)

Some analysts who follow Rank (1924) think that the separation of the baby from the mother's body at birth is inevitably a trauma, a foundational experience that influences mental health even more than the Oedipus complex. Certainly the mother's body pushes the infant out of the womb, down the birth canal and into the world, but this exit doesn't normally happen until the infant is mature. Then the birth is a shift from a no longer adequate environment to one for which the child is ready. The lungs expel a cry, the infant takes a breath, and life begins in a joyful welcome to the world. The infant is wired to latch on to the nipple and search for the mother's eyes as a great new adventure begins. But there are birth circumstances in which birth really is traumatic. Premature birth, induced birth, breech presentation, cord around the neck, and C-section come to mind. These certainly do make their mark on the child and on the mother.

Arminda presents four vignettes of children traumatized at birth like that. The vignettes are so rich I hesitate to comment on pieces, which will not do justice to the whole story. But Arminda responded to narratives of whole analyses, picking out the parts relevant to her exploration of birth trauma, so perhaps that gives me license to proceed. Marta was demanding, babyish, aggressive, enuretic, and had a fear of her feet being exposed; Daniel had a behavior disorder and tended to faint and sleepwalk; Diego was late speaking and talking; and the twins were still thumb-sucking and were polar opposites, Silvia the outgoing bossy one and Graciela the shrinking violet. Marta was born with the umbilical cord around the neck which had to be cut before her forceps extraction; Daniel with cord around the body was stuck; Diego, twisting in the canal was pushed out so fast that he had to be caught before falling on the ground, and the twins Silvia and Graciela arrived unexpectedly when their mother thought she was having a large, single male child. In every case, Arminda sees the story of the birth enacted in play.

The twins relived the birth process in a school performance when they had to emerge from a large box: Silvia, the bossy firstborn was out of the box right away while Graciela the timid one cowered inside hesitant to leave. While the twins worked through the birth and the weaning in therapy the mother realized she had been identifying Silvia as the lost boy. The power and timidity distributed between the two girls was rebalanced and they each became a more complete personality. Diego recreated his fast birth in the play of a twisting, turning, and careening racing bicycle and in his cutting of his finger, an association to his circumcision, the loss of the foreskin, and his fear of losing the analyst. Daniel represented his stuckness in the birth canal by playing inside a closet, doing and undoing that stuckness by opening and closing the door, and illustrating the cord and placenta in a pan with a twisted handle. Marta fought mightily to stay attached to her mother, grabbing and snuggling in her skirts and refusing to be pushed out into the analyst's room by herself until mother and analyst insisted, cut the cord as it were, and eventually one leg came out, then the other, the voice of the therapist serving as the midwife.

These are compelling examples of dedicated attunement and astute play interpretations. They remind me of the work of Piontelli (1992) who also treated disturbed young children (including twins like Silvia and Graciela) and had access to their pre-birth sonograms. Piontelli noticed that the majority of twin couples retain their pre-birth way of relating, so either Silvia and Graciela were in the minority, or more likely it was their therapy that allowed the rebalancing of their power dynamic. Piontelli (1988) described a girl who always got herself tangled up in the cords to her office curtains, a girl whose birth was complicated by her entrapment in the umbilical cord. At a time when Aberastury's work was unknown among Italian or English speaking analysts, Piontelli's story of that girl struck me with the same force as did this Chapter 10 and spurred my birth as a child analyst. But if I could have read Spanish, I would have got there much earlier!

At that time I was an adult analyst working with a depressed mother who as an early adolescent had been shocked to find her adored mother dead of a massive stroke and stuck in the bath tub. One day on the couch my analysand writhed in pain because she got her leg caught between the seat cushion and the back of the couch. I have no idea how that happened to this well-coordinated athletic woman. Her leg was painfully twisted, and it took some contorting to get it out of there. I worked on how she might be recreating the death scene of her mother being struck and stuck, but having read Piontelli, I also inquired about her birth history. She had been born feet first, with one foot out and one stuck until an internal maneuver was done. So the death trauma was also a birth trauma. This adult patient came back to mind when I read about Marta. I wondered if Marta's birth had been a foot presentation too. What goes against that is the early image of her hanging upside down from her mother's lap. But her way of approaching the analyst foot first with her head in her mother's lap is so striking it suggests an alternative that the mother might or might not have confirmed.

I conclude with gratitude that Arminda's skillful and imaginative access to the replay of birth trauma is helpful not only to the child analyst but also to the adult analyst in understanding various bodily communications and working through the associated traumatic memories in current experience in the consulting room.

Part IV

New perspectives on treatment and prevention of infantile neurosis

CHAPTER 11

The prophylactic effect of mothers' counseling groups and their relation to psychoanalysis of children

We have often pointed out that the analysis of children, like that of adults, must be conducted in a boundaried two-person relationship, and that interviews with parents are not agreed upon except under special circumstances, stipulations, and conditions. We also pointed out that young children are capable of adapting to the environment or changing it, and that we consider any technique that includes advice or environmental changes to be useless.

Through the detailing of a case, we will now show how a group of mothers, by allowing, without interference, joint action on the child and on the mother, facilitated the treatment of the index patient and served as prophylaxis for healthy development of her younger sister. Their mother suffered from a compulsion to destroy and then repair, and she repeated these destructive behaviors with her younger daughter, which in turn contributed to the elder daughter's illness. We will present fragments of the analysis of this elder daughter of a normal family, as well as detail the group sessions with her mother in which the interplay between individual and group, and the prophylactic action of the group is shown.

Nora, age three, was oligophrenic and came to the consultation with a diagnosis of epilepsy for which she had been prescribed phenobarbital two tablets with breakfast, and epamine two tablets with dinner and one tablet with breakfast. The therapist for the assessment, Susana L. de Ferrer, used the techniques for the initial interview with the parents and the first recorded hours of play—as laid out in Chapters 5 and 7—and concluded that the diagnosis was not correct. She reoriented the treatment approach by radically suppressing all medication and recommended psychoanalysis for the girl and placed the mother in my mothers' counseling group.

The three therapists—the one responsible for the diagnosis, the one who treated the girl individually, and myself, who treated the mother in the mothers' group setting—were all part of a study group where we discussed the evolution of the case. We were able to confront, step by step, the material offered by both mother and daughter. We compared this ongoing material with the first observations made during the diagnostic sessions. Our review of the data given by the parents in the first interview, and gathered from their responses to the child's later improvements and ensuing relief of guilt, confirmed our findings concerning the inaccuracy of the diagnosis and the validity of the recommendations.

The first parent interview

Nora was the elder daughter of a young couple and, according to the data provided by the mother during the first interview, was desired by both parents. The pregnancy was normal, as were the delivery and breast-feeding processes. As will be seen in the course of the case, this data was found to be only partially accurate. According to the mother, the girl developed regularly during her first three months. After these three months had elapsed, however, a congenital bilateral hip dislocation became evident. The doctor suggested they immobilize the lower part of the body, including the pelvis and the leg, in an *ad hoc* removable splint which was to be kept fixed for as long as possible but removed for occasional freedom. The parents were to maintain this treatment until the child was nine months old, but, due to her anxiety, the mother did not ensure the limited freedom the doctor had recommended. The child's splint was not removed the whole nine months.

At that time, due to Nora's anxiety, she was given two or three sedatives a day, which manifestly decreased her vital reactions without modifying her anxiety or the sleep disorder that she experienced. When she was one—according to the mother's report in the first interview (or at nine months according to the subsequent report)—Nora lost consciousness for two or three minutes while she was being bathed, specifically, as her head was being washed. She did not turn pale, and continued to breathe normally. The only real symptom that was observed, aside from the loss of consciousness, was a slight deviation of the eyes. She recovered with a simple alcohol rub. One trigger described by the mother appeared crucially important to our team: the girl's anxiety always shot through the roof when she threw her head back to wash it. We were later able to relate this situation to the difficult circumstances regarding her infancy.

When Nora was a year and two months of age, this episode repeated but this time it was more serious. Her loss of consciousness was more prolonged and it was accompanied by a hemi-lateral seizure. Nora's mother explained that while she was holding Nora, she dropped a package, knelt down to pick it up, and abruptly lowered her. It was at that moment that the child lost consciousness. Nora was taken to a hospital, where she underwent a series of examinations, including lumbar puncture, ventriculogram, EEG, and a fundus study. The results were negative and any serious danger was ruled out. The tests revealed no hematomas or traumatic injuries, and the parents were advised to bring her in for another electroencephalogram the following year. Epamines and daily sedatives, both in large doses, were prescribed for her treatment. The day after this episode, Nora developed whooping cough that lasted much longer than usual.

At one year and eight months of age, Nora's mother became pregnant. Coinciding with this, Nora began to show symptoms of irritability, anorexia, and constipation. She was taken to a hospital for a series of tests, after which the mother was informed that they had revealed that Nora had only 60 percent of the mental capacity expected for her chronological age. They also notified the parents that, due to the epilepsy, it would be necessary to double the doses of sedatives and epamines. On this occasion, they were again advised to return in a year and repeat the exams.

At two years and two months of age, when her sister was born, Nora's emotional and intellectual delay became glaringly evident. She hardly spoke, drooled continuously, refused solid foods, and suffered from an alternating pattern of persistent constipation and massive, unrestricted bowel movements. It was evident from what the mother described that Nora reacted to the birth of her sister with an increase in aggression that she had previously repressed. She said, for example, that the day they arrived from the hospital with her new little sister, Nora struck one of her cousins, for which she was reprimanded by being locked up in a dark room. The next morning, and after a prolonged period of sobbing, Nora shivered, screamed shrilly, then remained motionless. In the early hours of the afternoon, her fever began to rise, reaching 40°C.

During this health crisis, Nora rolled her eyes upward and fell backward, screaming "I'm falling!" as she threw herself back. A few hours later, she was stiff as a board, and would periodically break her thousand-yard stare to vomit. Upon awakening the next morning, she tried to get out of bed several times, falling during each attempt. A state of somnolence and prostration followed, accompanied by vomiting of clotted blood and severe dehydration. These symptoms once more led to her being admitted to a hospital. She was diagnosed with encephalitis. A lumbar puncture was performed and the administration of serum and specific medication was started. She was hospitalized for four days and her diagnosis was officially deemed encephalitis.

Her mother had thought that, for a long time, Nora's sedatives—especially the epamines—had been causing her a lot of damage. She insisted on the need for a urinalysis, which revealed drug intoxication. Epamines and sedatives were suspended, and an evident improvement was almost immediately observed. It was the mother's concern regarding her daughter's condition that led her to consult with a relative and demand that the girl be tested. Two months later, the hospital doctor, at the request of the mother, arranged for the analytic consultation. We want to remind our readers that, when this mother was a girl and played dolls, the games always included deranged children that she saved at the last minute. With Nora, she always repeated the same situation: When all seemed lost, her love for her daughter enabled the mother to save her.

Dynamic formulation

The interview with the mother and the observation of an hour of diagnostic play revealed a more optimistic picture than could be assumed from the preceding history and current signs. I think that the apparent severity of the symptoms was due to the fact that the child's mobility was restricted in the second half of the first year of life. This, compounded by the strong doses of sedatives, caused a blockage of the aggression. This resulted in both organic symptoms and an inhibition in sublimation. In this, as in other cases, failure in symbolization begets symptoms that can easily be mistaken for a state of impaired mental development. The suspension of drugs was indicated, and the psychoanalytic treatment of the girl begun immediately. She attended sessions for four hours a week.

The mother entered a counseling group that same day. She recalled her experiences regarding pregnancy, childbirth, and immobilization during one of the group sessions that we discussed in the previous chapter. We will later see how the confluence of the two treatments allowed the clarification of the case and the relatively quick recovery from the symptoms. What we know about the evolution of a child allowed us to understand that, for an immobilization to be this traumatic, it had to have happened between the third and fourth month of life, that crucial stage of development in which the child passes from the paranoid-schizoid position to the depressive stage. At that moment, the child's need for freedom of movement also begins to emerge and allows the child, when ready to do so, to walk and separate from the mother. Nora's immobilization, which lasted up to nine months, made the previous genital phase begin under these strenuous conditions. Not only was masturbation made impossible, but was experienced as prohibited. The mother understood the reason for her behavior, and immobilized her at that age and not before or after. This meant that she repeated the immobilization imposed on her between three and nine months of pregnancy, when they told her that because of the losses she had suffered, she ran the risk of miscarriage.

Nora's play session

Nora began treatment when she was twenty-eight months old. She was an adorable child, with a pleasant demeanor, and a restless and curious look on her upper face. This stood in stark contrast to the lower part of her face, where drool continually dripped out of her mouth and ran onto her clothes, with no awareness and no attempt to clean up. When Nora did begin to wipe the drool off, it became a signpost of her improvement.

Nora entered the consulting room with her mother and looked around at everything inside the room. She showed no signs of anxiety when her mother left the room. Once alone with the therapist, Nora approached the table, which was covered in toys that her individual drawer would eventually contain. The pile consisted of dolls, toy animals, cups, plates, cutlery, a ball, toy cars, toy airplanes, paper, thread, scissors, colored pencils, modeling clay, and buckets.

Nora grabbed the clay and gave it to the therapist, saying the word *tina* (bathtub). She did not symbolize the therapist, and notably her play during the first period used substances and clay exclusively, and did not include the usual use of toys of a child of similar age with normal development. During this first hour, she showed her unconscious fantasy of illness when she pointed to a small spot on her forearm that she called *nana* (nanny) and then proceeded to strike the underside of her head with the same arm. She thus showed us that her illness—*nana*—was somewhere in her head. She then added a series of noises that she called *radio*, describing what she felt inside her head. She linked her nanny to her head and the noises inside it. She started a game wherein she compared the two arms; one had a watch and the other a bracelet, the two objects looking very similar in that they were made of the same material but being different in purpose. Nora thus pointed out a difference between the therapist and the mother. The equality and difference of the two objects awakened her anxiety: She had symbolized the newness of the therapeutic relationship, as well as her latent distrust that the analyst would repeat her mother's behavior. For the rest of the hour, she made a series of *tetitas*—little breasts made of plasticine balls—which she later molded into a series of *patitos* (ducklings). Under the tail of the last duckling, she penciled a hole, filling it with new balls that she referred to simply as *caquitas* (poop).

We need to remember at this juncture that Nora had had a lumbar puncture after the seizure and experienced successful bowel movements only through the daily use of suppositories. During her game, she expressed this situation; how she felt attacked and full of waste, until she got sick. In later sessions, she dramatized the lumbar puncture more clearly, when, following a game in which she hit her head and fell down, she asked for injections in her spine. She repeated the original situation that caused the hospitalization, expressing fear that her treatment in our office would recreate her treatment in the past. The hypermobility shown in her sessions was interpreted as perpetual motion, a defense by means of which she could deny her paralysis and her fear that the therapist would also immobilize her. Nora's anxiety when remembering the immobilization of the lower part of her body—the same anxiety that emerged in the transference situation as a potential repetition of the original situation—is evident in her behavior upon entering the sessions: She took off her shoes and lowered her panties.

Progress and understanding of child and of mother

During her time in treatment, Nora has made remarkable leaps in language and vocabulary. Not only can she pronounce words more clearly, but she formulates sentences well. She hardly drools, and when she does, she tries to control it by sucking and swallowing her saliva or wiping her chin. Her constipation has disappeared entirely, and her eating and sleeping routines are normal. Her mother points out that she is pleasantly surprised by Nora's normal behavior during play with other children.

We believe that, when such rapid improvement is achieved, it is only because the interpretation and resolution of the conflicts during the child's treatment were combined with changes in the mother's behavior. When Nora's mother understood to what extent she was maintaining her daughter's illness, she was better able to assess her own role in the appearance of the symptoms and treat the condition more effectively. The improvement, by alleviating the mother's feeling of guilt, allowed her to become aware of the gravity of the previous situation. She began to remember fragments of her daughter's story that were totally repressed during the first interview (which we presented earlier), and that were fundamental to understanding the genesis of the disease.

Before the mother's pregnancy with Nora, which the mother had claimed was her first, she had actually had another. She had miscarried during the third month. The characteristics of her miscarriage had led doctors to believe she would never conceive again, let alone carry a child to term. During the third month of her pregnancy with Nora, she had suffered heavy blood loss, and the doctor advised her to reconsider, as there were no guarantees that she would reach term or that, if she did, a healthy child would be born. This threat of a possible sick child distressed her more deeply because it was the fulfillment of an old fantasy that she traced back to her childhood, specifically to her games where she was condemned to rescue "deranged" dolls. Perhaps for this reason, she decided to preserve the pregnancy, despite the fact that the probability index that her child would be born healthy was one in a hundred. Perhaps this is why she kept such a strict rest schedule from the third to the ninth month, just as she did for Nora in postnatal life. She immobilized Nora to cure her of a congenital defect.

During her first sessions, the mother might have consciously understood her daughter's symptoms as illness. But her actions, through which her own illness was brought to light, were never judged by her as anything but mischief or whims. One of the problems that she brought to her group was her inability to prevent Nora from hitting her little sister, who at that time was three months old. The blows were mostly on the head, and each time they were carried out, the fear that her second daughter would also be "retarded" surfaced. She became aware that not only did she not know how to stop Nora's aggression, but was, in a sense, using it as an instrument of her own aggression, just as she had done in following the doctors' prescriptions which had really been an assault on Nora, compelled by her long-standing need and fear that her children would first be tarred with defect, and then she would heal them. Her compulsion to transform the second daughter into a second sick child was shown when she did not know how to stop the blows that Nora gave her on the head, and when she cured her of a fantasized constipation by applying suppositories every morning. It was not until the mother understood the conflict between love and hatred—that conflict which drove her to destroy and then repair—that Nora's hitting disappeared. And thanks to the mother's evolution, her second daughter was free of suppositories and medications. The mother repeated an attack against that daughter, immobilizing her with a belt, but this lasted only one day. Realizing what she'd done, she replaced the belt with her arms to teach her daughter to walk. Had she not understood these conflicts, the mother would never have grasped and modified her behavior so quickly.

This case illustrates the perspectives of varying groups of mothers who are open to the therapy of infantile neuroses and to the prevention of future disorders.

Commentary on Chapter 11

Elizabeth Palacios (Spain)

Context and legacy

Arminda Aberastury, alongside her husband Enrique Pichon-Rivière and several contemporaries, profoundly shaped the clinical landscape of mental health practice and theory in Buenos Aires for decades. Their collective contributions influenced the clinical field within mental health institutions and permeated the broader conceptual framework for mental health. Of those fortunate to have trained in this influential milieu, our perspective on mental illness and human suffering bears the unique imprint of the rich and enduring tradition of the Río de la Plata region. Particularly in the field of child psychoanalysis, Aberastury's enduring legacy (Aberastury, 1959, 1962; A. Pichon-Rivière, 1946, 1950a, 1950b) exerts a significant impact within Argentina and beyond, particularly evident in the diaspora of psychologists, psychiatrists, and mental health practitioners who, amid challenging social and political circumstances, have carried forth her ideas, whether consciously or unconsciously, shaping the landscape of mental health across borders (Ben Plotkin, 2003).

Arminda privileges technique. For her, it is a tool to ensure that children are active in their own treatment and not passive recipients of an ideology based on a series of traditional premises. She supported her work for many years on Melanie Klein's propositions on child analysis. However, based on her own experience, Arminda carried out a series of fundamental technical and theoretical changes (Cipolatti, 2021). These changes are based on her interviews with parents and children, her appreciation for the value of playtime, and her belief that children understand their illness and desire to be well from the first session on. Klein described how the mother figure was structured in the child's mind. Aberastury argued that a similar process occurred regarding the father figure. For her, with the initiation of the Oedipus complex and the elaboration of the depressive position, the father figure took on a new meaning and a dual function: to spur the ability to separate from the mother and find an essential source of masculine identification for both girls and boys. Given the bisexual basis of early development, she believed that the integration of the mother–father pair was necessary for the harmonious development of personality.

Having worked with pediatricians and dentists, Arminda studied the process of teething and concluded that it pushes the child to separate from the mother (A. Pichon-Rivière, 1958b). She observed that teething drove the child to separate from the mother in order to avoid destroying her by the force of oral aggression. The appearance of teeth in the sadistic oral phase leads to fantasies of destruction gaining ground in the child's fantasy. This development urges the child to abandon the oral bond and recreate it in another part of the body. She believed that the child discovers their genital parts, prior to the anal stage, and that the mouth–breast union is replaced by the penis–vagina union, thus inaugurating an early genital stage. For Aberastury, the shift from mother to father is accompanied by a continuous shift from the oral to the genital. The teething process also leads to the development of language (Aberastury, 1964). Language allows for the magical reconstruction of objects to ameliorate depressive anxiety increased by teething. Insight about teething enabled Arminda to understand that symptoms of delayed speech acquisition develop during teething. Later, the shedding of the milk teeth ushers in the decline of the Oedipus complex.

Genitality is fundamental for Arminda and led her to devise an original scheme for the development of infantile sexuality, based on the existence of a genital phase prior to the anal phase (Aberastury, 1964). By proposing this new view of libido development, she was able to understand some "early childhood disorders" that occur during the second half of the first year and suggest an essential change by considering the infant's genital life and the resulting effect on adult genitality. Aberastury also proposes a modification of the aims and intensity of defense mechanisms acting in the paranoid-schizoid phase. She suggests that the dissociation of the maternal image into good and bad breasts ceases to function in this period, and that it is better conceptualized in terms of breast mother and genital mother. Building on Winnicott's idea of the baby hallucinating an object capable of satisfying its needs before the first oral experience, Arminda proposes that in this early genital phase, the child can hallucinate an organ capable of providing genital satisfaction in the emergence of the genital functions proper to this stage (Aberastury, 1970). Based on the model provided by the oral experience, the child can make the equation of breast with penis.

Mothers' orientation groups

In the early 1960s, Arminda's technique was developed in hospital settings, primarily departments of pediatrics and dentistry. Under her guidance, child psychoanalysis also reached the university where she introduced the importance of developmental issues and the need for preventive care in childhood. Intervention with parents was fundamental for her, although she believed the analyst–child–patient link must be carefully nurtured. She refrained from advising parents, believing that parental behavior was unconsciously motivated and could not be modified by conscious directives. Unlike the views of other contemporaries, for her, advice was detrimental, because the unconscious guilt felt by their parents for not being able to follow advice was transferred into aggression. As seen in Chapter 11, Arminda developed a novel complement to treatment: Mothers' orientation groups, to which mothers were recommended while pregnant or having a newborn. This idea for complementary groups for mothers of children in analysis arose from her conviction that the mother–child link could only be improved through the interpretation of unconscious conflicts that hindered the relationship (Aberastury, 1962). These groups, of which we have an example in Chapter 11, served in several ways:

- As a tool for the prevention of childhood neurosis
- As a space for mothers of children undergoing analysis, which supported the mothers and so enhanced the child's treatment
- As an alternative for mothers when fathers could not afford the child's treatment.

Aberastury's focus was on the child, not on the family. Mothers' groups could provide her with a means to overcoming the obstacles parents posed to her, when she was treating their children. The difficulty of managing multiple transferences (from the child, the mother, and the father) creates difficulties in treating the child. Another obstacle arises from the mother who pathologizes the child. In mothers' groups, Arminda interpreted mothers' ambivalence and envy towards their own mothers as an interference in raising their children. Mothers' feelings of guilt emerged in these groups and were deeply explored. For Arminda, it was fundamental that mothers could develop a good link with their children. In this sense, these groups also served a pedagogical and preventive function for childhood neurosis. They provided knowledge of pathogenic factors, introduced awareness of the baby's need, and provided group support among peers, all of which allowed understanding of infant development and the role of mothering to reach the mothers. In this and other chapters in this volume, we can observe Arminda's rich and adventurous creativity throughout her psychoanalytic productions, both theoretical and clinical. Arminda Aberastury is an author who deserves a special place in child psychoanalysis worldwide.

CHAPTER 12

Psychoanalytic perspectives on infant development

The process of expecting a child reactivates certain latent feelings in a woman, namely those primal anxieties she has felt since childhood in relation to the interior of her body. If the child is born healthy, it certifies that she is a healthy woman. The fears frequently found in pregnant women, mainly relating to the idea of having a defective child or of not carrying the pregnancy to fruition, are a consequence of these anxieties. This is why the child takes on the characteristics of an internal stranger, about which the mother's fears and actions are evidence of an ignorance that goes far beyond what we would consciously call lack of experience. Animals know how to feed and raise their children instinctually. When they don't, when they kill, abandon, or in some way mistreat their young, we consider it an unnatural aberration. As an animal, the healthy mother should also know, on a primordial level, how to care for her child, but as a human being subject to various deformations, she is unable to rely on primal drives, and needs education in mothering. The path by which we arrived at this knowledge was similar to the path required to transmit it, and it ranged from the pathological to normal.

Learning from child analysis and mothers' counseling groups

During the analysis of neurotic and psychotic patients, we studied pathogenic factors. The understanding we gained, combined with our research on primitive development, led us to know what babies consist of, what their needs are, how they must be satisfied so that they can evolve normally. Although we made great leaps in the prophylaxis of infantile neurosis through this method, we needed a way to convey this knowledge to mothers. Ideally, this would be achieved through *grupos de orientación de madres*, mothers' counseling groups.

In counseling sessions with mothers, we noticed that the feeling of strangeness in regards to the child manifested in each mother through multiple failures to comply with a proper childrearing routine. When analyzed in the counseling groups, this incompetence was shown to have deep roots in either childhood situations or in their relationship with their own mothers. Common to all the mothers was the sterile struggle of rescuing a genuine love for the child, which was impeded by uncontrollable forces and by the suffering in which this struggle plunged them.

Therapeutic success in groups does not consist of the mother getting to know the child, and it does not come from the mother being able to apply any acquired knowledge to the child. Instead, it stems from the woman getting back her sense of fulfilled motherhood. This is a source of joy for the child and for the mother, and allows love to flow freely between them. Like the free-flowing milk of a healthy breast, this gratification can be regulated and does not bend to impulses or momentary demands.

Due to the importance of establishing the mother–child relationship immediately after birth, the best time for a mother to enter the group is when she is expecting. During her sessions, the mother will learn about any potential problems, preparing her for her role as a caregiver. More importantly, she will learn to be tolerant of mistakes, know the life of a baby, and empathize with a child's feelings. When her child is born, she will be able to analyze any fears and anxieties associated with the childrearing process during her group sessions, more effectively preparing herself to face any difficulties that may arise in the future.

The process of preparing for painless delivery frees a woman from much of her suffering and brings her closer to living naturally.

The mothers' guidance groups, by preparing her for the relationship with the child and analyzing her difficulties with reality, fulfill a similar function. They allow the woman to effectively fight deeply ingrained habits or beliefs that run counter to the basic needs of both child and mother.

The same limitations that a mother encounters when attempting to understand her child's needs are often experienced on a larger scale by many adults who care for children. An example is the person who immediately separates the mother from the child upon delivery, sending the child off to a nursery or seeking to remove the baby from the mother in any way. In this, they are obeying the conscious idea that the mother needs rest, but ignoring the unconscious knowledge that the abrupt breakdown of an intimate, nine-month relationship affects both baby and mother, and that these specific circumstances and characteristics will never be repeated in life and the subjects will, thus, perpetually long for them.

At birth, the newborn's ego is engaged in the extremely complicated task of elaborating the trauma of birth. Indeed, many authors have studied the importance of intrauterine life and the trauma of birth. On our end, Arnaldo Rascovsky and his group of researchers have studied the fetal psyche. All this knowledge leads us to believe that a fetus that is separated from the mother needs to reestablish an intense bond with her as soon as possible and regain—even partially—contact with her body. This can only be achieved if the child remains with the mother for a significant amount of time, especially in the first days. Later, one can gradually adjust the distance in order to ensure a safe separation.

Infant needs: From feeding to separation

Experiences with infants show that, although the mouth is the most appropriate area for the child to establish contact with the world—after all, infants must feed themselves to survive—it is not enough. Nor is it enough to be fed. We can help the child overcome his separation anxiety by putting him in contact with the mother immediately after birth, and by encouraging the initiation of suckling. So long as the mother's offered breast satisfies the child's needs and relieves tension, the outside world will gradually begin to signify a pleasant atmosphere that is worthy of the child's curiosity.

The infant also needs the mother's warmth, her voice, her company, her handling, her touch, and her provision of appropriate clothing. These factors must be carefully studied, so that the babe is neither too hot nor too cold, and is thus helped in the task of thermo-regulation. For many years, it was believed that a child that is not nourished directly by the mother would have serious disturbances in their further development. Currently, we know that artificial feeding, provided with plentiful, affective contact and in physical conditions that are as close as possible to breastfeeding—including an adequate nipple hole, a cradled and well-supported position in the arms, and a feeding time that lasts the same as an average natural session—ensures the normal and adequate development of the child as much as its more organic counterpart. It is also worth noting that a breast might be overflowing with milk, yet still be introjected by the child as inadequate if it is not accompanied by sufficient emotional contact and gentle handling.

The first case to teach us a considerable amount of new information concerned a girl whose mother had breastfed her until she was nine months old. Despite this, the child presented very serious conflicts related to food, and her overall relationship with her mother was complicated. In theory, her breastfeeding stage was handled perfectly. However, we later learned that the mother, who suffered from severe asthma, had breastfed her daughter during a period in which her asthmatic episodes were occurring on a daily basis. We came to the realization that the breast that this child had introjected was loaded with the terror of this perpetually sick, drowning mother which the child had inhaled. Feeding was associated with subconscious memories of her mother in danger of death.

We stated before that the mouth isn't everything, and that oral gratification might be the first contact infants have with their mother, but it is not the only required one. Well, milk isn't everything, either. It takes more than full, physical nourishment for a breast to be introjected as a positive imago by the baby.

Our team was consulted about a child who cried continuously and expressed great concern. This occurred despite the fact that the mother's milk was plentiful and that she was breastfeeding at regular intervals. When I spoke to her, she mentioned how difficult it was for her to breastfeed every three hours. However, since she knew it was healthy for her son, she entertained herself during the boring ordeal by watching television. The tradeoff, as convenient as it sounds, illustrates for us what lack of contact can mean. This child received milk from an absent mother; one who had physically provided her breast, but who had also checked out psychologically. In addition, this lack of contact prevented the baby from understanding the generally unpleasant noises and shrill music blaring from the shows the mother watched. These unexplained and overwhelming stimuli were unhealthy and contaminated any healthy associations with the plentiful nourishment. In a sense, they spoiled any good milk the mother might have been providing.

All factors related to the first relationship with the child are essential for their subsequent development. In an attempt to return now to the initial situation, we can say with some confidence that, when a mother is separated from her child after childbirth, something is definitely lost in their relationship. When the baby is brought to her at twenty-four hours, some of the heat that bound her to him in her womb has already cooled down. If, on the contrary, the child is given to the mother immediately, they will both be able to reclaim some of the intimate union that they had through the umbilical cord.

Once contact with the mother is reestablished, it should be repeated at regular intervals. The first week should consist of careful observation, as it is crucial to identify the proper length of time each individual child can go without eating, and that can fluctuate between two-and-a-half hours and three-and-a-half hours. After the first week, the mother can know the rhythm that best suits the child's needs. Each baby, according to the conditions of their birth, handles frustration differently. This must be carefully studied, mainly because one of the first and most difficult tasks that the ego performs is that of coping with anxiety. If the external circumstances are positive, this ability to cope will be gradually bolstered. However, if the child experiences increasing anxiety and continuous frustration, the struggle of the self becomes more difficult. This is why we need to know what the child's needs are at birth, as well as which of these will gradually cease to be imperative in order to give rise to new needs and new stimuli.

Once the daytime feeding rhythm has been established, and fifteen to twenty minutes of suction at each feeding has been accounted for, the question of whether or not the babe needs a pacifier should already be answered. Of course, we do not recommend giving a pacifier to the child before knowing if it is necessary. If the proper feeding intervals of three-and-a-half hours have been established, and the indicated suction time is observed at each feeding, but the child still manifests anxiety, discomfort, or continuous crying between feedings, then it is advisable to consider a pacifier.

Each child is born with various needs, and the supplementary suckling provided by a pacifier can be useful, not as a replacement, but as a way to satisfy the remnants of anxiety that linger between feedings. However, it is important to understand that a child's cries do not always come from hunger or a lack of suction. Though we have delineated that they need to feed themselves to survive and that the mouth is of fundamental importance in this period, we reiterate that it is not the only crucial factor. Often, a child might cry and express unhappiness, and the solution might be as simple as a softly spoken reassurance, a few minutes in the arms, or a change in position. Only when a parent has exhausted all other resources, emotional or physical, should the pacifier be introduced. It is also acceptable to use it when circumstances relating to the family organization impinge on routine, or if the required time to learn and establish proper feeding rhythms is not available.

Psychoanalysis has familiarized us with the meaning of learning difficulties and inhibitions in general. During group sessions, we noticed that when a baby cries and the mother does not understand why, or somehow feels incapable of reasonably surmising the child's needs, she becomes so paralyzed by anguish that the situation devolves into nothing short of a total inhibition of function. This inhibition can be temporary, but can reach extreme degrees if left unchecked. It is common, for example, for a mother to interpret a baby's cries as hunger. This is a logical response. However, when the child is offered nourishment and this does not satisfy, yet the mother continues the attempt to feed, she is acting as if her child is simply a mouth to be fed. The message to the child is that she does not know how to offer anything else. It is common for a baby who is placidly installed at the breast and successfully suckling to abruptly leave the nipple and cry inconsolably. Interestingly, before this process, the mother usually reports feeling as terrified as the baby.

If the mother has positive contact with her infant, she will let the baby cry, at least for a time, while held against her. She will not force the child to eat, and she will wait for calm before offering the breast again. If, on the other hand, the mother has negative contact, or has not fully grasped the child's conflict, she will insist on forcing the nipple into the infant's mouth again, without thinking that—at that moment—the action of swallowing something scary and invasive might trigger feelings of suffocation for the child. With this force-feeding approach, a mother can create new problems in her child, including but not limited to vomiting symptoms.

Every need that is efficiently and properly met during the first year of a child's life is a step toward guaranteeing future independence, not only for the child but also for the parents. However, there seems to be a variable divide between the needs of a child and the potential for a parent to satisfy them.

During our research, we noticed that the close bond that bridges the child with the mother during intrauterine life—as well as the unconditional satisfaction of the child's needs—makes it necessary for the detachment from this exceptional situation to be gradual. During this detachment, infants must have their needs met, as they still do not know how to achieve this by themselves. This provision of care is also variable, and changes based on each mother's abilities. After all, a set of stringent rules that ignore the real demands of the parents' lives would always be doomed to failure. The life of a child cannot overwrite that of the parents. In fact, it can be as dangerous to subject a child to an entire life of obsessive and anxious care, as it can be to abandon the child altogether. The only result that can stem from this type of relationship is resentment. The child's rules should not invade the parents' lives, except to a reasonable and necessary extent.

The need for contact with the mother will gradually diminish, as the development of the functions of the ego grant the child new sources of enjoyment in relationship with the world. This will coincide with the growing well-being of the mother and her gradual reconnection to the interests that she lost during these last few years. We are referring, mainly, to her union with her partner, and through him, with the entire adult world. The ease of separation between a mother and a child is directly proportional to the rate at which the mother and child allow for initial, deep contact.

The first week in the clinic or hospital should be widely used for the establishment of intimate contact, which is why the use of the hospital nursery is so counterproductive. It's perfectly fine for a fifteen-day-old baby to remain in the nursery a few hours a day; but the infant should not be left alone in a nursery at birth, or even twenty-four or forty-eight hours after birth, or else there is a risk of major emotional and psychological impoverishment.

After birth, the child and the mother both need privacy, protection, and care. It is the worst possible time for a mother to try to socialize. If she does, much of the emotional charge that her child needs will be lost in interactions with others. When the child is brought back to the mother, the contact will most likely be disturbed, even more so if she insists on giving the child the breast or the bottle while surrounded by stimuli that drive them both away.

One of the more difficult moments for the average mother is the return home after the week at the clinic. Though she consciously yearns to leave the medical facility, the reality she encounters often disappoints her. The clinic—especially if the visiting cadre of friends and family is welcome—becomes an ideal place; one where others take care of the baby, while the mother is suffused in a manic climate of evasion that suits her lack of knowledge on childrearing perfectly. Her house forces her to confront the full responsibility of caring for her child, without the frequent opportunities to run away from it. It is common for a mother, especially one who is not aided by a live-in or visiting nurse, to feel very lost during those first few days. If she, on the other hand, has established an intimate bond of contact with her child while at the clinic, she has gradually become familiar with the child's needs. This means that her arrival at the house, though still difficult, is much easier to deal with.

Therefore, it is of crucial importance that parents take account of time. A routine must be established that adheres to the time of day the child eats and sleeps, as well as to the general parenting routine. This is important not only because the baby's anxiety is immediately checked and controlled by an established routine, but because the parents can then know, in advance, what their free time is and how much of it can be spent pursuing their own interests. This will better equip the mother to bear the burden of motherhood. Depending on the degree to which the mother allows herself to enjoy her relationships—both with her child and with the world at large—the impression of slavery disappears. It is instead replaced with an awareness of the responsibility and dedication that the child demands from her.

To the newborn, the mother's breast represents a source of food and life. Having formed the prenatal unit with her fetus, the mother creates within the newborn the distinct feeling that there is an object in the world that will give them everything they could ever need. After the trauma of birth, all the efforts and achievements of the newborn will be, in essence, attempts at reproducing that prenatal unit without success. The child feels the need for an ever-present breast that frees them from persecutory anxiety, but this doesn't exist either, and reality necessarily frustrates. However, the image of a real breast that satisfies the child at regular intervals, even if it disappears for a few hours, can help. If the child internalizes it through this lens, they can work out the loss and wait patiently for their feedings.

Sleep schedules must also be respected. The baby can sleep in the adjoining room, but only if they have already had sufficient contact with the mother during the time at the clinic, and only if the process of separation from the mother was gradual. Moreover, the child simply needs to sleep, and knowing how many hours they rest and the usual time slot they choose to rest is not only good for the child, but for the well-being of the couple.

Following the second week, a child that has been well cared for during the day can sleep six to seven hours without feeding. Little by little, that interval can reach up to eight hours. In an ideal situation, a one-month-old baby can be put to bed and the parents can sleep through most, if not all, of the night. The degree of adherence to a nightly sleeping routine will determine how long the child remains awake during the day, and how the child relates to external stimuli. This relationship to new aspects of the external world will facilitate the child's detachment from the unique bond with the mother.

The child's room should be as close as possible to the mother's, and the baby should sleep alone, if possible. Mothers who are very anxious, or who have demanding nightly social lives, often rely on a babysitter to care for the child. The anxiety or need to escape by a mother who delegates her functions to the babysitter is not a feeling we can modify with advice.

Sleep issues

Many mothers wonder what to do when the baby cries at night. The obvious response is to attend to the child, but the way in which attention is given is a decisive factor in the progression of the nighttime crying. Based on the research we conducted and the materials we gathered from our group sessions, we can confidently affirm that if either parent comes to the call with empathy, and driven by a willingness to understand the child's needs, the potential for the crying episodes to lessen—or cease entirely—radically increases. When a parent makes the decision to care for a crying, sleepless child, the necessary time must be taken to ascertain positive results. If the parent tries to solve the conflict quickly, it will only increase the tension, causing both the parent and the child even greater anguish.

Young children may dream of something that scares them, or they might have woken up with a start as a result of something that happened during the day. Their sudden and abrupt consciousness may make them feel lonely and fill them with a fear of abandonment. The mere appearance of the mother, smiling or simply looking calm, often results in the child returning to sleep almost immediately. If the crying continues, despite this calm attitude, the parents must consider the possibility that it is a symptom of greater concern, and seek diagnosis in order to ascertain the conflict that has produced the disorder, and how to solve it. In babies, any type of sleep medication is not only counterproductive and discouraged, but also completely ineffective. If a child does not sleep well, there is something wrong with the inner workings of the child and parents must seek out the reason for the symptom. The child's diet might be to blame; it might feel insufficient and the child might feel a deep hunger that they can't satiate. Perhaps the child's daily rhythm is not adequate for healthy development. Only direct patient observation can lead us to the cause, which can be subtle enough that it is not consciously suspected by either parent. When a mother attends a group session and is asked for the details of her child's daily life and a description of her attitude towards the child, we usually find the reason for the sleep disorder fairly quickly, and slight changes in her behavior immediately remediate the situation.

If the reason is insufficient nutrition, the mother must consult the pediatrician, who will indicate how to adapt the diet to better suit the child's nutritional needs. It is common for a child who has suckled to reject bottles at first, mainly due to the smell of the new plastic being drastically different from that of the mother's breast. This makes the new food less palatable to the child. There are mothers who try to solve this by delegating the role of feeding the child to a nurse or nanny. Only the mother's patient insistence will make the desire to eat triumph. If this is done properly, the new image of the bottle that relieves hunger will merge with the positive memories of the nourishing breast. The child thus configures the image of the breast in relation to her unconscious fantasies. These exist prior to any sort of relationship with reality, but later this reality modifies them. There is always an interaction between internal and external reality. It is essential to allow the child complete experiences. If the child is interrupted in this process, she cannot start and end the experience according to her needs. In this, as in all cases, forcing the child to accept something is counterproductive, and it is instead the patient and understanding attitude of the mother that overcomes any of these obstacles. The transition to a more solid diet or the inclusion of meat in meals can be difficult at first, and the refusal to chew and swallow, which is frequent in babies, is indicative of an inadequate handling of aggression.

In terms of food and nourishment, we often see children who have a positive relationship with food, but a negative relationship with their mother; or vice versa. If the relationship with the mother and/or the food is positive, it results in a healthy diet. If the relationship with the mother and/or the food is negative, it leads to disorders like physical or mental anorexia. When a child rejects food, or a parent notices a lack of engagement and enjoyment when eating, it can be accompanied by certain behaviors and thoughts. The child may express a fear of being poisoned, reject elements of the outside world, speak and think pessimistically, and inhibit sadism; all of which can lead the child to not eat in order to preserve the breast. This easily explains why problems with eating can have varying definitions and solutions, as we see on a daily basis in mothers' group counseling.

Movement and play

Movement and play are two basic factors as necessary for a child's development as physical nourishment. Around the three or four month mark, a baby will begin experimenting and playing with sound, as evidenced by his babbling. He will also play with his blankets or his own hands. The psychological mechanisms that govern the appearance of these games are the same mechanisms we observed in the playful activity of older children. The first game that a child plays is that of hide and seek, or peek-a-boo. In these sorts of games, the elaboration of losing and refinding is clear. The activity of the game is made possible by a mental process that occurs in the child in the middle of the third month, and is one of the consequences of the development of his depressive phase, that is to say, the symbolic function. If the baby did not have the ability to symbolize, he would not be able to project the symbols onto the objects and the play activity would be meaningless.

It is very striking that the first children's toy developed in most civilizations is the rattle, an object that, when moved, produces sounds that appear and disappear. Melanie Klein, during her clinical research, discovered masturbation fantasies underlying playful activity. Our team was able to observe that, underneath the anxiety that activates the ability to play, lie unsatisfied genital needs which arise from the early genital phase: Upon experiencing the eruption of the first tooth, the child must abandon her oral bond with the mother, and seek a genital one instead. The baby wants to bite before the teeth appear, and their appearance marks a fundamental stage in development. What, until then, was the mere fantasy of biting and tearing, becomes a reality. Feeding with solids is therefore essential at that time, not only for biological nourishment needs, but also to satisfy the need to bite and channel it through normal avenues. Movement is also a bodily and psychological need that, at that time, serves to further the child's exploration and knowledge of the outside world, thus relieving anxiety. When babies show a need for movement, they force themselves to sit up. They try to take objects and hold them close. These needs can appear in children at different times, depending on the child, and it is necessary to satisfy these needs. Only through affectionate observation of the child's reactions can we analyze the pattern of the stimulus that the child requires. As early as the second half of the first year, the child will need to explore the world and separate from the mother. The child does this in order to preserve the mother from her impulses to destroy her with teeth, nails, and all the means that are at the leading edge of their bodily development. This is normal for the age. By distributing her aggression, guilt, and desire for reparation on other objects, the child can keep her positive relationship with the mother intact. If these needs are not met, disorders arise, one of the most common being insomnia.

Language acquisition

Another achievement that helps the child relieve anxiety is the acquisition of language. At the end of the first year, children acquire the ability to pronounce their first words. This babbling constitutes a game of sounds, which allows them to name things that they have and let go or are taken away. Words—which are, at first, simple reconstructions of external objects in the child's mind—facilitate the elaboration of successive losses.

When the child walks, can move freely, and can speak a few words, he is in a position to elaborate and learn toilet training. This is not only because of freedom of movement which physically facilitates access to the toilet seat, but also because of changes in the child's perceived meaning of urine and fecal matter. Until then, the need to get dirty was satisfied with fecal matter and urine; elements that represented, for the child's unconscious mind, the instruments of his destructive sadistic omnipotence. Other objects and activities slowly replace these representations over time.

In the experience of child psychiatrists and psychoanalysts, every child with enuresis has had a similar, threefold experience with early toilet training: It deprived them of an instinctive need, it bolstered their notion of inner evil, and it distressed them due to the insecurity of not having sufficient muscular control to adhere to the demands of toilet training.

In general terms, we can safely claim that when a mother educates her child, she tries to instill a series of values that, naturally, run counter to everything the child feels she needs. Many of these demands are essential for the child's adaptation to reality, and if they are demanded at the proper time, and the child is given the necessary time to achieve them, there will be no disruption. If the learning of toilet training coincides with the internal demand for cleanliness—which is only possible when obsessive defenses are properly internalized and installed—the process will move forward smoothly and painlessly.

The first year of life, especially the months between the second half and the beginning of the second year, is characterized by multiple and convergent learning experiences. During this period, the rapid acquisition of achievements leads to a fundamental change in the face of the external world. This change is as significant as being born. Then, children stand up, walk, utter their first sentences, and, ultimately, begin weaning.

Weaning, teething, walking, talking, separating

Weaning is the consequence of an in-depth process of detachment. The most essential role of this process is the intensification of depressive anxiety. This intensification is produced by the appearance of teeth, instruments that make possible the concrete realization of destructive fantasies.

Weaning determines several things: First, it establishes the need to separate from the mother in order to preserve her, partially losing the communication achieved during the early stages; second, it births a need to find new ways of connecting with the world; and finally, it promotes the structuring of a genital phase prior to the anal and polymorphic phases. The fantasies of a genital link with the object, expressed as the act of penetrating and being penetrated, are supported by oral experiences that serve as molds. The fantasies associated with the image of a nourishing object being inserted into a welcoming, receptive cavity—a motion that is evident in the act of eating itself—begin to arise, creating an equivalence between the symbols of the breast and the mouth or the penis and the vagina. The child's fantasies of a dangerous genital union with an object charge the imago of their parents with a special destructiveness, and this is one of the reasons for the lens of intense fear and danger through which the child experiences the primal scene during that period of their life. Through the process described, oral and genital needs increase. This, in turn, precipitates the need for an organization to expel. The first anal phase, which serves to maintain the bond, ends up being structured by a mechanism with similar wiring to that of the interplay and cooperation between projection and interjection which we saw in the initial relationship with the mother.

Though oral, anal, and genital tendencies act upon a child from the moment of birth, the oral phase is organized and structured at a certain time and according to specific schema, due to its importance in allowing the child to overcome the trauma of birth. Without this structure, the child cannot survive the initial hurdle and grow. We believe that, once the teeth make their first appearance and the oral link with the object must be abandoned, a recovery of the link with the object is attempted through the genital organs.

Language, by allowing the magical reconstruction of objects, helps the child elaborate the depressive anxiety intensified by teething. Pronouncing the first word signifies, for the child, an attempt at repairing the simultaneously loved and hated object. Through the formulation of thoughts and their expression through speech, the child essentially rebuilds the object within and releases it into the external world. On a secondary level, the child experiences that speech has put them in contact with the world, and thus it is a means of communication that can be relied upon.

When the tooth erupts, the child experiences the alarming feeling of a hard, coarse, sharp object penetrating soft tissue. It crushes the skin around it and tears through it, mimicking the threat to the breast due to the need for solid food. This experience is at the core of the child's anxiety when he begins to eat solids and especially meat. The child can and does verify his ability to destroy with his teeth. The chewed rattle, the shredded sheet of paper, the solid food that he can now bite with ease, all symbolize a part of himself and a part of his mother. In this way, the child can confront the real effects of his destructive tendencies, and, depending on the degree to which this is achieved, both depressive and paranoid anxieties increase.

On the one hand, the development of movement and the increase in the ability to manipulate and grasp objects reinforces the child's depressive anxieties. On the other, they also serve to elaborate said anxieties, and are used as stand-ins for locomotion and language, holding the same meanings and purposes. Standing and walking arise from the child's imperative need to separate from the mother, so as not to destroy her. These same achievements then serve the child's need to recover her.

Summary

In summary, the genital organization, by virtue of failing to secure the reconnection with the object, mimics the rupture caused by birth. It causes communication systems to regress, in an attempt to restructure the link with the different partial, oral, anal, and genital objects of the polymorphous phase. In order to maintain the link with a good object, the primary anal phase of expulsion is structured, keeping the oral and genital features active.

These views support Melanie Klein's findings on the early stages of the Oedipus complex, specifically in regards to the emergence of genital tendencies in the second half of the first year. Based on our studies, I have attempted to explain why the genital phase arises, as well as why it fails as a permanent organization.

We wanted to make note of a factor, closely related to the anal phase, that drastically changes when the child first stands up. While the child is prone and tightly wrapped in diapers, the stool and urine are pushed up against the diapers, meshing with them and forming a whole. When a child stands up, they feel that fecal matter and urine can now be released from their body freely. The experience of detachment and loss that children experience during these moments contributes to an increase in separation anxiety and depression. Furthermore, the situation recalls the previously traumatic incident of the fetal membranes detaching.

The expulsion mechanism that serves to conserve the object is the principal acting force in a child's desire to move and walk. The child who walks conserves the mother, moving away from her and approaching her only when necessary. Locomotion and the acquisition of new symbolizations, as well as the free distribution, displacement, and elaboration of these anxieties, can facilitate positive relations between child and mother.

In this period of development, it could be said that children project themselves onto the external world, destroying the negative parts of themselves and their mother, in order to save both. The more aware they become of the potential for destruction that lies dormant in their teeth, muscles, newfound flexibility, and mobility—in essence, their natural weapons—the more afraid they will become of destroying the mother as a total object. And the more this fear takes hold, the more the need will arise to divide and discharge their fantasies regarding objects from the outside world, as they represent, through projective identification, the negative fragments of the father and the mother.

Movement, play, toys, learning tools, and even bodily functions are all essential in preventing the accumulation of destructive fantasies, as they might be directed at the mother's figure if the child is immobile. When an infant's needs for movement, exploration, and games are not satisfied, she will feel her aggressive impulses tugging at her, increasing by the second. This determines the increase in depressive and paranoid needs. Paranoid anxieties lead the child to explore the outside world, in order to verify the reality of the dangers that she feels surrounded by.

In normal development, the child feels the anxiety of displacing these feelings onto objects increasingly distant from himself, and we believe that the need to separate from the mother—so as not to destroy her—is what prompts the child to crawl, climb, walk, and play. We found, through clinical observation, that infants whose needs were misunderstood by their mothers, and who were forced by their parental unit into a routine of immobility and lack of stimulation, invariably developed neurotic disorders. One such disorder, we have studied at length: insomnia. All cases are characterized by the same factor: an immobile daily routine with a lack of stimuli to fill it. This condemns the child to kill the objects originating in fantasy, without having been able to divide or repeat the experiences in the external world. Consequently, they fear the repetition of feeling attacked, and retreat into themselves, immobile and defenseless.

Walking helps children overcome this depressing situation, allowing them a chance to recover and find new objects. But it is also the trigger for one of the textbook defense techniques of this phase—escaping the loved object. In normal development, this is followed by the restitution of objects through words, using the repair mechanism to overcome anxiety. The baby enters the depressive phase to overcome the depressing situation. The depressive stage is internalized.

How does language begin? Children create noises that symbolize something exiting their body. Behind these lie fantasies and hidden memories, and words give children an increasingly explicit avenue to transmit these. The genetic continuity and the original identity between sounds and words seems more and more evident. The word is, for children, the recreation of external objects within their internal world. They can choose to save them or release them into the outside world, with the latter option establishing an initially internal bond, externally. The anxiety that arises when they begin to speak is enormous, and this is due to the fact that their world has been enriched in a way that is disproportionate to their capacity for verbal expression. Children, thus, cannot be sure they should trust the new instrument's ability to repair them.

To pronounce the first word means several things for the child. First, it signifies the magical repair of the loved object. Second, the child experiences that words create contact with the outside world, and are thus a means of communication. In reality, it is the recreation of a link with the internal object, that the child then externalizes and reinternalizes in repetitive verbal games. This egocentric language is transformed into contact with the outside world and, through learning, into a social language. Little by little, language serves children, helping them construct their own communication systems. An object appears upon being named, the word links them to the object; and the environment reacts emotionally to their achievements of language. All these experiences and realizations fortify and ratify the child's belief in speech's capacity for true magic.

Conclusion

These theoretical conclusions are the result of the observations made during the analytical treatment of children and during mothers' counseling groups. Children will develop normally, so long as the mother knows their needs and meets them effectively. The importance of the first year of life has proven to be transcendental. A child's literal first steps are the blueprint for metaphorical first leaps into the external world, and all first experiences moving forward will serve as road markers for the child's further development.

Commentary on Chapter 12

Jeanne Magagna (UK)

This chapter reveals many ways in which parents and professionals can more deeply understand parent–infant interactions, which I shall highlight. Once a baby is conceived, the woman and her partner begin to shift their identifications into that of being a mother or father. Identifying now as a parent arouses deeper connections with one's internalised mother and father. Problems arise in the new parents' relationship with their baby if there is a lack of capable internalised mother, father, couple relationships. Counseling sessions with mothers reveal how a mother's lack of "good enough" inner capacities is revealed through the way the baby's emotions are not understood and not responded to appropriately. One of the problems in the parent–child interaction is that both partners can project their own dependency needs and hostility into the baby and then the baby's feelings overwhelm and threaten the parents. This chapter, "Psychoanalytic perspectives on infant development" places a lot of stress on how the mothers can obtain emotional understanding and support from both a mothers' group and from individual psychotherapy.

The importance of the father

Nowadays we would also like to emphasize the valuable therapeutic aspects of helping fathers develop their emotional sensitivities to mother and baby so that they can support the arduous task which mothering a newborn baby involves. Most importantly, the author, way before the current trend in creating parents' groups for pregnant couples, suggests that mothers' groups should begin as soon as the mother is pregnant, for she then has sufficient time to develop both reflective functioning and tolerance of difficulties in herself, the baby, and her partner. Also important is the suggestion that the fetal psyche is developing through the interaction with the mother's mental state. Most importantly, she stresses that the newborn needs to remain emotionally and physically close to the mother as much as possible as soon as born. What is impressive is the author's highlight on what is crucially important: not simply an adequate maintenance of the baby's physical needs, but also an attentive, emotionally healthy mother who does not project her own unhappiness about physical or emotional difficulties into the baby. All this is later elaborated upon in the concept of the "no entry defence" in which Williams (1997) suggests that the baby who refuses food builds defensive structures against a mother who projects her own pain into the baby.

Acknowledging issues regarding attachment, separation, and loss

Bowlby's ideas presented in *Attachment and Loss* (1973) were in the process of becoming more widely known at the time Aberastury, the author, was writing about the necessity for an attachment bond to be formed and not prematurely ruptured by both emotional and physical separations from the mother, and the importance of the mother's emotional receptivity to her infant for the healthy development of the baby's personality. What is wonderful about this chapter is that it speaks to parents in a language which they can readily understand, reminding the reader of Winnicott's very clear and helpful radio talks for parents in the 1960s.

Introjection of containing parents

The author suggests that the baby needs to have "good enough parents" to hold feelings and give them meaning. Good enough parents recognize that the baby's beckoning for someone when alone and distressed is not just because the baby is tired, in pain, hungry, or needing changing, but because the baby wants and needs the presence of the external emotionally supportive and interested parents. Recommended is the gradual transition of the baby's environment from the constant presence of the parents to a rhythm of presence and absence, titrating the times alone depending on the baby's emotional capacities to gradually feel connected to mother even in her absence. I suspect many parents today would not necessarily feel that a one-month-old baby can sleep through the night, but most parents understand that the parents' good emotionally attuned care of the baby during the day will facilitate the baby's capacity to be alone for longer times at night. What is written between the lines in this discourse is that parents should not simply delegate too much of their parental roles to nannies. Fulfillment of parental roles by the parents facilitates an essential bonding between the infant and his or her parents. One criticism about this chapter is that, in 1962, neglected was the knowledge of how a good father's close bond with the baby positively influences the baby's social, emotional, and intellectual development throughout life! Nowadays we would put it in the following way. What matters is the introjection of an internal couple of containing parents who are deeply receptive to the baby's emotions and capable of bearing the baby's dependence, love, and hostility and who thereby facilitate internal security and gradual independence.

The importance of detailed observation of interactions

Aberastury refrains from relying too much on giving generic advice to parents and instead advises: "Only direct patient observation can lead us to the cause, which can be subtle enough that it is not consciously suspected by either parent." What is impressive in this work is that, without having access to Esther Bick's (1968) thesis that detailed *observation of interaction* between baby and the parents is essential to deeply understand issues such as difficulties in eating or sleeping, Aberastury arrives at this idea independently. In a gentle way she suggests that underlying anxieties regarding transitions from breast, to bottle, to solids, to meat may represent some hostility directed to the internalized and external parents. The baby needs to internalize parents who bear love, dependence, and hostility and resulting anxieties so that the infant can move from the need for repetition of sameness to tolerating all sorts of changes in the parents' caregiving.

Movement, play, and language acquisition

Freud (1920g) thought that a child's play tends to convey the child's emotional experience and attempts to come to terms with it. By observing the young child's spontaneous play we can see a version of the child's significant relationships with parents and siblings and we can perceive the workings of the child's unconscious. Freud and Klein describe how play portrays the child's loving and destructive feelings and phantasies. Susan Isaacs suggests that unconscious phantasies of love, hate, and longing are present in all the child's activities (Magagna & Pasquini, 2014). If there is no possibility for the mother and father to bear the child's hurt, aggression, dependence, and love and the resulting anxieties, then problems in the young child's development will be shown through repetitive play, failure to sleep, eat, think, and develop linguistic capacities.

Conclusion

While different psychoanalytic theoreticians may differ today from the author in their interpretations of the meaning of the infant's psychological development, there is a shared assumption among most of them that the baby is searching for meaningful, deep relationships with the parents, siblings, and the outside world. Each step in the infant's development heralds anxieties about separation on the part of the parents and the infant, while simultaneously the infant finds the pleasure of developing effective ways of joining significant others through walking, talking, and engaging in symbolic play. When hurt, frustration, or hostility are not sufficiently contained by the parents, persecutory anxieties abound and interfere with the baby's physical and emotional development. For parents and professionals alike this chapter illustrates how important it is to give meaning to each parent–child interaction by looking *through an emotionally receptive* lens in order to promote repair of *ruptured loving links* with the parents.

Bibliography

This bibliography section gives the author's list of resources she consulted but did not cite.

Aberastury, A., & Alvarez Toledo, L. G. (1961). La música y los instrumentos musicales [Music and musical instruments]. *Revista de Psicoanálisis, 1*: 185–200.

Campo, A. J. (1957). La interpretación y la acción en el análisis de los niños [Interpretation and action in the analysis of children]. *Revista de Psicoanálisis, 14*(1–2): 121–128.

Campo, V. (1957). La interpretación de la entrevista con los padres en el análisis de los niños [Interpretation of the interview with parents in the analysis of children]. *Revista de Psicoanálisis, 14*(1–2): 19–136.

Campo, V. (1958). La introducción del elemento traumático [The introduction of the traumatic element]. *Revista de Psicoanálisis, 15*(1–2): 4–9.

Chaio, J. (1958). Algunos aspectos de la actuación de las interpretaciones en el desarrollo del insight y en la re-estructuración mental del niño [Some aspects of the role of interpretations in the development of insight and in the mental restructuring of the child]. *Revista de Psicoanálisis, 15*(1–2): 10–15.

Evelson, E. (1958). Una experiencia analítica: análisis simultáneo de hermanos mellizos [An analytical experience: Simultaneous analysis of twin brothers]. *Revista de Psicoanálisis, 15*(12): 16–21.

Freud, A. (1927). The theory of child analysis. In: *The Writings of Anna Freud, Vol. 1* (pp. 162–175). New York: International Universities Press, 1928.

Freud, A. (1949). *El Yo y los Mecanismos de Defensas* [*The Self and Defense Mechanisms*]. Buenos Aires: Paidós.

Freud, S. (1905d). *Three Essays on the Theory of Sexuality. S. E., 7*: 123–246. London: Hogarth.

Freud, S. (1912–1913). *Totem and Taboo. S. E., 13*: vii–162. London: Hogarth.

Freud, S. (1943). *Obras Completas* [*Complete Works*]. Buenos Aires: Americana.

Freud, S. (1948). *Obras Completas* [*Complete Works*]. Madrid: Biblioteca Nueva.

Freud, S. (1956). *Obras Completas* [*Complete Works*]. Buenos Aires: Santiago Rueda.

Garbarino, M. F. de (1958). Dramatización de un ataque epiléptico [Dramatization of an epileptic attack]. *Revista de Psicoanálisis, 15*(1–2): 22–25.

García Reinoso, D. (1958). Reacción de una interpretación incompleta en el análisis de un niño psicótico [Reaction to an incomplete interpretation in the analysis of a psychotic child]. *Revista de Psicoanálisis, 10*(4): 433–438.

Garma, E. G. de (1953). La masturbación prohibida y el desarrollo psicológico [Forbidden masturbation and psychological development]. *Revista de Psicoanálisis, 10*(2): 149–171.

Gesell, A. (1946). *Embriología de la Conducta* [*Embryology of Behavior*]. Buenos Aires: Paidós.

Goode, E. (1949). Aspectos de la interpretación en el psicoanálisis de niños [Aspects of interpretation in child psychoanalysis]. *Revista de Psicoanálisis, 7*(3): 221–248.

Goode, E. (1950). Un cuento en al análisis de un niño [A tale in the analysis of a child]. *Revista de Psicoanálisis, 7*(3): 402–414.

Goodenough, F. (1951). *Test de Inteligencia Infantil por Medio del Dibujo de la Figura Humana* [*Children's Intelligence Test Using Human Figure Drawing*]. Buenos Aires: Paidós.

Grinberg, R. (1958). Evolución de la fantasía de enfermedad a través de la construcción de casas [Evolution of the fantasy of illness through the construction of houses]. *Revista de Psicoanálisis, 15*(1–2): 26–30.

Harlow, H. F. (1959). Love in infant monkeys. *Scientific American, 201*(6): 68–74.

Homburger, E. (1948). Configuraciones en el juego [In-game settings]. *Revista de Psicoanálisis*, *6*(2): 347–432.

Huizinga, J. (1959). *Homo Ludens* [*Man Playing*]. Buenos Aires: Emecé.

Klein, M. (1929). Personification in the play of children. *International Journal of Psycho-Analysis*, 10: 193–204.

Klein, M. (1940). El duelo y su relación con los estados maniaco-depresivos [Grief and its relationship with manic-depressive states]. *Revista di Psicoanálisis*, *7*(3): 415–449.

Klein, M. (1948). *Contributions to Psycho-Analysis*. London: Hogarth.

Klein, M. (1952). *Developments in Psycho-Analysis*. London: Hogarth.

Klein, M. (1952). The origins of transference. *International Journal of Psycho-analysis*, *33*: 433–438.

Klein, M. (1955). The psychoanalytic play technique: Its history and significance. In: *Envy and Gratitude and Other Works, 1946–1963* (pp. 122–140). London: Hogarth.

Lamana, I. L. De (1958). La asunción del rol sexual de una melliza univitelina [The assumption of the sexual role of an identical twin]. *Revista de Psicoanálisis*, *15*(1/2): 98–102.

Merleau-Ponty, M. (1957). *Fenomenología de la Percepción* [*Phenomenology of Perception*]. Mexico: Fondo de Cultura Económica.

Morera, M. E. (1958). Fantasías heterosexuales subyacentes a una histeria de conversión [Heterosexual fantasies underlying a conversion hysteria]. *Revista de Psicoanálisis*, *15*(1/2): 36–44.

Pearson, G. H. (1953). *Trastornos Emocionales de los Niños* [*Emotional Disorders in Children*]. Buenos Aires: Beta.

Pearson, G. H. (1954). *Psychoanalysis and the Education of the Child*. New York: W. W. Norton.

Perestrello, M. (1950). Consideraciones sobre un caso de esquizofrenia infantil [Considerations on a case of childhood schizophrenia]. *Revista de Psicoanálisis*, *7*(4): 487–540.

Pichon-Rivière, A. A. de (1947). Indicaciones para el tratamiento analítico de niños. Un caso práctico [Indications for the analytical treatment of children: A practical case]. *Revista de Psicoanálisis*, *4*(3): 467–491.

Pichon-Rivière, A. A. de (1951). Como repercute en los niños la conducta de los padres con sus animales preferidos [How parents' behavior with their favorite animals affects children]. *Revista de Psicoanálisis*, *8*(5): 398–401.

Pichon-Rivière, A. A. de (1951). Trastornos emocionales en el niño vinculados con la dentición [Emotional disorders in children linked to teething]. *Revista de Odontología*, *39*(8): 357–359.

Pichon-Rivière, A. A. de (1952). La transferencia en el análisis de niños, en especial en los análisis tempranos [Transference in child analysis, especially in early analysis]. *Revista de Psicoanálisis*, *9*(3): 265–310.

Pichon-Rivière, A. A. de (1957). La inclusión de los padres en el cuadro de la situación analítica y el manejo de esta situación a través de la interpretación [The inclusion of parents in the framework of the analytical situation and the management of this situation through interpretation]. *Revista de Psicoanálisis*, *14*(1/2): 137–146.

Pichon-Rivière, A. A. de (1958). La dentición, la marcha y el lenguaje en relación con la posición depresiva [Teething, walking and language in relation to the depressive position]. *Revista de Psicoanálisis*, 15(1): 41–48.

Pichon-Rivière, A. A. de (1961). La dentición, su significado y sus consecuencias en el desarrollo [Dentition, its meaning and its consequences on development]. *Sección Psicológica del Boletín de la Asociación Argentina de Odontología para Niños*, *3*(4): 41–48.

Pichon-Rivière, J. (2009). *E & A, Enrique and Arminda*. Buenos Aires: Capital Intelectual.

Racker, G. T. De (1958). El cajon de juguetes del niño y el cajon de fantasías del adulto (medios de actuación—juego frente a la realidad angustiosa interna—transferencial) [The child's toy box and the adult's fantasy box (means of acting out—play in the face of internal, distressing reality—transference)]. *Revista de Psicoanálisis*, *15*(1–2): 49–54.

Rascovsky, A. (1960). *El Psiquismo Fetal* [*The Fetal Psyche*]. Buenos Aires: Paidós.

Rascovsky, A. (1993). Consideraciones psicosomáticas sobre la evolución sexual del niño: paralelismo entre las expresiones psicológicas, fisiológicas y estructurales [Psychosomatic considerations on the sexual development of the child: Parallelism between psychological, physiological and structural expressions]. *Revista de Psicoanálisis*, *50*(3): 637–684.

Rascovsky, A., & Rascovsky, L. (1960). Consideraciones psicoanalíticas sobre la situación actual estimulante en 116 casos de epilepsia infantil [Psychoanalytic considerations on the current stimulating situation in 116 cases of childhood epilepsy]. *Revista de Psicoanálisis*, *2*(4): 626–640.

Rascovsky, A., & Salzman, J. (1940). Estudio de los factores ambientales en el síndrome adiposo genital en el varón [Study of environmental factors in genital adipose syndrome in men]. *Archivos Argentinos de Pediatría, 14*(6): 501–516.

Rascovsky, A., Pichon-Rivière, E., & Salzman, J. (1940). Elementos constitutivos del síndrome adiposo prepuberal en el varón [Constituent elements of prepubertal adipose syndrome in men]. *Archivos Argentinos de Pediatría, 14*(4): 331–342.

Ribble, M. A. (1950). Infantile experience in relation to personality development. In: J. McV. Hunt (Ed.), *Personality and the Behavior Disorders* (pp. 621–652). New York: Ronald.

Rolla, E. H. (1958). Análisis contemporáneo de un padre y un hijo [Contemporary analysis of a father and a son]. *Revista de Psicoanálisis, 15*(1–2): 55–64.

Saz, C. (1958). Comunicación y destrucción [Communication and destruction]. *Revista de Psicoanálisis, 15*(1–2): 65–69.

Scolni, F. (1958). Psicoanálisis de un niño de 12 años [Psychoanalysis of a 12-year-old boy]. *Revista de Psicoanálisis, 4*(4): 664–704.

Segal, H. (1950). Some aspects of the analysis of a schizophrenia. *International Journal of Psycho-Analysis, 31*: 268–278.

References

This reference section includes all texts cited by the author, editors, and contributors.

Aberastury, A. (1959). La filosofía del hecho consumado y su repercusión en la formación psicoanalítica [The philosophy of the fait accompli and its impact on psychoanalytic training]. *Revista de Psicoanálisis, 16*(4): 381–387.

Aberastury, A. (1962). *Teoría y técnica del psicoanálisis de niños* [*Theory and Technique of Child Psychoanalysis*]. Buenos Aires: Paidós.

Aberastury, A. (1964). La fase genital previa [The early genital phase prior to the anal phase]. *Revista de Psicoanálisis, 21*(3): 203–213.

Aberastury, A. (1970). La importancia de la organización genital en la iniciación del complejo de Edipo temprano [The importance of genital organization in the initiation of the early Oedipus complex]. *Revista de Psicoanálisis, 27*(1): 5–25.

Ben Plotkin, M. (2003). *Freud en las pampas. Orígenes y desarrollo de una cultura psicoanalítica en la Argentina (1910–1983)* [*Freud in the Pampas: Origins and Development of a Psychoanalytic Culture in Argentina (1910–1983)*]. Buenos Aires: Editorial Sudamericana.

Bick, E. (1968). The experience of skin in early object relations. *International Journal of Psychoanalysis, 49*: 484–486.

Bion, W. R. (1970). *Attention and Interpretation*. London: Tavistock.

Bloj, A. (2014). Introduction to the life and work of Arminda Aberastury Pichon-Riviére (1910–1972). In: N. Lisman-Pieczanski & A. Pieczanski (Eds.), *The Pioneers of Psychoanalysis in South America: An Essential Guide* (pp. 449–452). Hove, UK: Routledge.

Bollas, C. (1987). *The Shadow of the Object: Psychoanalysis of the Unthought Known*. London: Free Association.

Bowlby, J. (1973). *Attachment and Loss. Vol. 3: Loss: Sadness and Depression*. New York: Basic Books.

Chartres, B. de (1904). *The Proverbs of Saint Bernard*. Whitefish, MN: Kessinger, 2010.

Cipolatti, M. C. (2021). Las ideas más significativas de Arminda Aberastury con respecto al psicoanálisis de niños y adolescentes [Arminda Aberastury's most significant ideas regarding psychoanalysis of children and adolescents]. *Revista de Psicoanálisis, 78*(2): 429–438.

Erickson, M. H. (1941). On the possible occurrence of a dream in an eight-month-old infant. *Psychoanalytic Quarterly, 10*(3): 382–384.

Fairbairn, W. R. D. (1958). Observations on the nature of hysterical states. *British Journal of Medical Psychology, 27*: 105–125. [Also in: D. E. Scharff & E. F. Birtles (Eds.), *From Instinct to Self: Selected Papers of W. R. D. Fairbairn, Volume 1* (pp. 13–40). Northvale, NJ: Jason Aronson, 1994.]

Ferro, A., & Basile, R. (2006). Unity of analysis: Similarities and differences in the analysis of children and grown-ups. *Psychoanalytic Quarterly, 75*: 477–500.

Freud, A. (1927a). *Einführung in die Technik der Kinderanalyse* [*Introduction to the Technique of Child Analysis*]. Berlin: Internationaler Psychoanalytischer Verlag.

Freud, A. (1927b). *Psicoanálisis del niño*, L. Rosenthal (Trans.), from *Einführung in die Technik der Kinderanalyse* [*Introduction to the Technique of Child Analysis*]. Buenos Aires: Editorial Imán; Paidós, 1949.

Freud, A. (1928). *Introduction to the Technic of Child Analysis*, L. Pierce Clark (Trans.), from *Einführung in die Technik der Kinderanalyse*. New York: Nervous and Mental Diseases Publishing Company, 1927.

Freud, A. (1947). *The Psychoanalytical Treatment of Children*, N. Proctor-Gregg (Trans.), from *Die Psychoanalytische Behandlung des Kindes*, 1942. Thame, Oxon, UK: Imago.

Freud, S. (1897). Letter from Freud to Fliess. October 15, 1897. *The Complete Letters of Sigmund Freud to Wilhelm Fliess, 1887–1904. 42*: 270–273.

Freud, S. (1901b). *The Psychopathology of Everyday Life. S. E., 6*: vii–296. London: Hogarth.

Freud, S. (1905e). *Fragment of an Analysis of a Case of Hysteria. S. E., 7*: 1–122. London: Hogarth.

Freud, S. (1907a). Delusions and dreams in Jensen's *Gradiva. S. E., 9*: 1–96. London: Hogarth.

Freud, S. (1909b). *Analysis of a Phobia in a Five-Year-Old Boy. S. E., 10*: 1–150. London: Hogarth.

Freud, S. (1920g). *Beyond the Pleasure Principle. S. E., 18*: 1–64. London: Hogarth.

Freud, S. (1925d). An autobiographical study. *S. E., 20*: 1–74. London: Hogarth.

Freud, S. (1925h). Negation. *S. E., 19*: 233–240. London: Hogarth.

Freud, S. (1926d). *Inhibitions, Symptoms and Anxiety. S. E., 20*: 75–176. London: Hogarth.

Garma, A. (1948). *Psicoanálisis de los Sueños* [*Psychoanalysis of Dreams*]. Buenos Aires: Nova.

Garma, A. (1949). El origen de los vestidos [The origin of dresses]. *Revista de Psicoanálisis, 7*(2): 191–220.

Heimann, P. (1950). On countertransference. *International Journal of Psycho-Analysis, 31*: 81–84.

Hug-Hellmuth, H. (1921). Zür technik der kinderanalyse [On the technique of child analysis]. *Internationale Zeitschrift für Psychoanalyse, 7*(2): 179–197.

Jarast, S. G. de (1958). El duelo en relación con el aprendizaje [Grief in relation to learning]. *Revista de Psicoanálisis, 15*(1–2): 31–35.

Jones, E. (1959). *Vida y Obra de Sigmund Freud* [*Life and Work of Sigmund Freud*]. Buenos Aires: Nova.

Kennedy, H. (1979). The role of insight in child analysis: A developmental perspective. *Journal of the American Psychoanalytic Association, 27*(Suppl.): 9–28.

King, P., & Steiner, R. (1991). *The Freud-Klein Controversies 1941–45*. London: Routledge, 1992.

Klein, M. (1927). The psychological principles of infant analysis. *International Journal of Psychoanalysis, 8*: 25–37.

Klein, M. (1932). *El Psicoanálisis de Niños* [*Child Psychoanalysis*]. Buenos Aires: Biblioteca de Psicoanálisis.

Klein, M. (1945). Letter from Melanie Klein to Arminda Aberastury, April 27, 1945. Personal communication.

Klein, M. (1952). Some theoretical conclusions regarding the emotional life of the infant. In: *The Writings of Melanie Klein, Volume 8: Envy and Gratitude and Other Works* (pp. 61–94). London: Hogarth.

Klein, M. (1955). The psychoanalytic play technique: Its history and significance. *American Journal of Orthopsychiatry, 25*(2): 223–237. [Reprinted in *The Writings of Melanie Klein, Vol. 3*. London: Hogarth, 1980.]

Kris, M. (1959). En la discusion sobre problemas de neurosis infantiles [In the discussion of problems of childhood neurosis]. In: *The Psychoanalytic Study of the Child, Vol. 15*. London: Imago.

Lisman-Pieczanski, N., & Pieczanski, A. (2014). *The Pioneers of Psychoanalysis in South America: An Essential Guide*. London: Karnac.

Losso, R., S. de Setton, L., & Scharff, D. E. (Eds.) (2017). *The Linked Self in Psychoanalysis: The Pioneering Work of Enrique Pichon Riviere*. London: Karnac.

Magagna, J., & Pasquini, P. (2014). *Being Present for Your Nursery Age Child*. London: Routledge.

Mayes, L. C., & Cohen, D. J. (1992). The development of an imaginative capacity in young children. *Psychoanalytic Study of the Child, 47*: 23–47.

Merriam-Webster Dictionary. Definition of pioneer. Merriam-Webster.com. https://merriam-webster.com/dictionary/pioneer (last accessed on April 29, 2024).

Morgenstern, S. (1937). *Psychanalyse infantile: Symbolisme et valeur clinique des créations imaginatives chez l'enfant* [*Child Psychoanalysis: Symbolism and Clinical Value of Imaginative Creations in Children*]. Paris: Edición Denöel.

Pichon-Rivière, A. A. de (1946). Psicoanálisis de niños [Child psychoanalysis]. *Revista de Psicoanálisis, 4*(2): 200–219.

Pichon-Rivière, A. A. de (1950a). *El juego de construir casas. Su interpretación y su valor diagnóstico* [*The House Building Game: Its Interpretation and Diagnostic Value*]. Buenos Aires: Nova. [Also reprinted in the name of Aberastury, A., Buenos Aires: Paidós, 1961.]

Pichon-Rivière, A. A. de (1950b). Fobia a los globos en una niña de 11 meses [Balloon phobia in an 11-month-old girl]. *Revista de Psicoanálisis, 7*(4): 541–554.

Pichon-Rivière, A. A. de (1951). Algunos mecanismos de la enuresis. *Revista de Psicoanálisis, 8*(2): 211–221.

Pichon-Rivière, A. A. de (1958a). House construction play: Its interpretation and diagnostic value. *International Journal of Psychoanalysis, 39*: 39–49.

Pichon-Rivière, A. A. de (1958b). Dentition, walking and speech in relation to the depressive position. *International Journal of Psychoanalysis, 39*(2/3): 167–171.

Pichon-Rivière, A. A. de (1958c). Una nueva psicología del niño, a la luz de los descubrimientos de Freud [A new psychology of the child, in the light of Freud's discoveries]. *Revista de Psicoanálisis, 13*(4): 220–226.

Piontelli, A. (1988). Prenatal life and birth reflected in the analysis of a 2-year-old psychotic girl. *International Review of Psycho-Analysis, 15*: 73–81.

Piontelli, A. (1992). *From Fetus to Child: An Observational and Psychoanalytic Study*. London: Routledge.

Racker, H. (1967). *Transference and Countertransference*. New York: International Universities Press.

Rambert, M. L. (1938). Une nouvelle technique en psychanalyse infantile: Le jeu de guignols [A *New Technique in Child Psychoanalysis: The Puppet Show*]. *Revue française de Psychanalyse, 10*: 50–65.

Rank, O. (1924). *The Trauma of Birth*. New York: Harcourt, Brace.

Reichenbach, H. (1938). *Experience and Prediction: An Analysis for the Foundations and the Structure of Knowledge*. Chicago, IL: University of Chicago Press.

Sandler, J., & Freud, A. (1980). Discussion in the Hampstead Index of "The Ego and the Mechanisms of Defence" 1: The ego as the seat of observation. *Bulletin of the Anna Freud Centre, 3*(4): 199–212.

Scharff, D. E., Losso, R., & S. de Setton, L. (Eds.) (2017). Pichon Rivière's psychoanalytic contributions: Some comparisons with object relations and modern developments in psychoanalysis. *International Journal of Psychoanalysis, 98*(1): 129–143.

Scharff, J. S. (2017). Case study: Analysis of a traumatized hemophiliac boy. *International Journal of Psychoanalysis, 98*: 71–90.

Schilder, P. (1958). *Imagen y Apariencia del Cuerpo Humano* [*Image and Appearance of the Human Body*]. Buenos Aires: Paidós.

Stern, D. N., Sander, L. W., Nahum, J. P., Harrison, A. M., Lyons-Ruth, K., Morgan, A. C., Bruschweiler-Stern, N., & Tronick, E. Z. (1998). Non-interpretive mechanisms in psychoanalytic therapy: The "something more" than interpretation. *International Journal of Psychoanalysis, 79*: 903–921.

Sugarman, A. (2003). A new model for conceptualizing insightfulness in the analyses of young children. *Psychoanalytic Quarterly, 72*: 325–355.

Sugarman, A. (2008). The use of play to promote insightfulness in the analysis of children suffering from cumulative trauma. *Psychoanalytic Quarterly, 77*: 799–833.

Sugarman, A. (2009). Child v. adult psychoanalysis: Two processes or one? *International Journal of Psychoanalysis, 90*: 1255–1276.

Wakefield, J. C. (2007). Little Hans and attachment theory: Bowlby's hypothesis reconsidered in light of new evidence from the Freud archives. *Psychoanalytic Study of the Child, 62*: 61–69.

Williams, G. (1997). Reflections on some dynamics of eating disorders: "No entry defences and foreign bodies". *International Journal of Psychoanalysis, 78*: 927–941.

Winnicott, D. W. (1947). Hate in the countertransference. In: *Through Paediatrics to Psycho-Analysis* (pp. 229–242). London: Hogarth.

Index